LAST CALL

Sweat, Tears, and Beers:
Thirty Years at the Firehouse

CHARLES E. RICE

Cover Photo: 4 a.m. February 27, 1949. Kenyon College student volunteers use a small hose from the basement of Old Kenyon dormitory. Nine students died and twenty six were injured. (*Greenslade Special Collections and Archives, Kenyon College, Gambier, Ohio. Used by Permission.*)

This is a work of nonfiction, but in some instances names and details have been altered to protect the privacy of individuals.

Copyright ©2009
Charles E. Rice
All rights reserved
ISBN: 978-1-880977-28-6
Archives: *Greenslade Special Collections and Archives, Kenyon College, Gambier, Ohio. Used by Permission.*
Orders and Inquiries: lastcallfd@yahoo.com

To Hobe, our Chief

TABLE OF CONTENTS

Acknowledgments

Preface

Part One: Why Our Community Needed an Effective Fire Department

   1. The Village, the College, and Their History of Tragic Fires
   2. The Tragedy at Old Kenyon and the Failure of the GFD
   3. How "Repeal" Helped Create CTFD

Part Two: Behind the Locked Door of the Firehouse

   4. The Chief with the Cast Iron Ego
   5. At the Firehouse Morning, Noon, and Night
   6. The Feedgrinder Teaches the Professor: Lesson One
   7. High School Physics and Math Saved the Firefighter
   8. When the Village Siren Wasn't Sounding
   9. The Final Exam Wasn't Oral or Written
   10. Firefighters, Church Bells, Sirens, Beebeeps, and Rats
   11. The Handwriting on the Wall Spelled EMS

Part Three: The Mutation of the Fire Service, and The Related Changes in Law Enforcement, and Medicine

   12. EMS is Born: It Was a High-Risk Pregnancy
   13. At CTFD Squad Runs 90, Fire Runs 10: Squad Runs Win.
   14. Is There A Doctor in the Hospital?
   15. What We EMT's Did Not Want To Know: Lesson One
   16. Fools Rush In
   17. PK, The Last of the Old-time Sheriffs

Part Four: Scars No One Else Can See

   18. Critical Incident Stress Debriefing (CISD) Rediscovered
   19. The Best Volunteer of All
   20. I Did Not Know What Evil Lurked
   21. Images That Will Not Disappear From My Head
   22. Local Boys Make Good
   23. Good Friends Who Have Moved North On Gaskin Street
   24. Farewell

ACKNOWLEDGMENTS

The College Township Volunteer Fire Department (CTFD) in Gambier, Ohio, did not rise to excellence in isolation. Many individuals deserve recognition for their roles in the development of Knox County emergency services. I can name only a few here, but the contributions of all should not be valued less.

The College Township Trustees Jim Kunkle was the first CTFD Chief. Later, his dedication as a trustee of College Township found him at the firehouse Sunday inspections for years. Barry Bowden, Jim Ingerham, Doug McLarnan, and Harold Burch provided heroic leadership as Trustees through good times and bad.

The Kenyon College student volunteers Their service was as dedicated, skillful, and intense as that of any local native. They have continued to be outstanding citizens after graduation.

The Danville and Bladensburg Volunteer Fire Departments Both were our close neighbors and assisted us in emergencies on many occasions. The essence of their volunteerism is personified by Bladensburg's Kenny Heisterman and Art Ward. That department has accomplished more with fewer resources than any I know. The Hammond family of Danville, Dale as patriarch, and John and Mike, as his successors, led their department from the beginning. Donnie Rogers gave them a polished granite rock of support for decades.

The Centerburg Volunteer Fire Department It is the oldest volunteer fire department in the county. Robert Whited, Ed Dick, Gary Durbin, and Tom Stewart were among its leaders. Some of its volunteers are now career officers in large urban departments, while the "new" guy, Joe Porter, has assumed command.

Distance meant that I had less contact with the volunteers of the Fredericktown Volunteer Fire Department and Fredericktown Emergency Squad. Bill Whaley was a dedicated long-time stalwart, and Don Wilson and Alice Campbell were the pros I knew best. Departments in neighboring counties, especially those of Utica, and Homer in Licking County, and Marengo, in Morrow County, participated in many of our emergencies, training sessions, and pioneering experiences.

At Knox Community Hospital and its predecessors, the nursing staffs helped us get hands-on experience and advanced training. Barbara Noonen, Alice Campbell, and Margaret Frederick held us to rigorous standards.

Drs. John Drake and Richard Smythe provided the encouragement and endorsement of volunteer emergency medical care necessary for its rapid advancement. Tracy Schermer, M.D., tenaciously lobbied politicians and fought the stagnation of established traditions to advance emergency medicine in the county. All the while, he was available to respond to fire and medical emergencies with CTFD, twenty four hours a day seven days a week. (24/7).

In this book I poke fun at the conflicts CTFD had with the emergency medical teams of Mount Vernon. In fact, they were pioneers as professionals in EMS and excelled in victim care. Some of those early members were Duane Shaw, Randy Orsborne, Don Wilson, Jake Fredericks, Carol Eckle, Michael Cronin, and Rick Cantrell. They are among the best medics in the United States.

The College Township Fire Department is indebted for its position as a leader among volunteer departments to L. Hobart Brown who built its buildings, trained the firefighters, and created the leaders. He even supported me as his helper in spite of my temperamental management style. Richard "Dick" Baer served the department in various capacities for fifty years. As mayor and village manager he established the infrastructure that resulted in a first rate fire service. Carl Holmes provided wisdom and maturity that stabilized the department in good times and during turmoil.

I do regret that, to protect the guilty, such as Asst. Chief David E "Lightning Williams, and Lieut. Gail Stenger I could not include such tales as those about CTFD Christmas parties, house demolitions, a swimming pool frolic in the burning house, "donations" of Christmas trees, and countless other incidents that might horrify a prim and proper reader.

But the greatest frustration in writing this book was the knowledge that I could not mention, by name, all the CTFD volunteers who served loyally and heroically and never received the recognition they deserved.

My research for the book was aided by Carol Marshall in the Kenyon College Archives, and by Kenyon College through permission to reprint archival photos. "Mayor" Dick Baer, Bill Baer, and Dick Ralston provided indispensable factual data and recollections. Bruce Haywood, Harry Clor, Chuck and Pat Leech, Jon Williams, Jo Rice, Lizz Forthofer, Don Bateman, Brenda Howard and Mike Harden provided helpful criticism and suggestions. I am especially indebted to Jerry Kelly who guided me through the technical morass of publishing the book. Wayne Larsen at Southern Illinois University did a splendid job as copy editor. But the flaws of the book are solely mine.

PREFACE

An ancient legend tells of a supernatural bird, the Phoenix. It lived for a thousand years and at the end of its life it built its own funeral pyre and jumped into the flames. Instantly, it was reborn and arose from the ashes to fly off and live another thousand years. The history of volunteer firefighters goes back a thousand years, too, but in 1971, when funeral directors suddenly stopped providing ambulance service they lit the fire that ended the ages old volunteer fire service. Almost instantly it was reborn, but the relevance of fires waned as the new fledgling flew to the rescue at medical emergencies, hazardous materials spills, and terrorist attacks. It remains to be seen whether the new form of volunteer organizations, more appropriately labeled emergency services, will live for the next thousand years.

As members of a small volunteer fire department my colleagues and I were pioneers in the era of that change even though I never once heard them discuss it by comparison to the legend of the Phoenix. I know they would have seen the validity of the metaphor but come to think about it, we didn't talk about metaphors either.

My "other life" was lived at the College Township Volunteer Fire Department (CTFD) in Gambier, Ohio. My family knows that for certain, as do my colleagues at work and a lot of the people who live in the village. Writing observations and reminiscences about the people who served with me, and about our adventures at the "firehouse" allowed me to extend that thirty-year period a while longer. I also want others to learn how being volunteers changed our relationships with the people of the community in ways that would not have happened if we had minded our own business.

During my years of service most volunteer fire departments (VFDs) underwent immense change. In a few short years their dominant activity became emergency medical service (EMS), not fire protection. Most of us were not prepared for that responsibility, and things did not always go well. Describing the development of EMS at my VFD is one example among hundreds that took place across the country over the same period. It is important to record such events, because that era began the last chapter in the history of the purely volunteer fire service.

The book is written in four sections. Part One provides the history of fires in the village of Gambier and it makes clear the need for a fire department capable of fighting major fires. The village had few permanent residents but hundreds of transients and was full of large buildings. Those two facts posed a major problem for fire protection. An effective volunteer group was finally established, and the second part of the book depicts its people, culture, and activities during the years when the fire service was almost exclusively concerned with extinguishing fires. It was a FIRE department. The third section describes the infancy of EMS at CTFD. EMS invaded fire departments throughout the nation and began pushing the traditional volunteer firefighters out. Emergency medical responses immediately dominated activities at CTFD, and we began to witness emotionally traumatic incidents. The fourth section of the book tells of the effects of some of those emergencies on us.

When CTFD was founded the milieu of the village, the culture that finally evolved inside the firehouse walls in the 1960s, the characters who made up the roster, the training requirements, the olio of motivations that sustained membership, and the entailments of what being a volunteer meant in those days were all typical of traditional volunteer fire departments throughout the country. Knowing about those years is essential to understanding how EMS affected the volunteers and their traditions when it was shoved in the fire house doors.

Almost as soon as EMS began many of the long-time firefighters became as obsolete as their 78-rpm record players, but they did not know it right away. They ignored the signs that beckoned them out the door, and their continued presence assured that the traditional fire house culture would endure for a few years. I am indebted to a couple of those old-timers who, before they were gone, tried to teach me the basic principles of fire fighting. There were a few other notable guys who were fire house regulars but not as likely to be seen holding a nozzle at a fire. Some of them were more likely creating the horse play that exceeded by a wide margin the number of fires we extinguished. For readers not familiar with the centuries-old volunteer fire department traditions, I hope the depiction of that genre will prove interesting, because it is now gone.

When I was elected to membership, CTFD was a FIRE Department, but within a year it began to change. Soon it almost seemed as if all the fires were out. They weren't. They were just lost amidst the noise of ambulance sirens. The third part of the book documents the transition by presenting examples of the new adventures awaiting the neophyte emergency medical technicians.

As I wrote about the learning experiences of our emergency squad, I had the nagging feeling that there was an implicit theme I could not bring to awareness. Finally, after many drafts of the preface I realized what it was. We, along with our counterparts across the country, became the pioneer emergency medical technicians. It is likely that we were the first to conduct a successful cardiopulmonary resuscitation outside a hospital; start an intravenous line in a victim in the bedroom or barn at their home; and use the first model "Jaws of Life" to tear apart a vehicle in order to extricate a trapped victim. We naively approached and treated victims of criminals, with no law enforcement officers or SWAT team to "secure the scene" before we arrived, and we were among the first to make a fatal mistake due to our ignorance of medical knowledge.

We began the EMS work before there were formal courses, state certifications, emergency medical technicians (EMTs), or paramedics. Our efforts were based upon little or no experience, and our instruments and supplies were primitive. In our department, for example, the ambulance carried dressings and scissors declared surplus after World War II. The fact that we demonstrated enough success to impress the medical community resulted in our being given more medical responsibilities, and then more training and even more responsibility. Today people take for granted that fire department personnel will arrive at their emergency after being prepared by a rigorous government sanctioned-technical training curriculum. No current day volunteer or professional EMT will ever engage in pioneering experiences such as ours.

We were not alone in our pioneering. In the 1970s the medical schools had not yet invented the medical school specialty of emergency medicine. We found that neither the doctors nor the emergency rooms were consistently competent to treat the patients we brought to them.

Almost as remarkable is the evolution of communications within and between the agencies. In our first decade or so there was no 911, central dispatching, or direct communication to hospital emergency rooms from the emergency squads. Law enforcement was also primitive by today's standards, and there was little coordination among the various emergency organizations.

There is another aspect of that thirty years unlikely to be duplicated by our successors. As volunteers we saw our fellow villagers on a daily basis, at work, at play, and in commerce. It was "Hi, how are you." "Give me a quarter pound of the ham salad." "Are you going to the school play tonight." "Can you folks come over for dinner Saturday?" The fourth part of the book documents the sudden changes in many of those informal relationships as soon as we began to respond to medical emergencies. The veneer of personal privacy that insulates family affairs from friends and neighbors vanished when we were called to help in a medical emergency. Suddenly, I needed to know the private medical history of someone at that house. Sometimes I inserted catheters into their veins or bared their chest to try to restart their heart. Once in a while I had to tell relatives that their loved one is dead. Whether or not I had previously known the victim or the family, an emotionally charged memory became indelibly linked to the occasion. Then I returned to my daily routine.

Some of those experiences resulted in images we volunteers carried for the rest of our lives. I take the liberty of sharing some of mine in the last section of the book so the reader can appreciate that not only were we not paid for our work, we were assessed an emotional price for doing it. As volunteer EMTs my colleagues and I have responded to more than 60 percent of the homes in the village.

Today, fewer members on the department roster live or work in the community, and they know fewer villagers and fewer of the victims they help. They respond to help strangers and seldom see them again. They return to the station and finish their shift. They even pick up a paycheck that encourages them to continue as a "volunteer." They do collect emotional images as we did. But because most of them do not live in the village, the emotions are not triggered by everyday contact with people they aided. In contrast, almost every day my eyes met those of a person we had been called to help. Sometimes there was a reflexive change in facial expression that led me to know that I had initiated a replay of an incident each of us wished had not happened. Even nearly ten years after retirement as an EMT, those meetings still occur as I walk in the village.

This is my personal memoir, but a similar book could have been written by hundreds of others who were volunteers across the country during this time period. We were the pioneers of EMS and made today's paramedics possible.

PART ONE

WHY OUR COMMUNITY NEEDED AN EFFECTIVE FIRE DEPARTMENT

In small rural communities major fires seldom occur and the economic resources available for fire protection are so limited, that damaging fires may be viewed with a sense of helplessness. A brief history of Gambier Village and its Kenyon College in rural central Ohio reveals that it was uniquely vulnerable and a list of its many fires provides tragic evidence that creation of an effective fire department was essential. Its first attempt to form one failed when it was needed most. The community leaders did not comprehend that in addition to firefighters an array of infrastructure and equipment was necessary to provide adequate fire protection. Even if they had known those requirements, the money needed to purchase them was not available. It took well over a hundred years of seeing death and destruction before the village achieved its fire protection goals.

That first fire department was comprised of local men who volunteered to respond to fires. They responded to an alarm but there was little training, no assignment of responsibilities at a fire and no preplanning for fighting a fire in its buildings. There was no professional expertise to inform the community about the resources required to prepare for major fires. In its first decade, the second fire department was better organized and funded but its members did not equate being a volunteer firefighter with a motivation to strive for professional competence. The core group was comprised of self sufficient long time residents who were bound to the firehouse by the social culture they formed behind its locked doors. Until a leader instilled in them the motivation to develop professional firefighting skills fires were often devastating.

Part One reviews the history of fires in the community that echoed again and again the call for a competent fire service. The first two chapters should convince the reader of that need. The story of how it reached that goal fills the remaining chapters and is based upon my observations as a volunteer during its journey to excellence.

1

THE VILLAGE, THE COLLEGE, AND THEIR HISTORY OF TRAGIC FIRES

The College Township Fire Department (CTFD) did not spring forth full-blown from ashes like the legendary Phoenix of ancient Greece. More than 150 years of incidents of human tragedy and economic loss preceded its founding. The history stored in the Archives of the Kenyon College Library reveals how much a competent fire department was needed and why its absence took such a heavy toll. The history also provides the perspective required to understand why it took so long to develop effective fire protection and sets the scene for the memories that I chronicle. Actually, CTFD did rise out of ashes, a lot of ashes, but it was a slow ascent.

When a fire suddenly destroys property and kills people, there is a search for the cause. If it is discovered, there is a sense of closure for those not enduringly affected. Then it becomes an event of interest in a page or two of history, and much later it is recalled only in the reflections of the senior citizens who witnessed it. Some catastrophic fires reviewed here were unavoidable in the era in which they occurred. Smoke and fire flare up often in any history of Kenyon College and the Village of Gambier.

The Village of Gambier is a very small dot on maps that show it at all. If Kenyon College had not been built, the little hill on which it stands in eastern Knox County, Ohio, might have remained an anonymous, vegetation- covered, glacier-formed, geological bump, notable only as a warning that Appalachia is nigh. The College was put there in 1826 by Episcopal Bishop Philander Chase. He purchased four thousand acres, about 2½ square miles, which became College Township. Chase's college would educate young men. He placed it up on that hill five miles east of the nearest city, Mount Vernon. He chose the remote knob because it was far from those distractions and temptations of urban life that seduce college-age students away from the joys of intellectual inquiry. The first and most prestigious building was called "Old Kenyon." Its corner stone was laid in June of 1827. It was a 170-feet-long, four-story building made of large sandstone slabs, some of them four and one-half feet thick, that were quarried east of the village.

Chase begged money from wealthy nobility in England and honored them by naming things for them, like Kenyon and Gambier. However, his management style caused a near revolt, and he did not stay long. Some of his faculty probably thought it fitting that the street leading north out of town bears his name, Chase Avenue.

The founding of the college resulted in the creation of a village and a local economy. Tradesmen and their families arrived to construct the buildings, locals distilled whiskey, and professors came to teach. Enough students enrolled to keep it alive. The College nearly died in the Civil War when its president enlisted as soon as war broke out and other faculty and students followed, starving the college of money and students.

At first the College's dug wells and springs provided the drinking water. Later its deep wells and pumps provided tap water for the whole community. After the mid-1800's, the tradesmen and their families needed some things that the college didn't supply, like a public cemetery and eventually flush toilets.

In the late nineteenth century, private preparatory schools also opened in Gambier and expanded the educational offerings in the tiny village. For almost two centuries, schools have attracted workers to live in and around the village to prepare food for the students, resole shoes, cut hair and grass, sort the mail, and sell groceries, books, and beer. A village government was eventually born. Jobs and local population waxed and waned with the relative prosperity of the educational institutions. A railroad came with coal-fired steam engines and left in the age of diesels. The neighboring farms prospered early on but gradually declined in number and some were replaced by homes on a couple of acres with horses and llamas in residence.

Today, the college strives to preserve the adjacent farm land. It is still almost as isolated as Chase intended, but the pandemic of twenty-first century sinful teenage temptations has found its way to the top of the hill, and Chase would not have approved the admission of female students in 1969. Some students have hated the remote rural confinement, while others have developed a strong affection for the place.

Fire, on the other hand, has never wavered in its love of the small isolated town. It licks its lips when it finds such a village, with its buildings loaded with huge amounts of fuel and no means to inhibit its being sated. Gambier and Kenyon College provided some of its favorite entrées.

Fire has also played havoc with the local economy. The Farmer's Co-op grain elevator, the "pole yard," the airplane hangar, a restaurant, and the hardware store went up in smoke. But it was the burning of buildings dedicated to the education of young people that could have returned the hill to nature. The entities of college and village have always been symbiotic. That interdependence of "town and gown" is no more dramatically evident than in the history of the fires that took lives and destroyed vital buildings.

It can even be argued that those fires were predestined by the era in which they occurred and by circumstances created in the pursuit of a noble cause.

The explicit consideration of fire hazards was probably in the consciousness of all who lived in College Township from the outset. In its first few decades both urban and rural fire fighting was primitive, and vulnerability to fire was implicit in everyone's thinking. People recognized that, once freed from containment, fires created desperate, often hopeless, circumstances. Before technology such as pumps powered by engines and protective gear for firefighters were available to help fight fires, the likelihood of extinguishing a damaging fire in the cities was not much greater than in the country. The cities, however, had one advantage over villages that soon allowed them to advance their firefighting ability as technology came available. That advantage was money.

For 150 years fire arrogantly overwhelmed Gambier's primitive defenses, confident in its ability to reduce its buildings to large mounds of rubble and ash. The village's great disadvantage was the lack of money. When fire-fighting technology became available, the town could not afford it. The community existed only because of tax-exempt private educational institutions and therefore was financially vulnerable to disaster by fire.

Fire, Friend and Foe

Fires are physical phenomena. They are dependent on the simultaneous presence of adequate amounts of heat, oxygen, and fuel. Those essentials are present in some quantity almost everywhere and all the time. Simplistically, therefore, fires are potentially an ubiquitous danger. To extinguish them, however, one has to avoid combining the required quantities of the three components. Remove one of the essentials, and a fire will go out. Doing that isn't always easy.

The problem is to limit fire to its beneficial purposes while preventing the unleashing of its destructive potential. Fire in some form remains essential, especially where there are winters. Fire is a fickle friend. Chase's initial college building, Old Kenyon, had four huge chimneys to vent the many fireplaces that provided warmth to the earliest students. In 1907, the building was remodeled, and the fireplaces were walled over, as a central heating system rendered them unnecessary. There were new fireplaces built that vented through the original chimneys. They were intended to provide a homey ethos for the students who lived there. "Lets have a fire in the fireplace tonight" evoked visions of relaxed pleasure for the student residents. If, however, a chimney has not been properly maintained, it can be waiting to kill.

The Elements of Fire Protection

Urban governments provide the tax income to fund the basics of fire protection. Those include water reservoirs with underground delivery systems to hydrants, powerful fire engines and pumps, and people paid to

The original "firehouse" built in 1902. It housed the "hose cart."

standby around the clock to initiate rapid attacks on fires. The concentration of population, business, and industry in the cities yields tax income for fire protection resources.

Small villages, however, often do not have adequate water supplies, adequate water lines to hydrants, adequate fire apparatus with high volume pumps, or paid firefighters twenty four hours a day seven days per week. (24/7). They are so limited by the lack of tax income that important firefighting assets cannot be afforded and so fires often win.

The fire risks and potential costs of fires are magnified when boarding schools occupy an isolated rural village. The population of permanent residents and employees is sometimes a third of the number of young transients who live there only during the academic year. The student population within the campus is densely housed in large dormitories. The college buildings are larger, taller, and more expensive than those found in typical small towns. All of the buildings are loaded with flammable contents. But educational institutions pay no property taxes and hence provide no financial support toward their own fire protection.

That the educational institutions were exempt from paying property taxes magnified the vulnerability of the Gambier community. The proportion of tax-paying citizens and businesses, relative to the total population living in Gambier, has always been small. Even if the college had been willing to contribute to fire-fighting resources, it was on the verge of economic collapse for much of its history. Often it was barely possible to see the tassel atop a professor's mortar board hat in the college's sea of debt. It was almost 150 years before economic security arrived.

Lack of money, flammability of large academic buildings, inadequate water supplies, inadequate firefighting apparatus, untrained or minimally trained firefighters, and time delays between ignition and the arrival of firefighting men and equipment <u>predestined</u> catastrophic fires in the first century and a half of the Gambier/Kenyon community. It was a matter not of whether there would be disastrous fires, but when.

When

For several decades around the end of the nineteenth century, the college operated a residential grammar school, the Kenyon Military Academy (KMA). Today, only those who have studied the history of the college and village would be aware of its importance to the survival of Kenyon. Inadequate enrollment was a chronic threat to the college's existence. It was reasoned that the presence of KMA would result in many of its graduates entering Kenyon. Although its effect on enrollment at the college never matched expectations, the school was a success. It was housed in two brick buildings, Delano and Milnor Halls, northeast of the Kenyon campus.

On May 7, 1889, Milnor Hall was destroyed by fire. Delano Hall was connected to Milnor by a breezeway, but it was saved. The college newspaper reported that there was a bucket brigade passing water from a nearby pond. Kenyon students, theological students from Kenyon's divinity school, and the "ladies of Harcourt" (the school for girls), all joined with faculty members to pass the buckets of water to fight the fire.

The positive reputation and solid enrollment at the academy motivated the construction of a new and larger brick building to replace Milnor. There was great optimism that the school would feed students to the enrollment-starved college. In 1891, the college had forty three students, while KMA was attended by 134. Whether Kenyon would ever have derived significant value from KMA would also be determined by fire.

In 1897 Rosse Hall, the Greek Revival auditorium and former chapel was lost to flames. There was no insurance, because the rates quoted to the business manager were judged to be too high. It took three years to raise money and rebuild it. When it was finished, things began to look hopeful again for Kenyon. If students began to flow in from KMA, the college would be on more solid financial ground.

The new KMA thrived until February 24, 1906. In the middle of the night, it again caught fire. This time, the fire started in Delano Hall, where students slept in a third-floor dormitory. Those students who were awakened by the commotion struggled to flee the building. Two students burned in their beds, and one went back into the burning building to recover belongings and never came out. Many more were seriously injured. Both Delano and Milnor Halls burned to the ground. Shock and sadness darkened the mood of the whole community. The effect of the loss may be indicated by the fact that the site of the fire was never completely cleared, and bricks from the buildings are still uncovered by residents of houses that stand on its site. KMA was not rebuilt. For the rest of his life, one resident who witnessed the fire as a child spoke with great emotion whenever he discussed the tragedy. He was Harold "Shoppy" Parker, a life-long resident of Gambier. As an adult he helped organize its volunteer fire departments and remained a firefighter into his eighties.

The embers of KMA had hardly cooled when in 1907 the "French House," a frame structure sometimes used to house students, burned.

Three years later, in 1910, Hubbard Hall, which served as the college library, burned. The college lost many valuable works of art and important documents related to its history. Fortunately, an attached building designed with a wall to stop the spread of fire held most of the college's library books. Volunteers prevented its ignition by extinguishing embers that fell on its roof. Their water may have come via the hose cart brought over from the fire house. A hose cart is an axle between wagon wheels with hose wrapped around it. It can be pulled by people to a hydrant and then provide water. It was stored in a fourteen by twenty eight feet brick building standing just north of the college cemetery. The sturdy structure contained the hose cart and fire-extinguishing chemicals in anticipation of a fire. It likely represented the college's response to the devastating fires that had plagued it for years. That first fire house remains firmly in position 106 years after its construction, but few people today know its original purpose.

Fires struck other important buildings in the village. Some of the oldest residents still recall fires that destroyed houses and businesses. In 1931, a popular restaurant, located where the current post office now stands, was destroyed, and in 1950, Doolittle's Hardware was consumed by flames at the site where the Village Inn now feeds students and visitors.

Depending on who is asked, Kenyon is known for The Kenyon Review, Rutherford B. Hayes, Paul Newman, E. L. Doctorow, or the Old Kenyon dormitory fire. Newman, a senior at the time, could have told the story of the last from first-hand experience. Around 4 a.m. February 27, 1949 following the sophomore dance weekend festivities, the nightmare began.

The dance theme was billed as "Sophomore Shipwreck." The previous evening there had been a wood fire in a parlor fireplace in the middle of Old Kenyon. As the parties began to wane, someone threw a box of trash paper on the embers. They flared up brightly but briefly and appeared to be out. The students could not know that the paper had ignited ancient residue between the first and second floors. It glowed there for hours, gasping for air. When it finally found unlimited oxygen, it exploded into flame, and then ended the lives of nine students and injured twenty six others. Most of those who died probably were killed by thick black smoke that rose from the fire's place of origin and into the rooms above where the students slept. Those who were awakened ran downstairs, climbed onto fire escapes, tried to climb down the thick ivy vines that clung to the building, or jumped out of windows. Some were burned while escaping their rooms into blazing halls. By daylight the fire had destroyed the huge building.

A volunteer fire department had been organized some years before the tragedy. A little fire truck, a 1941 Chevrolet, was purchased jointly by the village and college. In 1942 a fire brigade of eighteen men was formed and became the Gambier Fire Department (GFD). The engine was stored in an unheated frame building that was used as a garage for college vehicles. The inadequacy of those measures can be grasped by viewing news photos of the attempts to fight the fire and by reading the transcripts of the investigating panel. No one understood the magnitude of the resources required to fight such a fire. It was a catastrophe. The study of the Old Kenyon fire in chapter two provides evidence that effective fire fighting on a college campus requires much more than a few volunteers and a fire engine.

After the deficiencies of GFD had proven fatal at Old Kenyon, it was about fifteen years before the community tried again to form a fire department. Initially, the second group of volunteers was not much more successful than the first. There were more major fire losses. The largest of those was the destruction of a telephone-pole processing factory located adjacent to the railroad in 1966. Logs saturated with creosote ignited and sent smoke into the air that was visible from thirty miles. The financial loss was estimated to be $1 million, a significant amount in those days. A fire that lit the whole village in the middle of the night destroyed the Gambier Farmers Co-op lumber and building supplies structure in 1970 and its associated hardware store in 1975. Those fires claimed victory over the volunteers because fundamental resources required to augment their efforts were still not available. For that first 150 years, too little water, too little technology, too little money, too few trained firefighters, and too much time before responding to alarm brought tragedy and financial disaster. Hindsight clearly shows that the tragedies and destruction were predestined by the lack of those vital components of successful fire fighting.

More than 175 years later the resources for fighting fires are available, but some things have not changed. When a fire such as the one at Old Kenyon kills nine students, disables others, and destroys the hallmark building of the campus, it becomes the Old Kenyon fire. In a college such as Kenyon the immediacy of the tragedy to the students who witnessed it will last for the rest of their lives. One student generation later, four years, its influence on fire safety awareness had dissipated. By then all students who witnessed the fire had graduated or left the college. Subsequent students have learned about the fire as a legend, but it has not inhibited the behavior of some who lived in the resurrected dorm. Many later student generations continued to confirm the fire hazard of housing large numbers of teen-age men. In 1983, a student survived a jump out of the window of his third-floor room in Old Kenyon when fire and smoke awakened him. That fire was accidental, but alcohol probably impaired his awareness of the danger until almost too late. He survived. Not all fires, however, have been accidental.

Arson and the Male Kenyon Student

The long history of fires at Kenyon provided plenty of justification for the creation of a local fire department, but the case is underlined several times by the characteristics of the students who lived in the dorms. A unique demography of humans has repeatedly confirmed the need. Reporting evidence to support that allegation risks singling out a subset of the population at a time when college communities decry any negative attribution based on gender. The group was almost all Caucasian and male.

I know of no one who suggested that any of the major fires that occurred in Gambier and Kenyon College before 1949 were cases of arson. Conversely, many of those after that date meet the technical definition. No one, however, questions that students "played' with fire in the dormitories before and after the Old Kenyon fire. There are suspicions that over the years since that tragedy several students have started major fires in the community. Most likely, they were products of disturbed students expressing anger or emotional instability. Others were "pranks" by young men who had no intention of doing harm to the structures or people they endangered. They did, however, purposely start fires that did result in property damage and could have injured others. People in that college age group, almost always men, seem to push the limits of risk to themselves and others without gauging the potential implications.

Watching fires, no matter how large or small, tempts one to attribute viability to them. In the movie Backdraft, the flames and the sounds associated with intense heat take on the qualities of an angry beast. The metaphor is not original with Hollywood. Firefighters come to regard fire as a dangerous living organism that is to be hunted and destroyed before it attacks and kills its prey. For firefighters it is like lion hunting in Africa or wrestling alligators. The challenge is there. The thrills are there. Pride in killing the beast is luscious. People who set fires have strong feelings about fire too, but theirs are more nurturing. A few of them have even attended Kenyon

There have been fires on the Kenyon campus that were the work of arsonists. Students who survived the Old Kenyon fire reported that many men paid little attention to shouts of "fire" at that early morning hour. They had been desensitized by the number of times pranksters had set fire to paper in waste baskets to create panic late at night. It was funny.

In the period from 1953 through 1955, several small fires were the result of lighter fluid being squirted on the doors of dormitory rooms and lit. Others were the result of carelessness. George Hallock, a student in the "new" Old Kenyon recalls extinguishing a fire there and receiving a note of thanks from President Chalmers. A 1955 memo to the head of maintenance from Dean of the College Frank Bailey urged the purchase of a couple of oxygen masks for the firefighters after fire caused several thousand dollars damage to Old Kenyon. There were six separate fires set between 1953 and 1955, most of them in Old Kenyon. Photos in the college archives show smoke-stained walls above a dorm room window from one fire. Another popular fad was to squirt lighter fluid under dormitory room doors and light it. The catastrophic fire of 1949 had occurred only four years before, one college generation, but it did not inhibit some students from using fire as a prank; or was it just a prank? Those lighter-fluid dormitory incidents could have been ignited by disturbed students, but probably were a product of the risky behavior characteristic of teen-age men in their self-perceived age of immortality.

The fires at the Farmers Co-op, near the college's airplane hangar, and the one that destroyed the college storage building in the 1970s were of suspicious origin, according to the fire chief, but lack of evidence prevented prosecution. It was certain that students were observed in the area at about 2 a.m. when one of the fires was reported. Later the hangar burned.

In 1974, an arsonist, believed to have been a specific student, set fire to a barn east of the eight story dormitory on the north campus. Ironically, it had been built to serve as the drill hall for the Kenyon Military Academy. The barn was destroyed. Several other fires were also set during the same period, one near the studio of the college radio station. Those fires stopped when the student left college.

Set fires have caused damage to buildings, but there have been no serious injuries since 1949. Except for the vacant barn, no college building has been destroyed by fire since 1974. Some years after the barn fire, however, another arsonist targeted the dean of students office in the Student Affairs Center (SAC), a frame structure in the center of town. While repairs were being made, the offices were relocated to Sunset Cottage, another frame structure on campus. Shortly after the move, an attempt was made to burn that building, but it too, failed. The fire starter had flunked his arson practicum exam.

There have been a number of other minor arson fires on campus in recent years. Most have been in trash cans or paper set on fire on bulletin-boards. It is assumed that these types of incidents are done as mischievous pranks, but obviously, they were potentially dangerous. Alert students and security personnel have extinguished most of the bulletin board and trash-can fires. False alarms in dormitories, set in the middle of the night, continue to be all too common. Though mainly a source of irritation, they create a hazard to those who are aroused and those who must investigate the alarm as a potential emergency.

That there are alarm and sprinkler systems in most buildings and a water supply available to fight any size fire has reduced but not eliminated the likelihood of another Old Kenyon tragedy. The steady decline in the number of fires since the 1970s mirrors the gradual development of a first-rate fire department.

Fires at Kenyon that did not kill people or destroy buildings may quickly become a vague memory. The fire that threatened to destroy Pierce Hall, the classic dining hall and student center, during the summer of 1999 almost escaped notice. It was caused by students who had abandoned a lighted burner on a stove. It occurred in the summer when few students were on campus, it was away from the busy village streets, and it was largely repaired before students arrived back in the fall. A large dining room in the lower level of the building was fully involved in flames when the fire department arrived. With an additional few minutes to grow, it could have destroyed the whole building and crippled the college's ability to feed its students. If that fire had happened a decade or so earlier the building would have been rubble. It was saved because, finally, there were trained campus security members to initiate a quick alarm, well trained firefighters with excellent engines and equipment, and adequate water to fight the fire. The CTFD firefighters responded with all their engines two minutes after the alarm was sounded and carried out a courageous interior attack on the fire under the leadership of Chief Craig Shira and his volunteers. They were supported by seventeen engines and forty seven firefighters from every fire department in the county. Only a few townsfolk and the firefighters remember it. The rapid response time saved the building. It marked the first major test of the department after it had acquired all the essentials of firefighting. To progress from bucket brigade to hose cart, to little engine, to water system, to a professionally trained volunteer fire department with modern engines took 175 years.

No small reason for this success was that, once the college was prospering financially, Kenyon, through action of its Board of Trustees, contributed a financial subsidy to the fire department. That decision paid off in several ways. It enabled the fire department to achieve a better rating from the insurance industry thus substantially lowering fire insurance costs in the community. Donating the money significantly enhanced the department's fire fighting assets. Therefore, the department had the resources necessary to stop the fire in Pierce Hall, and the college did not suffer the cost of rebuilding it or the many inconveniences that would have ensued.

If Chase, or any of the subsequent college or village leaders, ever conducted a thorough study of fire hazards and how to combat them, we do not know. For the most part it would not have made much difference, because the resources required to address the problem were neither available, nor affordable. College officials tried to provide some protection when they built the little 1902 brick firehouse, but that measure proved inadequate. Later, they must have believed that by buying the 1941 fire truck and assigning the responsibility for operating it to a few men, the college would finally be protected. But officials did not understand that fire protection for large buildings requires an ample water system, multiple engines, rescue equipment, continuous training for firefighters, fire-prevention programs, preplanning for possible fires in each building, and organized leadership.

Alarm systems and sprinkler technology are only now reaching their potential to reduce the likelihood of another Old Kenyon fire. Certainly by 2008 there is recognition that fire-prevention measures such as alarms and sprinkler systems are essential, yet not all college buildings have them. It has been a long time since there was a dorm fire at the college. It would be very unwise to say, "It cannot happen here again."

The evidence pointing to the need for a first-class fire department is documented by the history related in this chapter. No news media were at Old Kenyon in 1949 assigning blame while the flames still blazed, and no politicians were there to milk publicity with their own "independent investigation." In some ways that sort of limelight might have helped identify explicit needs. It should have been clear that the GFD was not the answer. Its successor, CTFD, was the solution, but today's media would love to have exposed its origins and liability attorneys would have drooled in anticipation of its fires.

2

THE TRAGEDY AT OLD KENYON AND FAILURE OF THE GFD

In the nineteenth and early twentieth centuries fire fighting technology in Gambier consisted of buckets of water passed from person to person and thrown on the fire. Those were succeeded by the hand-drawn hose cart. The hose cart is now a treasured relic justly preserved in a collection of historic fire memorabilia.

Well after motorized technology was commonly available elsewhere, village and college leaders combined their meager financial resources to purchase the 1941 Chevrolet fire truck from the American Fire Apparatus Company for $2,290. Maybe the reasoning of those who bought it was "Now we have a fire truck and firefighters, and they will surely put out any fires we have." The little truck was better than the buckets and better than the hose cart, and in fact would put out any fire on campus but only if manned with skill and at the fire in _time_.

In 1942 eighteen men completed the Ohio Trade and Industrial Commission fire fighter training course sponsored by Kent State University. They were the firefighters who would respond to alarms and man the new truck. They became the Gambier Volunteer Fire Department (GFD). Charles Carpenter, an elected official of the village and a supervisor in the college maintenance department, was appointed its leader. The state-sponsored training course taken by the group was valuable but there is no indication that the group met regularly to maintain the truck, review their instruction, practice their skills, or more important, formulate plans for fighting a fire in any of the college's buildings. Evidence suggests that the brigade was, at best, loosely organized. They were also individualists, and just because Carpenter had been designated to be in charge did not mean that all the members would welcome his orders nor that he was prepared to organize and direct them in a catastrophe. Labeling the group a fire department did not necessarily signify that it could function as one.

The time from alarm until the engine arrives at a fire determines whether a fire truck can save lives and property. In Gambier during daytime there were GFD firefighters on campus and in the village. Lots of people were also around to discover a fire before it was out of control. In the middle of the night a fire might not be discovered as quickly, and the firefighters would have scattered to their homes. One wonders if the group had considered questions that might determine their effectiveness. If there is a fire at night how can we be sure enough of the firefighters learn about it? How long is it likely to take from discovery of the fire to the time the firemen are alerted? How long does it take firefighters who are at home in bed to get dressed, into their cars, and to the engine? Is the engine easily accessible to the firefighters? Who will be responsible for assuring the engine is always ready to respond? It is doubtful that the GFDers had any gear to protect them from the hazards of firefighting. By 1942, the truck was ready and resting in a maintenance garage down the steep hill behind Old Kenyon. Or was it ready?

The truck was capable of pumping water to a fire from hydrants in the village and on the campus, and it carried a small supply of water in its tank. The amount of water available from some hydrants, however, was inadequate because the inside diameter of their water lines was so small they could not supply enough water to meet the demands of the truck's pump.

The college's deep wells supplied water for the college and village. Water from the wells went into the 320,000-gallon reservoir near the maintenance buildings. A pump elevated the water from the bottom of the hill behind Old Kenyon to a water tower on the north boundary of the campus. When supplying fire engines, an additional pump located at the maintenance power station could be turned on manually to keep maximum flow to the storage tank. Maintenance personnel were aware of that need, but it was not always recalled as a top priority. There is no doubt that the Chevy was capable of arresting a fire in its early stages, or quenching a fire in a vehicle, but it could not provide enough water to extinguish a significant fire in any of the college's academic or dormitory buildings. It had to arrive at the fire <u>in time</u> to be effective.

The new fire department was publicized in the <u>Kenyon Collegian</u> student newspaper. The article announced that no students would be allowed to join it because of their inherently temporary residence in the community. That rationale might have been reasonable, but it was emphatically refuted by the actions of students at Old Kenyon in 1949. Twenty years later, two or more members of each new class of Kenyon students were being trained as volunteer firefighter/EMTs in the College Township Fire Department and routinely providing skilled assistance.

The Old Kenyon Fire

The events of the night of February 27, 1949, can be reconstructed from the stories of those who were there and the analysis of the investigating panel.

A student testified that he went to bed after the Sophomore Shipwreck party at around 3:50 a.m. and detected no smoke or anything unusual. At 4:10 a.m. that student arrived at the "power house" to report the fire. Several other students testified that it was fifteen minutes after the fire was reported

Many students trying to control the fire stream of a 2 ½" hose.

before the GFD engine arrived at the top of the hill, though an exact time could not be verified. It was agreed that the fire originated after 3:50, and we can assume that it took the student less than five minutes to reach the boiler room. The Mount Vernon Fire Department was notified at 4:20 and arrived in about ten minutes.

What cannot be disputed is that when the GFD truck arrived, the fire had advanced beyond its ability to extinguish the blaze. In testimony before the committee maintenance employee Generous Nell, who was on duty firing the boiler at the power station, reported that a student ran down from Old Kenyon to report the fire (about two hundred yards through woods). Nell stated that he got the truck out and up the hill with "no problem." He observed fire at the second floor, south side as he arrived at the top of the hill and at the front on the same floor when he arrived on the north side of the building. He stated that after parking the truck at a hydrant, the lower floor "lit up." Nell said students in front of the dorm were already pointing a stream of water at the second floor fire from the small hose they found in the building's ground floor hallway. Other GFD firemen arrived and Nell then returned to the power house to start the back-up pump to supply extra water to the storage tower.

The "little engine that couldn't" had been parked in the unheated frame garage adjacent to the college power house at the bottom of the steep hill behind the dorm. According to some, the battery was dead and the pump frozen, but Nell denied that. Others, including GFD firefighter and village mechanic Harvey Matthews, disputed his story and claimed the truck's battery failed. Students' testimonies tend to support Matthews, but panic in operating the engine might also have resulted in temporary failure. Students reported helping shove the engine into position. The engine and pump did eventually function. Nell's testimony suggests that however long it took to get the engine to the fire it arrived too late to be effective. He had seen fire on the second floor of both the north and south sides of the building and then the lower floor. It is almost certain, therefore, that the fire had extended beyond the capability of the engine even if there had been an interior attack by well equipped firefighters. Students immediately took the ladders off the truck and used them on the front of the building. None were ever used at the rear, where students had already leaped to their death and others died in their beds.

The fire had suddenly exploded into destruction and death. It spread rapidly once it had access to unlimited oxygen, and an accelerant assured its rapid advance. The building's floors were soaked with the oils used to clean them. The oil-soaked pine floor boards sent thick deadly smoke up into the rooms of sleeping students well before flames reached them. After staying up to the early hours of the morning and then retiring, almost all students would have been in a deep sleep. Many in the dorm had consumed alcoholic beverages during the preceding party. Some who were reported to have been drinking died in the fire, but some who had not also died. The state arson investigator asserted that the smoke and gases would have made no distinction and were quickly lethal.

There is a likely explanation for why the fire was out of control when the engine arrived. In part it may also account for why it seemed to take the engine so long to get there. The rapidity of the fire's spread was probably due to a backdraft. Two of the essentials of combustion, fuel and heat, were in ample supply and were burning in a confined space. The heat was there, the fuel was there; all that was needed for explosive ignition was enough oxygen. For a long time there was not enough oxygen. The fire had been kept alive and spreading by a small amount of air sucked from the parlor fireplace, where paper had been burned at 8 p.m.

When Old Kenyon had been remodeled forty years earlier, the chimneys were not completely rebuilt. The 1826 chimneys were constructed before there were fire bricks that could endure the heat over many more years. The disintegration of the old bricks created an opening in the chimney and allowed flaming paper from the parlor fire-place to pass out of the chimney and into spaces between the first and second floors. The fire ignited material

Old Kenyon fully involved. (Greenslade Special Collections and Archives, Kenyon College, Gambier, Ohio. Used by Permission.)

in there and up between the walls. As it captured a small draft from the parlor it gradually extended further through the closed spaces. It was very hot but gasping for more oxygen. The heat was there. The fuel was there. When it finally burned through its containing materials and access to unlimited oxygen, there was an explosive ignition, a backdraft. The fire spread at a rate making escape tenuous. That it grew in those spaces for eight hours after the paper fire is quite possible, as there were just enough air, fuel, and heat to maintain its smoldering spread. The addition of the oil soaked floor boards was a perfect guarantee of rapid acceleration that quickly exhausted the response time available to the GFD. As soon as the fire broke into rooms, it had books, desks, clothing, bedding, and much more to add to its fuel. When students opened the windows to escape, the draft from outside air fueled a blow torch type acceleration. Had there been a crew of volunteers sleeping by the engine maybe lives and the building could have been saved, but even that is doubtful given the assumption of a backdraft. The testimony of students who escaped referred to the breath-like puffing of smoke prior to flames. That phenomenon is the gasping of the fire for more air before breaking through the wall and floor barriers. The puffing of smoke is a strong correlate of an impending backdraft.

Students in their rooms above the second floor might well have been dead before the flames burst into the open because of thick smoke and carbon monoxide. Their lives may have ended before they could awaken. Getting out of the building and into the freezing night air was essential for those students on the upper floors of the building's south side, and many students did make it out. Several died in their rooms. Two who were aroused from the sleep into the hell of the fire jumped to their deaths from upper-story windows.

There can be no doubt, however, that some students were heroic in their firefighting and rescue attempts and more effective than the members of GFD. It was clear that deaths and rescues were occurring before Nell arrived with the engine. The horrific scene being witnessed by the students must have made it seem an eternity for the engine to arrive. Prior to its arrival the students had rescued many of their comrades. Edward Collins stood on a fire escape and caught others who jumped to him even though he suffered severe burns. Several others ran to the lower level of the building, grabbed the small fire hoses kept there, and climbed the stairs to conduct a dangerous interior attack on the fire with the little hoses. Robert Levy carried a mortally burned student out of the building. Other students, too, dashed past flames to rescue those trapped above and were singed in the process. Donald Rothchild, who lived in a front room of the building, grabbed a fire hose and "worked it for a while" but reported that water pressure from the hose was not strong enough and that someone told him the well was dry. He complained that the Gambier fire engine did not come for a long time and its battery was dead. Warren Sladky, a blind student who lived on the first floor, simply heard the commotion and found his way out of the building. His room was below the level of the fire and he exited before it ignited.

Thomas Hill's well-written letter to his parents after the fire provides autobiographic insight into the situation faced by the students. He was aroused by the shouting around 4 a.m. and went out of the building, more from curiosity than alarm. At first he thought the fire would easily be contained, but it was not long before he realized the whole building would be destroyed. Interestingly, he too observed students take a ladder from the fire truck to try to rescue those in the upper floors of the building. The first ladder was too short, and they had to return to the engine to obtain the longer one. That observation tends to confirm that there were no GFD firefighters engaged in ladder rescues. Hill stood at a distance and watched the weak hose streams from the engines. His use of the word <u>ridiculous</u> to describe their effect communicates his fatalistic assessment. College historians of the fire are fortunate that his typewriter was one of the few possessions saved from the inferno.

Many faculty and administrative staff members soon arrived at the fire. They organized procedures to account for all students and help those who were still in night clothes in the freezing night air. Photos of the fire show one stream of water coming from each of two engines. They were from

2½" diameter hoses leading from the pumps for about fifty feet and ending in straight stream nozzles. In those pictures the water exiting the nozzles appear in strong streams. As many as twelve students are hanging on to the lines and directing the water at the flames. A 2½" fire hose emitting water from its nozzle under high pressure exerts a mechanical force in the opposite direction from the water being ejected from the nozzle. Under high pressure it may require several inexperienced persons to control and direct its stream. After the water leaves the hose's nozzle it is a powerful battering ram that assaults anything in its path. One student was struck by that force and painfully injured. The fire ignored the exterior attack and left the huge building a pile of smoking rubble.

In reading the testimony of students after the fire, it appears that many of them demonstrated extraordinary heroism and that some behaved with maturity of judgment and intelligence beyond what might have been expected of college-age students. They gambled their own lives to save those of their friends. Others gathered up the injured and drove them to the hospital in their cars.

The Old Kenyon disaster revealed the inadequacy of the GFD and the shortage of essential infrastructure. Two members of the GFD were engaged in rescue attempts. None, however, are visible in any of the photos of fire fighting, nor are their actions mentioned specifically in testimony. Joe Carpenter, brother of Charles lived in an apartment in the village business section. He was observed by Rothchild in the building. Joe reported that he tried to rescue boys and that one he encountered was in fact on fire while trying to escape. Charlie Carpenter reported that he arrived quickly and urged students in unaffected areas to evacuate.

After the engine arrived at Old Kenyon, Matthews and Charlie Carpenter engaged in a verbal dispute. Harvey, refused to comply with his commander's orders and persisted in doing things his way. He was a talented expert in operating engines and working with mechanical devices, but he sometimes had difficulty accepting direction from others. Raising the topic of his conflict with Carpenter rearoused Harvey's anger toward that "chief" for fifty years. The incident suggests that there was not the discipline or teamwork needed to provide a coordinated attack on the fire or organize rescue operations. There is little reference to the GFD in the investigators' report. How many of the GFD firefighters were at the fire is not clear, but only four are mentioned, none of them was equipped to perform rescues. In pictures taken during the fire only students are seen manning the hoses. It is doubtful that any of the GFD firemen anticipated being faced with such a catastrophic blaze. With no protective gear the firefighters would have been no more effective than the students as rescuers. In retrospect, lack of water would have led to a failure to save the building, regardless.

All those interviewed agreed that from the start, the fire trapped students on the South side of the building. Its first victims resided in rooms on that side of the building. A basic rule of fire fighting is to have an officer circle a structure upon arrival to get an assessment of the priorities for attack and assign equipment accordingly. Given the critical circumstances visible from the front of the building when the engine arrived, that may have been irrelevant, but according to Chief Carpenter he did not do that.

Mount Vernon fire Chief Carroll White said that the east and west wings of the building might have been saved had there been an adequate water supply. That seems doubtful, given the rapidity of the fire's spread through the interior and the lack of manpower equipped to get inside and attack its origin. There was a fire wall between the middle part of the building and the east and west wings, but the fire spread across the roof to each side. Several students bemoaned the fact that the water pressure on the two fire hoses mounted in the lower level of the building waxed and waned and then stopped.

The water tower at the North end of the campus could hold a maximum of forty thousand gallons of water. The two fire engine's pumps, plus the fire hoses inside the building, would have used well in excess of one thousand gallons per minute. The pumps from the power house reservoir to the water tower could not have kept pace. Together they could supply 825 gallons per minute. After the fire, an engineer claimed that the tower had been kept full and the reservoir only partly depleted. Whether or not that was true, the water lines to the hydrants apparently did not keep pace. The building was therefore doomed before the engines arrived. Even if there had been additional fire engines, there was not enough water to supply their pumps. If, however, several engines were available, a relay of water from a second reservoir could have helped. A couple hundred yards from Old Kenyon was the college swimming pool. That fact would have been a part of a well-rehearsed preplan for fires on campus.

Unreported at the time were the Gambier firefighters' assertions that the response of the Mount Vernon Fire Department was inadequate and negligent because it dispatched only one truck and two men to a disaster causing loss of life. The GFD complaints about the Mount Vernon effort marked the beginning of a long antipathy between the departments that began to abate only in 2006. It seems likely that regardless of the response times of the two engines those who perished would have died before their arrival. In retrospect a well-organized and drilled group of firefighters would have discovered the water supply problem by performing fire training that required the testing of maximum water flow from hydrants at Old Kenyon.

Too much accelerant, too much time in reporting the alarm, lack of an efficient means of notifying firefighters, too long a response time, too few fire engines, too little manpower, no protective gear, a balky engine, inadequate water supply, inexperienced firefighters, the time of day, and residents deeply asleep, all combined to assure failure. The human and technical resources simply were not there. People mourned and responded with determination to rebuild Old Kenyon, but little was done at that time to create a more effective fire department. It was almost as if the failure of GFD left a sense of helplessness and a fatalistic view of the ability to intervene in major fires. There will be anger and recriminations after a disaster such as the Old Kenyon fire. GFD was not an effective fire department, but it was not atypical for the era. It would be another thirty years before firefighting would be sufficiently advanced by technology and knowledge to prevent or control a dormitory fire at the college.

Perhaps understandably, the college's publications and news media's attention turned toward the determined effort to rebuild Old Kenyon as it had appeared before. That commitment and the decision to return to classrooms immediately after the fire reflected the resolve of the college community not to allow the tragedy to destroy morale and undermine their reason for being there.

Perhaps too, the college leaders felt that by including all available fire protection measures in the reconstruction of the building, concerns about future fires could be abated. As it turned out, their assumption would be tested on numerous occasions within four years, a college generation. The fact that Dean Bailey had to request purchase of masks for firefighters four years after the fire suggests that little had been done to improve firefighting capabilities. GFD firefighters must have responded to those set fires in the "new" Old Kenyon without protective gear. At GFD the people and leadership problems persisted for well over a decade.

The need for better fire protection remained in the minds of local officials. It had been evident that major fires were beyond the capability of local volunteers and that aid from elsewhere should be assured. In 1950, College Township passed a levy and entered into a contract to pay the city of Mount Vernon to respond to fires in the area. It was reasoned that the arrival of trained professional firefighters and their larger engines would be a major asset in serious fires. One inference of the decision was that the volunteers were amateurs and not capable. The firefighting resources to be provided by the City consisted of a single engine and two firefighters. The contract may have eased the fears of some, but to others who witnessed the Old Kenyon fire it seemed no better. The only difference was that a contract assured that the Mount Vernon Fire Department had an obligation to respond but with the same size crew, an engine and two firefighters, that had eventually reached the Old Kenyon fire. It did not specify a response gauged to the relative severity of each incident, and the water-supply problem had not been corrected. In any case the distance traveled from Mount Vernon to Gambier, and the consequent delay in arriving, still allowed time for a blaze to do major damage or destroy a structure.

It would be the goal of the next local fire department to demonstrate that volunteer firefighters can be as professional in their competence as those who make the service their careers.

The community still had inadequate resources to protect life and property from fires for years after the Old Kenyon fire. Citizens were aware of the problem, but the economic and human requirements for operating an effective local fire department were not present.

A Second Chance: One Step at a Time.

News of the Old Kenyon tragedy spread nation wide. One person who was deeply affected was 1899 Kenyon alumnus Carl R. Ganter. He was a successful New York attorney, a graduate of KMA and Kenyon, who had received an honorary degree from Kenyon and was an emeritus member of the Kenyon Board of Trustees. He had entered the college after graduating from KMA and therefore was aware of the Milnor Hall fire before his arrival and of the tragic fire that ended the academy after his graduation. While a student at Kenyon he was a leader of Alpha Delta Phi fraternity, which was housed in the East Wing of Old Kenyon. The living quarters of the group were destroyed, but his strong loyalty to the fraternity never waned.

The tragedies at the college motivated Ganter to contribute a new (1955), 140 horsepower Ford fire engine, with a three hundred gallon tank for water, and a five hundred gallon per minute front-mount pump (Over the years it came to be known as #1, pumper #1, and Old #1). It came equipped with a Bangor ladder, a long extension ladder that requires stay poles to support it while being extended. It could be raised far enough to allow firefighters to reach the top of any college building of that period. The truck was also equipped with two breathing masks that provided pressurized 100% oxygen to protect firefighters from inhaling heated smoke and gases. The air masks were an important first step in safety and rescue, but without practice drills, GFD volunteers probably did not know how to don them quickly. There still was not an organized and rehearsed group of firefighters who could assure competent use of the engine. There would also have to be additional engines, personnel, and an adequate water supply before "fire department" was an appropriate attribution.

The new Ford truck and equipment were the seeds that eventually grew into the College Township Volunteer Fire Department; but not yet.

Ganter's truck, like the 1941 model, was housed in a college maintenance building, again at the bottom of the college hill. Its presence there left it accessible to Kenyon employees, but it is not clear that there was any regular training with it. It was a better engine than the '41 Chevy, but it could not provide the water required to extinguish a major blaze. A number of individuals knew how to start it, drive it, and get the pump into gear, but no well-led group was schooled and practiced in firefighting, nor was there a crew always available to respond.

That contention is supported by my first half hour long career as a "volunteer." In 1957 as a college admissions counselor, I was walking along Middle Path in my sport coat and slacks when the fire siren sounded. Shortly, maintenance supervisor "Till" Davidson, driving the '55 Ford engine, came to a stop across the street. "Do you want to go with me to fight a fire?" I supposed that volunteering was like the call to form a bucket brigade. The alarm sounds, and people are supposed to join others to fight the fire. I had no idea that knowledge, formal training, or skill was necessary. Why not go? It would be a lot more exciting than looking at grade transcripts of high-school-student applicants for admission. I hopped in, and we drove with lights flashing and siren screaming to a small village east of Gambier. The fire was out by the time we arrived, and we turned around and drove slowly back. I jumped off the running board at Middle Path, across from the post office, and Till took the little engine back down the hill. Long after, I reflected on the fact that no other member of the GFD had shown up to join Till. Neither he nor I had on any kind of protective gear. I did not have the slightest notion what to do if the fire had required me to take some action, but I would have been the best dressed firefighter at the scene. Ganter's truck, and appointing people to operate it, did little to protect the community without a water-supply infrastructure, constant training, maintenance of engines and equipment, and effective leadership.

Finally, with the encouragement and participation of Kenyon Vice President for Finance Samuel S. Lord, Dean of Students Thomas J. Edwards, and village and township officials, a plan to form an effective fire service began to take shape. It was decided that the College Township trustees, who could put a tax on the ballot in the village and township, would be the political subdivision to administer a fire department. The passage of a tax levy assured about five thousand dollars per year to invest in the project.

Attracting volunteers was no problem. The leaders were willing to cast their net widely, and there was a democratic willingness to consider anyone who wanted to help, except women. The college was eager to contribute Ganter's gift ("Old # 1") and to construct a fire station behind the Kenyon Alumni House, beside the village meeting hall on Scott Lane, about a hundred feet from Chase Avenue in the center of town. By 1963, a thirty foot by sixty five foot fire station had been constructed for $13,476 and old #1 and an eleven hundred gallon tanker truck were in the equipment bays. Fifteen volunteers received twenty eight hours of training from a state approved fire instructor. Now it was the College Township Volunteer Fire Department (CTVFD). Later "Volunteer" was dropped from the title in order to stifle any connotation that volunteers are not really professionals at firefighting. It became CTFD. It took a few years to find an effective leader.

Volunteer departments already existed within small communities throughout Knox County. The Danville and Fredericktown departments were governed by their villages. They offered fire protection contracts to their villages and neighboring townships. There had been a fire department in Centerburg since the 1880s. Therefore, experience in organizing and training volunteers was available in the county, and from state-certified instructors. The neighboring departments provided the potential for the mutual aid agreements essential to fighting major blazes.

Acquiring equipment, engines, and good people does little to improve matters unless there is an infrastructure that can support them. In this case a fundamental requirement was a water system. It took an additional fifteen years after the formation of CTFD for the village's 250,000-gallon water tower and larger underground water lines and hydrants to be ready. The system can now replace water to the tower at fourteen hundred gallons per minute and maintain a steady flow to engines for four hours. Firefighters can have confidence that water will be available wherever they go in the village. Credit for that goes to volunteer firefighter and long-time mayor Richard Baer, whose terms in office extended from 1966 to 1989. His service to CTFD still continues but now as the "fire house cook."

By the mid 1970s, the department was gaining recognition as one of the county's best and had taken on the challenge of making me a firefighter. It was rising to that status because it finally had the leader with the talents necessary to engineer all the components into an effective working whole. He was a brilliant manager of people who was respected, even by Harvey and the other old-timers who had served in the GFD. He was an unequalled salesman in getting the college and local officials to recognize the wisdom of his requests for financial support. He was a scholar of the fire service and masterful instructor for all aspects of fire training. For the first time, the CTFD had a professional's knowledge and skills at its helm. He was L. Hobart "Hobe" Brown, midlevel executive at a local manufacturing plant, farmer, mechanic, and fire fighter. Everyone in the department wanted to work hard to please him, and he tried to instill pride in each firefighter's accomplishments. Under his leadership the department became well known and respected throughout the state. It earned the financial support necessary to replace the little cement block starter set on Scott Lane with a first-class building. It earned the best fire insurance rating in the county. It acquired powerful engines, modern equipment, and could staff them with people who knew what to do at a fire. It put out fires before they destroyed property and killed people. Hobe had the intelligence to let the guys have fun at the annual Christmas party and the courage to stand up to the "competition" in Mount Vernon. His one goal, before all others, was to have firefighters who could put out fires quickly. In its very first years CTFD had on its roster a few local residents who had appropriate skills and experience. They were available at any time to respond to the town fire siren. Why they were so available, however, might alarm readers and therefore deserves some elaboration.

3
HOW "REPEAL" HELPED CREATE CTFD

A fire department needs skilled people who can operate and maintain fire engines, have the physical strength to fight fires, and the agility to climb ladders to rescue people from burning buildings. A volunteer fire department needs people who will do all those things for no pay. A liberal arts college faculty is an unlikely place to find many who qualify. In the early 1960s, more than half the male population of Gambier consisted of academic savants or the teenage student transients. Others were eager to volunteer, but they had no relevant experience.

The organizers of CTFD were faced with finding recruits from the male population of Gambier who could put out a fire, right away. The pool of those candidates was small.

One place seemed immediately obvious to those who really knew the village population. The uninformed observer, however, might anticipate some potential drawbacks. The best candidates were among the patrons of the one and only local bar. To the founding officials, it had immediate potential to produce the needed talent: certainly far more potential than the "halls of ivy."

That bar is where they were found, and some even had some directly relevant experience. A social stratum had developed there that made the responsible authorities comfortable with seeking recruits from off those bar stools. The beer was not the only reason the group was there. It was the one place in the village where local people of common interests and experiences could sit around and talk and laugh and escape from the solitude of a day of hard labor.

That culture likely was in its second generation by the time the call went out for CTFD volunteers. "Dorothy's" had opened a few years after the social revolution that swept the country from 1920 to 1933. I suspect that Gambier had been relatively unimpressed by the Eighteenth Amendment. Except for the Dillinger gang's 1933 robbery of the People's Bank, during which banker J. Ray Brown was shot in the hand, the village was pretty quiet and it was almost as remote as when Bishop Chase had caused it. It did need a place for people to socialize, spread rumors, and discuss events much less exciting than the bank robbery.

My theory about Gambier's ease of recovery from prohibition is based upon comparative observations during the twenty years after the repeal. Specifically, some communities recovered (or regressed, depending on your convictions) more quickly than others.

I grew up in the 1930s. Before I was born, making and selling alcohol had become not only a sin but a crime. It became a crime because politicians who did not vote to outlaw "demon rum" could not be reelected. Back then, politicians wanted to be reelected more than anything else. The Eighteenth Amendment placed alcoholic beverages in ICU on the critical list for a time, but Prohibition soon resulted in a profitable speakeasy industry and a thriving canning jar business. It was quickly evident that people drank anyway, and only outlaws made a profit on the stuff. It became politically prudent (politically safe) to make booze legal again. Prohibition could, after all, be sustained just as ineffectively from the pulpit. Repeal was the last great victory for the principle of separation of church and state and should receive some credit for the early success of the CTFD.

Recovery from the effects of not drinking booze during the thirties and forties was more rapid in some communities than in others. At my house, it was gradual but steady. All through the 1940s my boyhood was dominated by the superego inhibition to sin via alcohol. Some of my friends endured those pangs of guilt courageously. My superego prevailed. Then I went to college. My beer drinking had a sudden onset but was tempered by the threat of vomiting and expulsion. I attended Denison University as an undergraduate. It was still very much a Baptist college, and even its village of Granville was very, very, dry, except of course, in my frat house.

At the same time, twenty-five miles north of Granville, a different culture prevailed. Most residents of Gambier had long stopped discussing whether drinking was bad and agreed that only too much was not good. Among the liberal academics, "too much" was best defined by the drinker. I arrived there three years after graduating from Denison in 1952. Kenyon was different from Denison in many ways: it was all-male, far from anywhere, and a place where almost everyone drank. It was Episcopalian, not Baptist.

I was hired as Kenyon's assistant director of admissions. I quickly discovered that even some of the Gambier residents who shared my conservative Protestant upbringing, drank. There were some who never had been uncomfortable mediating their social lives with a beer. Do not get the impression that the whole community was made up of alcoholics; some, but no not everyone. Typical of academic communities it depends upon how one defines the term. For example, legend, and good authority hold that the entire maintenance staff enjoyed a little nip from time to time during the work day.

The Kenyon faculty and their families comprised about half the village population. I doubt that abolition had ever inhibited the flow of the grape or the grain for them. They were mostly from preFranklin Roosevelt, heavily Catholic, Blue states or had gone to school at an Ivy League school, or to Oxford in England. Alcohol was an integral part of their sophisticated lives.

They knew with certainty that abolition would not work. I am told that they ignored it, but their source of the illegal stuff is still a secret.

I got over the culture shock, but the vestiges of inhibitions spawned by my Methodist and Baptist acculturation were now a liability. The surrounding county and township were solid Red state, but the two groups could share the same bar without fighting. The social glue of the community was beer and booze.

Kenyon students got "smashed" and acted crazy, like when they led a horse up to the fourth floor of a dormitory. At the same time, they were very comfortable talking philosophy, literature, and science with faculty and administrators while sipping a martini. That seemed odd at first, but I concluded that it was what people expected if you were to fit in at Kenyon. I tried for a while but eventually realized that I was not a martini or manhattans guy and reverted to beer. If I had not, I would never have become a firefighter at CTFD. The firefighters were beer drinkers.

The Stem Cell That Created CTFD

Half way down the hill from the college was a cosmopolitan group of social drinkers. The diplomatic genius of Dorothy should be credited with creating that thriving commerce. She was Dorothy, as in "Dorothy's Lunch." She required that the entire span of local social and intellectual strata meet peacefully and enjoy genial conversation at her establishment. She had the power to enforce that goal because it was the only public place to get a drink in town, and if you did not behave, the nearest relief was five miles away. Peace was also encouraged by the fact that Dorothy's husband, Gene, kept a gun under the bar. The core group of evening patrons was composed of men of the college, village, and township.

It could be argued (by me) that Dorothy had made drinking an asset not only to those constituencies but ultimately to local fire protection. The ethos for democratic consumption of alcoholic beverages for the whole community evolved there. The establishment was three doors east and down hill from the Methodist Church and a block from the college campus. The entry was at the side door of the basement under Dorothy's two-story frame house which eventually would be only three blocks from the new fire station.

College folks, village folks, and residents of the townships surrounding Gambier and College Township frequented Dorothy's Lunch. It had become an institution long before I arrived and not long after repeal. My friend Don was a student at Kenyon before he went off to fight in World War II. He met his life-long love, Marion, while he was not studying. She was born in Gambier and fondly recalls Dorothy telling her to "scat" when, as a young girl, she entered the bar unaccompanied by an adult. That dates Dorothy's as thriving in the early 1940's, less than a decade after repeal and a couple of decades before Granville got wet.

Dorothy told many others to leave, too. It was her strict code of bar room conduct and motherly caring for old timers, college students, professors, and kids that had erased any latent psychology of abolitionary sin in Gambier long before the ethos of WCTUism vanished elsewhere.

Families and anyone else were welcome to order from the food menu through dinnertime. Students from the grade school across the street had to have a note from principal L. E. "Buck" Law before Dorothy would allow them to buy lunch there. But in the early evening, the all-male students of Kenyon, the almost all-male faculty, and the working men of the village and township took to their regular table, booth, or bar stool in a room that was only about twenty feet wide by fifty feet long. There were few women at Dorothy's, and almost none of them considered young. That demographic almost eliminated the biggest source of behavior problems: no women, no male fights.

I did not go to Dorothy's often during my initial three year stay in Gambier which ended in 1958. When I returned ten years later to teach at Kenyon, the bar had not changed. I think the same local guys I had seen before were there still happily talking about crops, or presenting their views on international, national, state, county, township, or village political issues, and gossiping.

Once in a while a small class or a seminar session left the Kenyon campus and held a less formal session there. Their intense concentration on the topic of the day censored the background cacophony. A stranger who came to town and wanted to know about the village and college needed only to take a booth at Dorothy's and listen in on conversations for an hour. The subjects of conversation spanned the price of corn to elegiac pentameter. Bob Gorsuch, brother of Dorothy and known as "Feedgrinder" at the Gambier Co-op feed mill was the authority on the former. His audience at the bar would be a different subset of folks from those toward the middle of the room. At tables beyond the bar, from the 1940s into the 1970s, it would not be surprising if an English professor was discussing literature and poetry with the eager participation of Kenyon students such as E. L. Doctorow and Robert Lowell while gathered around joined tables. Carl Djerasi might have been there, too, but he delayed writing much poetry until he had succeeded with his research that led to "the pill." It is certain that Paul Newman was there conversing with Dorothy or with students whose motivations were more recreational than scholarly. He and Dorothy became close friends, and he returned many times to visit her after he perfected his craft. Jonathon Winters was at Kenyon long enough to find Dorothy's, too, but not much longer. Her ability to gain the respect of all

Dorothy's Lunch. Students at the table, locals at the bar. (Greenslade Special Collections and Archives, Kenyon College, Gambier, Ohio. Used by Permission.)

who entered the side door reveals how special Dorothy was. She was more than proprietor, more than bartender, more than cook. The people who came there were more to her than just customers.

In a way, one could say that Dorothy and her establishment lived long enough to assure the village of an effective fire department. The culture of Gambier and the college changed when both were gone. After Dorothy died, the building remained empty for a number of years. Most of the volunteers who were regulars at the bar are gone, too. Ironically, none of them was around when the CTFD of the new millennium burned Dorothy's Lunch to the ground as a training exercise. By coincidence, Don and Marion were in town and watched the blaze. He was the only old timer there to watch. Marion was now old enough to pass Dorothy's intuitive "carding" eye.

The durable relationships formed among the locals at Dorothy's eventually provided a solid core of volunteer firemen who respected one another's talents. Anyone who knows volunteer fire departments also knows that the social culture of the members is what determines the strength and durability of the group. Without that cohesion, the rewards do not exceed the cost in time and effort. Some of the guys at the bar had the manual skills that are essential to effective fire fighting. Not all the volunteers who served CTFD were Dorothy's veterans, but there was a nucleus of talents, a core group. Whether they liked each other or not, the time shared at Dorothy's allowed them to know what they could expect from each other. They knew who was competent, who was bluff, who would be easy to work with, and who not. Without such knowledge it might have taken years to build the relationships necessary for an effective fire service. Getting the pieces in place and cemented together was another matter. The jovial banter at the bar was one thing but beneath that, the men were independent prideful individuals. The first problem would be to get any of them to agree that someone else would be qualified to lead.

It was clear to the community and college leaders that GFD was inadequate. Creating a publicly funded fire department required that a group of enlightened college officials and local civic leaders cooperate to make it happen. In 1961, they committed their time and influence to provide the resources of money, building construction funds, and a governmental structure to make it possible. If it worked it would be the first time in nearly 150 years that the community had effective fire protection.

Village councils, township trustees, and college executives usually do not know how to operate the engines or the pumps, use a fire axe, climb a ladder safely, or direct a combative hose stream at a fire. They could supply the money, and encouragement but without volunteers with specific talents to do the firefighting no amount of earnestness could solve the problem. The guys who could do those jobs right away were on the bar stools at Dorothy's.

"Feedgrinder"; Matthews, the village mechanic; Jim "Fergie" Frye; Davey Clark; Bill Lahmon; Chuck Imel and the young Mayor Baer were regulars at Dorothy's in the 1960s. Banker Charles William "Bill" Smith, Homer Keller, Carroll Dial, and Pete Woolison came in from time to time, if only for a good meal.

All those guys had family roots in the community and either lived in the village or within a mile or two. That meant that they knew most of the people who lived in the area and worked at the college or in the village. They also knew all the local roads and where almost everyone lived for a mile or more from Dorothy's in every direction. Knowing the roads, landmarks, where people lived, and the quickest route is essential to any emergency service. The CTFD'ers from Dorothy's had none of that to learn. They had lived and worked in the community all their lives. If you called for help, a map was never needed to get to you. The problem was how to get them off their gossipy bar stools to spend enough time to become an effective firefighting unit.

From Bar Stool to Firehouse Turned Out to be a Short Distance

I do not know who came up with the idea, but it worked. The leadership group furnished the new firehouse with a beer dispenser. The collegiality of

Dorothy's establishment was magically transferred, undiminished. There were now two places in Gambier where you could sit and have a beer among old friends. One great advantage of the fire department was that the dispenser would open on Sundays.

Maybe the most important factor in fighting fires is the time from alarm to the time the engines roll out the door. Gambier had the quickest-responding volunteer department in the county. A crew was never more than three blocks or ten feet from the engines seven days a week. That must have been a sobering thought for the rest of the village.

PART TWO

BEHIND THE LOCKED DOOR OF THE FIREHOUSE

Every volunteer fire department develops a unique social culture. At first, the new College Township Volunteer Fire Department (CTFD) was mainly staffed with long-time local residents. At its core was a small group of men who shared competence in the mechanical trades, familiarity with the local geography, a little experience with fire engines, and a knowledge of the local families whose generations had populated the community.

They were supplemented by "newcomers" whom they could teach some skills of firefighting. It was a <u>FIRE</u> department, and other types of emergencies were of little interest. The best way to envision the dynamics of the group is to become familiar with some of its central figures. That small clique established the pattern for day-to-day activities at the station. They could do that because some of them were at the firehouse almost all day every day, Sunday through Saturday, and in the evenings, sometimes quite late. If one among them was missing, the next best guess was Dorothy's Lunch. That small group asserted its leadership and established a hierarchy based primarily on a single criterion: "How long you've been <u>on</u>." They would not have regarded themselves as a social culture, but they were. Impartial observers might have said it was a private club with an exclusive membership.

4

THE CHIEF WITH THE CAST IRON EGO

One of the first challenges for the new CTFD was to find a chief who would not be intimidated by the self-reliant individualists from Dorothy's that would staff his department. A chief has to be a respected leader and able to gain the support of the community. Gambier residents Jim Kunkle and Leo Wolfe were the first chiefs and had those important qualities. After a year or so, however, they were unable to continue as the department leaders. Their replacement, Chuck Imel, was very good at putting the department in the newspaper but had some problems gaining the respect of his firefighters and, in fact, many others. Fortunately, he either did not notice or wasn't concerned. He was quite self confident, highly motivated, and on balance the department benefited from his term as chief.

Imel, (he was always referred to by his last name) was fairly short, about five feet eight, and had an ample girth, salt-and-pepper hair, and a ruddy complexion. He was not really handsome, but not homely either. A few seconds in his presence and it seemed certain that no one had ever heard him whisper, and no one had ever been unable to hear him.

As I listened to long-time residents of the village, I gathered that Imel was regarded by many of them as a buffoon for his management style in many of the various positions he had held over the years. He had been swimming and basketball coach at the college in the early 1940's. Later, he was coach of all sports at Gambier High School during World War II, then village constable, owner of a summer camp for children across the road from his detox center for alcoholics, township trustee and fire chief. As town constable his decision to cite students for jaywalking led to placarded parodies, and student protests. But those and other reactions to his authoritarian initiatives bounced off his deaf ego. Some people thought he did a fairly good job in those activities, but they still thought he was a buffoon

Before going on the wagon, Imel had been awarded a dedicated bar stool at Dorothy's Lunch. In that sense he had the appropriate lineage for membership in the new department. As Kenyon basketball coach, he loudly criticized his student athletes who came in with friends to have a social beer. His players saw irony in their well-oiled coach loudly taking offense at their enjoyment while occupying his perch at the bar. Eventually his problem became a problem for the President of the College. His fondness for alcoholic beverages was better tolerated by subsequent employers.

During World War II he took over the coaching reins of the Gambier High School Pirates. Dick Ralston, son of Paul Ralston, who was head of Kenyon maintenance at the time of the Old Kenyon fire, remembers his coach well. Dick was on the Gambier High basketball team coached by Imel. At the county tournament, Imel showed up with an inspired addition to their uniforms. The team ran onto the court in their Gambier Pirate-logo warm-up jackets, but those were supplemented by a pirate's feather-plumed hat. The innovation was not well received by many fans and somewhat embarrassed the team, but their reactions did not temper Imel's booming voice as he issued mandates from the bench.

Around the time he became fire chief, he stopped drinking.

Still, Imel's loud voice spoke with authority on most matters. Its amplitude was not sensitive to the likely response of his audience. He was, however, an energetic public relations man for the department. The Mount Vernon News carried story after story about the accomplishments and progress of the new department, accompanied by photos of Chief Imel. An action photo shows him gesturing and issuing orders at a grass fire while dressed in shorts and a tee shirt. It must have been a hot day.

Toward the end of his term as chief, Harvey and some of the other old-timers played pranks on Imel. Once, they set a little trash can on fire in the village and listened to him bellow out orders to board all the engines and race to quench the minute conflagration.

His arbitrary management style once led to important trouble for the department. Imel refused to send engines and firefighters to assist the neighboring Danville Fire Department with a fire one mile east of Gambier. It was in the township protected by the Danville group but was much closer in time and distance to Gambier. It was a matter debated in the local paper and it embarrassed CTFD.

Members of CTFD were critical of that decision. The grumbling in the department may have implicitly contributed to Imel's decision to retire. His successor, Hobe Brown, was quick to solidify a relationship with the Danville group and it has remained one of mutual respect ever since. In the twenty first century, automatic response policies are rapidly converting those territorial disputes into pride in cooperation at emergency scenes.

Imel was approaching retirement age when I met him in 1970. I learned that as a trustee of College Township he had been instrumental in advocating the creation of CTFD. I was told that he had been chief for all but a year or so of its existence and had recently resigned to become head of the Knox County Civil Defense Agency. (Today the organization would be called the

Chuck Imel hearing Kenyon students protest his decision to give them tickets for jaywalking while he was Gambier's law enforcement officer.

EMA, Emergency Management Agency.) Imel remained loyal to CTFD, in that position. It provided each county resources dedicated to disaster preparedness. The primary benefit to us was access to the military surplus center in Columbus, where acres of emergency gear were made available to volunteer fire departments. As our former chief, Imel encouraged us to go to the warehouse and pick up anything we could use. The stuff was not free, but could be claimed for token charges.

Imel was sure, for example, we should claim the helicopter that was sitting at the surplus center, available for the asking. It was a tantalizing prospect, but upon reflection and discussion, it was concluded that since no one in the department knew how to fly a helicopter and there was no place to land or house it, we should regretfully pass up the opportunity.

Chief Brown and I did find a number of items that were useful. As his new assistant, I picked up a field dental office complete with a foot-pedal-driven drill. A parachute priced at five dollars was a steal. In fact these were not completely frivolous acquisitions. The dental office included dozens of stainless-steel medical instruments, tweezers, antiseptics, and so forth. Instruments we could not use were given to the Knox County health department.

Remnants of the items that were not used in emergency work could be adapted to the members' personal needs. The miles of dental floss were important to my dental hygiene for about twenty years. After the parachute's lines were removed to supplement our rope supply on the rescue truck, the chute was put to use under my big old apple tree. I tied it to the lower lateral limbs and cut out its center. As apples fell in the autumn they rolled down to the hole and into a basket, thus saving the trouble of bending over to pick them up by hand, and freeing me to spend more time at the firehouse.

Major acquisitions from military surplus came in the form of a khaki-colored tanker truck and a former army field ambulance. The versatile skills of the firefighters turned those into vehicles of enormous value. They served for several years until we could afford genuine used fire engines.

After it was decided that Knox County was not a likely target for a nuclear attack, the state ordered counties to disband the civil defense bomb shelters. Imel saw to it that we "scored." The shelters were established after World War II and were merely rooms in the basements of public buildings. The Gambier shelter was under the post office. It yielded heaps of medical supplies, cots, splints, and other materials. The five gallon buckets filled with hard candies and chocolate were not as obviously relevant to our mission, but everyone in the department agreed they would have come in handy at a fire scene to nourish exhausted fire fighters had they not been consumed before the next fire.

Age finally caught up with Imel, and we seldom saw him. He was controversial in almost everything he did, but if he had not been willing to take the lead and aggressively promote the department's needs, no one else seems likely to have done that. He was, in a way, courageous to try to lead the individualists that comprised that first roster of volunteers. He ignored their abuse and never flagged in his dedication to CTFD. Like the rest of the volunteers he was a good person with some flaws. His style just made his flaws more obvious. For all his bluster, he provided aggressive leadership and fuel for the meeting-room culture. The department was really ready to welcome Chief Hobe Brown and help him create a model volunteer fire department.

5

AT THE FIREHOUSE MORNING, NOON, AND NIGHT

Forty years ago most volunteer fire departments, including ours, did not fight fires very often and emergency medical services had not been invented. Each person had some relevant talent to contribute to the department's mission but was not required to exhibit the skill often. The fact that the members met regularly under the firehouse roof led to formation of a unique social climate. That culture was not well known to the public, and in some ways, that was probably a good thing. In truth, the activities that go on in a small volunteer fire department are most accurately revealed by knowing its members rather than by reporting on the one or two major fires each year. Some members could create excitement without any flames. The "fly on the wall" at CTFD saw pretty much the same subset of individuals, and the same interactions played out in the meeting room every day.

It took several years after its formation to organize CTFD and train enough new members who could be depended upon to respond to fires. At first the roster listed about thirty names, but only a dozen or so would in fact attack a fire. There was a gap in the perception of many new untrained volunteers as to what was expected. For some, their preconceived idea was of coming to the station only when the town's siren sounded and then holding a hose to squirt water on a fire from a safe distance. Then they found out that there was regular mandatory training, and after one experience of wrestling a 2 ½" hose line under 125 pounds of pressure that is acting like a boa constrictor on amphetamines, they were either gone or contributed in other ways.

The core group was made up of long-time residents who knew the people of the village, township, and surrounding areas. They knew who was related to whom, who lived where, the first names of everyone's previous generations, what church the families attended, where the men worked, where the kids went to school, which cemetery housed the family plots, and who was already in them. In that sense the "mature" members, provided an immediate "data base" of local information. Those local natives had learned all that information as they grew up. Locals form the bedrock of every volunteer fire department. Their knowledge made them assets to the department even if some of them did not fight the fires.

Similar to other volunteer departments a diverse bunch of guys entered the CTFD doors at the 1970's firehouse, not in the contemporary sense of diverse, because there were no women or ethnic others, except for former Minneapolis Lakers star Bob Harrison. Bob was the Kenyon basketball coach and an active member of the original CTFD group in 1963. He may have become a Native American later but at that time he was an Indian. Diversity was based upon talent and occupational status. Some were in manufacturing at local plants, some were farmers, tradesmen, college employees, a couple of professors, one or two mature Kenyon students, an occasional would-be Episcopal priest from the divinity school, a mid-management manufacturing executive, a banker, retired guys, and so on. All but a few had a couple of things in common: being reared on the farm and/or manual skills. Some were "characters" in the sense of being memorable personalities. They were like one of firehouse cook Harvey Mathew's soups, a uniquely appealing blend, but sometimes difficult to understand how the ingredients resulted in a laudable end product. A minority were the real firefighters and leaders in the department's mission. Others were never regulating the pressure at an engine's pump, ventilating the smoke from a hole they had chopped high on a roof, or holding the nozzle at the end of a hose while charging through a door that had been busted open, but they all contributed in their own way. Volunteer fire departments had been like that for decades, if not centuries.

If one dropped in at CTFD any day of the week between 8 a.m and midnight, two or three Gambier natives would be present. One could drop by but not enter. Nonmembers had to knock at the side door, since the door was always locked. That fact communicated an aura of a private club that was not entirely in error. After 4 p.m. there was a bigger assemblage when some members got off work.

People preferred to stand or sit and talk across the top of the kitchen/pinochle table from their favorite vantage point in the room. Each of the regulars had staked out a two-square-foot area that was understood to be deeded to their footprints. In that sense anyone who came looking for a specific person just had to look toward his reserved space. Sometimes there was serious discussion echoing around the room but mostly there was good-natured joking at each other's expense.

In addition to the table, the room's furnishings included well-worn chairs for seating at the card games, and a tan leather couch on the west wall. The chairs were made of vinyl-covered plywood seats mounted within a frame of chrome-plated metal tubing. An old oak desk chair, that could both pivot and rock, sat in front of the homemade communications table in the northwest corner. The microphone and the two-way "fire band" radio transmitter sat waiting for a disaster. It constantly monitored the emergency "traffic" of departments over a thirty mile radius. Everyone enjoyed vicariously criticizing the actions of those neighboring volunteer departments from the uninformed vantage point of the radio room.

The call letters of our radio had been designated by the Federal Communications Commission (FCC). All our transmissions were supposed to

Davey Clark on duty in the firehouse kitchen getting ready to end training with "Last Call."

include that identification: KIZ 484. There were, in fact, a lot of FCC rules to be followed when transmitting emergency "traffic." The only one I was ever told was NO SWEARING.

On winter afternoons, Shoppy Parker's tall slender frame would enter by the side door and his "yep, yep, yep" greeting went out to the assembled group. Since most of the fire house regulars were less than five feet nine inches in height, he looked really tall. He stood in front of the radiator in his long brown overcoat, his hands lifting up its tails to let some heat rise up and warm his skinny, nearly eighty-year-old, butt. He had been in elementary school when he witnessed the tragic KMA fire, and as a life long resident, he had accumulated all the important facts and gossip from the community ever

From left: Hobe Brown, "Grandpa" Gorsuch, and Harvey Matthews celebrating a new batch of "Old Firehouse" mustard.

since. He did not initiate rumors or discussions of early Gambier history, but was respected as a reference who could supply information, or correct errors, but only if asked.

Shoppy was a widower and lived alone in a house on Ward Street, a couple of blocks from the station, so relief from his boredom and loneliness was only as far away as his key in the firehouse door. His daughter Jane, who is now ninety, was raised in Gambier. She married a Kenyon student who became a physician. The couple checked on Shoppy regularly by phone, but they lived in Michigan when they were not doing medical missionary work in South America. In 1970 he was still working in the chemistry department at Kenyon. He and Fergie Frye were lab assistants, but Shoppy's job was in jeopardy because of his age. Shoppy had once been the town shoe repairman and almost always an elected public servant. He and I served on the village sewer board after my election to that post. It was my only venture into politics, which one could say started and ended at the bottom.

Don't get the idea that we at the station were babysitting an old codger who could no longer make a useful contribution to the fire service. Although not fighting fires anymore, Shoppy would still drive a vehicle if no one else was at the station to bring it to the emergency scene. There were other ways he participated, too. When a young guy in his twenty's tried to crash the Christmas party, Shoppy reached across the bar and decked the guy with a good right cross. The "kid" left without another word.

Whenever I entered the kitchen, Harvey Matthews was presiding over conversation from behind the serving counter. It was actually a four-foot-high two-foot-by-six-foot bar rescued from some tavern. Occasionally it served its original purpose but only in special circumstances. The room could get crowded, around 4 p.m. The two square feet of floor dedicated to Harvey were located where he could lean on the bar and relieve his back pain. The bar also provided some safety while he was refereeing a verbal dispute he had started. Harvey was chief cook for the weekly meals. Fergie Frye had his dedicated footprints an arm's length east of Harvey. Fergie assisted with the cooking in a relationship that was kind of like kitchen helper to the executive chef. Fergie was a bit younger and shorter than the chef and knew better than to get involved in Harvey's trouble making plots. In fact he mostly stood silent but occasionally vocalized a single, long, modulated, "yeaaah." The "yeaaahs" were not relevant to the topic at hand or, as far as was obvious, anything else. At the end of every school year, Fergie and Shoppy could be observed carrying out the leftovers from the chem lab. They dumped them over the edge of the hill behind the lab and down the slope toward the river.

The other retired native who was present all day was Bob Gorsuch. He sat in the oak desk chair and participated in all the conversations. He was an active fire fighter within his physical limits. Very few in the room called him Bob.

Who else was in the room varied with the day and time of day, but there was a hierarchy, much like a pecking order, that prevailed with unspoken rigidity. It regulated speaking order. It was based first on who had been "on" the department longest. Those who were born here and on the department when it started were at the top of the pecking order. The rule meant that Harvey, Bob, and a few others, like Mayor Baer, held the stage most of the time. Fergie could have chimed in, but he didn't say much besides "yeaaah." Another of those with privileges was one-legged Bill Lahmon. He was Bob Gorsuch's son-in-law and arrived at CTFD after work, too. He was not much handicapped by his handicap. He was a real terror at the square dances and always eager to grab a hose line and help out at a fire. The only time his absent leg caused a problem was when he jumped out of bed as the fire siren sounded and started to run before he strapped on his wooden leg. There were only minor injuries.

Chief Brown usually arrived after the rest were assembled in the kitchen. He said very little but stood in the doorway to the equipment bay and chuckled non stop at the conversations going on around him.

There were occasional ego wars within the group, some disputes, and an occasional member who turned out to be a bad apple. Those problems got resolved without combat behind the closed fire house doors. Marital and extramarital problems were no big deal and in some cases okay to bring up in the presence of the male principal, if he could take a joke.

Those members who were new on the department, or "at the college" were peers at the bottom of the pecking order and were expected to listen, learn, and not speak unless asked an embarrassing question. Professors, especially those new to the fire service, were phantoms not to be acknowledged as present until they did something that was deemed either valuable or fodder for ridicule.

Being noticed could be achieved by a new member in a number of ways. One volunteer, a young professor who taught in the Kenyon Religion Department, qualified when he came to the station for first-aid after being bitten by his newly adopted stray German Shepherd. The stray had objected to having its teeth brushed. That event was accepted as empirical verification that college professors were spiritual beings ignorant of the consequences of living on earth.

The side door opened and closed many times each day from early morning to near midnight, but Harvey and Robert B. "Bob" "Grandpa" "Feedgrinder" Gorsuch spent their waking hours at the station. It should not be assumed that the two were only idling their time away. Each provided useful services to the department when not idling. They were retired from their occupations but still played important roles in emergencies for the first few years after I became a member.

Davey Clark usually arrived about an hour after the regulars were assembled. He was employed at a factory in Mount Vernon. His weekday routine never varied. The hour before he arrived at CTFD was spent five miles away at the Moose Lodge (the "Moose") which was a handy one block from the factory. Eileen, his wife, sometimes worried about his whereabouts in late afternoon and maybe, too, about his responsibility to keep the firehouse beer dispenser filled. The plus side of his habits was that she never had to make more than two phone calls to find him. The "business" phone at the station was often ringing around five thirty but someone other than Davey had to answer it.

Eileen was very patient with Davey and he with everyone. Actually, one could never tell when Davey was excited, or depressed, amused, or irritated. His temperament was set at "even," and it enabled him to remain calm and under control at all times. Around the meeting room table there was some allusion to the easy chair just off the production line at work where Davey could contemplate getting up after break. Eileen was the nurse at a different local factory, and their governors were at compatible settings. At fires, Davey's pace was not noticeably accelerated. He was fine with pump operations, unflappable and reliable, but not the guy for an interior attack at a structure fire.

Years later, Davey took over as firehouse cook when Harvey departed and his own days as a firefighter were over. His face now smiles down from a plaque with a copper likeness of him hung over the sink at the new (1978) station. Beneath his portrait are the words "Last Call." For many years Davey's "last call!" reverberated out over the engines and signaled that the evening meal was ready and that it was time to end Tuesday night training or Sunday inspection. His voice still haunts the station at meal times. A few of us were there when Eileen summoned us to what turned out to be the "last call" for Davey. It silenced that welcome shout that had always ended a work session at the station and hastened us to dine in warm fellowship at the firehouse. As long as the plaque is there, his call will echo in our memories. I would contend that the Tuesday evening when Davey shouted his final "last call" was also the last call for CTFD as a FIRE department. Davey was almost the final link to the old-guys, beer-cooler department of the 1960s thru 1980s. It was securely on its way to its new role as an emergency medical service.

Some Volunteers Contribute Much But Fight No Fires.

One might assume that a fire department would require that every member be ready to brave the dangers of every blaze; not so. The fact that a person had taken the required basic fire training course sometime in his life and yet did not actually fight fires was seldom a subject for discussion. It was a cooperative enterprise that earned an attribution of noble public service. Besides, if there ever was an emergency when too few firefighters were available, the "backups" would pitch in and do the best they could. Curiously once one passed the basic fire course the certification lasted for a lifetime. Roger Hite passed the course with distinction and left the department in the late 1960s. When he came back almost forty years later, his certification was still valid.

When I came on in 1970 there were two volunteers who did not brave the flames and the heat but supported the department in very different ways. Harvey Mathews was one of them. He and banker Bill Smith were examples of citizens who, in those days, did not go out the door on an engine often but played an important role in support of the department's mission.

Harvey.

In the early 1970s, Harvey Mathews was the most valuable man at the firehouse. The reasons were not all related to fire fighting. Harvey was not only indispensable during emergencies but the cook, a gossip, a ruthless agitator, and the arbiter of the cultural milieu. He ruled the room, ran the show, gave the orders, and stimulated the humor. He had been a member of the old GFD, a regular at Dorothy's, and a basic building block of talent that formed the new CTFD. He was bright, perfectionistic, hard working, and prideful in whatever he did, but in no need of praise from others. He was his own judge. He was at the fire house every day, and he did much more than stand around, drink beer, and agitate others.

When an emergency was phoned to the department it was Harvey who answered. He knew exactly where the caller lived and the best route to get there, and anticipated the need for help from other agencies. He knew department policies on burning brush, pumping basements, and getting cats out of trees. He was <u>the</u> reference source. He diagnosed all the problems of the fire engines and knew the history of everything local.

Harvey's profession had been as the only auto mechanic in Gambier. Before he was pained by his years of wrestling with every kind of auto that lived in the village he was as physically engaged as anyone in the department. His customers recognized him as their brilliant automotive general practitioner and surgeon who never charged too much. The wear and tear of working on autos had resulted in back problems that kept him off the engines at fires. He never complained. When CTFD was created, however, he performed major surgery on a fire engine that had broken down en route from the manufacturer to another fire department in Ohio. The builder said CTFD could have it if we could tow it to Gambier and restore its heart. Harvey did. He also reconditioned the 1959 Cadillac hearse; painted it red, and it became the department's first ambulance. The fact that he could drive it one hundred miles per hour to the city limits of Mount Vernon and then coast a mile to Mercy Hospital was a great source of pride to him and of terror for those tending the victim in the back.

He was also a multitalented craftsman who constructed and operated the two-way radio console in the northwest corner of the kitchen. But his recreational love was mischief and controversy in the firehouse kitchen. He stood behind the bar with a pipe stuck in the corner of his mouth, eyes searching for a soft spot in the ego of whoever was there. His genius lay in remaining completely untouched by the flames he ignited in the psyche of his targets. Someone would comment about what had happened on the old Dial property out on Big Run Road twenty years ago, and Harvey would start a verbal fight over who lived there in 1931. Once he got some heat generated in the dispute, he would withdraw to the sidelines with a twinkle in his eyes and let the fireworks flare. His other joy was relating the latest gossip. His eyes projected laser beams of delight when he learned that a former sheriff was spotted climbing out the rear window of a home occupied by a couple, while the man of the house was supposed to have been at work longer than he was.

It is not an exaggeration to assert that there is not a more important factor in establishing a positive culture in a fire department than sitting down together and enjoying a social meal with comrades. In the department' early days, Harvey prepared the 10 p.m. meal for Tuesday night training session and breakfast after Sunday morning inspection. The meals inverted the recommended food pyramid, but they were perfect in the eyes of the rank and file.

Harvey was indispensable for other reasons, too. He invented "Old Firehouse Mustard." It was his secret recipe. He and a selected few helpers, Fergie, Davey, and Mayor Baer would gather in the kitchen with all the raw materials on an early weekend morning and work all day producing a big batch of the stuff. In the evening another crew was brought in to seal the Ball canning jars, stick "Old Firehouse Mustard" labels on the quart jars, and place them in cardboard cartons. The mustard was a better public relations tool for the department than putting out fires, and it brought in more money than the chicken roasts. "Harv" ruled the kitchen for many years and then he left. It was not completely clear why. His next venue was on Middle Path of the village selling his canned pickles. People bought them by the case.

Harvey the legend lives on, but firehouse mustard is gone. When he left CTFD he gave the secret formula to Mayor Baer and Davey Clark, who succeeded him as cooks. They kept producing it for a few years. The mutation of the old department forecast its demise. With the emphasis on emergency medical service, the increased demands of training, and the decline in the number of old-timers in the department, fewer people were willing to participate in the social event of mustard production. When the State of Ohio found out that the department was producing and selling a food product but did not have a state-inspected kitchen, and the Fire Association did not have a tax exemption number, the hassles increased the inertia of the mustard crews and production finally came to a halt. Old Firehouse Mustard is still recalled fondly by old folks who live in the village.

<u>Banker Bill</u>. There were other members of the department who, like Harvey, were physically unable to be in the heat of a fire. Shoppy, because of his age, and Homer Keller whose World War II injuries remained painful were notable examples. There were also members of the department who stood ready to assist around the station in any way they could but, for reasons unique to their own lives, did not play a major part in firefighting. If asked specifically to assist within their capabilities, they would gladly do the best they could when they were available. Membership for them was important as a way to show their genuine concern for the well-being of their community. They found other ways to contribute to the mission of the fire department. One such person was the town banker.

I had met Bill Smith during my brief period of residence in Gambier in 1955 to 1958. Back in 1957, before consolidation of schools, each of the little high schools in the county fielded a six-man football team. When the Gambier Pirates took the field in 1957, led by coach Mat Media, it was obvious that the physical potential for a championship team was there. There were at least nine hard-muscled young men whose physiques had been tempered by pitching hay and doing chores ever since they could lift a double tree or shift gears on the family's John Deere. But within that group there was also a young man who could have been, and was, easily overlooked.

There were only twenty or thirty boys in the whole high school; therefore, every willing soul had to be enlisted if six were to be found who could play well and, more important, who could be spared from field and barn often enough, to learn the plays.

No matter how realistic the tackling dummies, every team needs to practice against real opponents. So with the six starters the team needed at least six others who were willing to try. Those young men did not always have a passion for the game and often were motivated more by the adolescent terror of appearing less than the archetype of rural manliness. When all the boys in the school can sit in one classroom, there is no anonymity, and the prescribed gender role for the rural male was unambiguous. The shortage of less talented tackling dummies was critical at Gambier High, so bad in fact, that Principal L. E. "Buck" Law suited up to fill in, ONCE!

At away games, as the Gambier Pirates exited the bus after the long ride half way to the other side of the county, it was not unusual to hear snickers from the home team fans as, mixed in with the five-ten to six feet tall linemen, there appeared, now and then, a head barely visible above the waist heights of others but, yes, wearing a team helmet. The presumption was, of course, that here was one heroic little guy who <u>was</u> willing to serve as tackling dummy for the varsity during weekday practice. One hoped, for mercy's sake, that the varsity had "gone easy on the little fella." "Give him the respect he deserves for sacrificing himself for the team." The trip to the "away" game and dressing with the regulars seemed the likely reward for being willing to practice with the big boys. Any humane coach would never put him in the game, and everyone knew that coach Media was a first rate guy and attended mass at least once a week in the city of Mount Vernon.

When the teams lined up for the kickoff and Gambier was to receive the ball, suddenly the partisan home-town crowd became quiet and a murmur spread through all ten rows of the home bleachers. Every face communicated puzzlement except for those most rabid locals who detected the first clear sign that their boys would win big. There, standing alone back on the Gambier fifteen yard line was number 23. The number, though clearly visible on a jersey, appeared below a helmet, but both were close to the ground as if waiting to be occupied by a Gambier player who perhaps had been delayed until kickoff time by his obligation to finish the milking. But occupied it was. The crowd was soon to find out that it was worn by a boy by the name of Charles William "Bill" Smith, listed as a generous five feet tall on the mimeographed program and soon to become a legendary member of the undefeated 1957 Gambier High School six-man football team.

Barely visible under the helmet, his face communicated a deadly serious mood, though it was impossible to deduce what mood that might be. It could have been fear, or determination, or an absence of mood altogether, but it never changed throughout the game. No elation, no frustration, no anger. But what he felt, or didn't feel, made no difference, because Bill had two assets that made him the most feared running back in all the villages of Knox County and perhaps among all the six-man teams in the whole state. He had size, and he had legs. When the team was at the scrimmage line and ready to center the ball to Bill, the opponents had to stand almost straight up to find him, thus rendering them in perfect position to be blocked. And when the ball was centered and Bill had it, those short legs began to operate. There is a cliché oft used by broadcasters to describe powerful running backs: "his legs are like pistons." Bill's were not, and it is doubtful, if anyone were ever to broadcast a Gambier Pirate's game, that the play-by-play commentator could have described how Bill's legs worked, because few people had heard of the Wankel rotary engine. But that's the way his legs appeared to be powered. Rather than moving up and down they appeared to be rotating at a high r.p.m. Given the speed he quickly attained and the blocking his lack of height made possible, hundred-yard games and multiple touchdowns were routine. The mystery of his impenetrable countenance was revealed by those legs in their determination to reach the goal line. He did that with such success that he became the record holder for touchdowns by a member of a six-man football team.

Many years later, when I returned to the community, I once again found Bill in what seemed to me to be another improbable context, and once again his determination to reach a goal would prevail. As cashier of the Peoples Bank of Gambier, Bill had achieved all the status that position can command in a village of five hundred, plus twelve hundred Kenyon students, nine months of the year. He had not, however, achieved greater height. It was sometimes difficult to see that his teller's window was open if you were a step or two away from the counter. Gone, though, was the impenetrable countenance. Now he smiled and greeted customers as a banker should. Every local patron was greeted by Bill with a question that reflected his warm interest in his or her health and happiness. Once he found an empathetic topic, Bill would greet a customer with the same inquiry about the same subject, every time he or she arrived at his window. After a few repetitions one could predict his first words and hence be prepared to offer the reply always proffered in response. Because Bill was a member of CTFD and we shared that experience for a few years, his invariant greeting to me was "Had any good runs lately?"

As Bill grew older, he filled out. And unlike the high school speedster, he was rounder. When we got reacquainted after my return to Gambier, he never spoke a word to me about those days of athletic heroism. Now, in contrast to his days of staring at you in silence with defiant "no one can tackle me" determination, he was quite chatty. I noticed too, for the first time, that he stammered ever so slightly. I speculate that the little problem might have been why he was so quiet in high school. A college faculty member remarked that, when looking at his now rounded face and then detecting that little stammer, it was irresistible not to expect "Th Th Th That's all folks" to conclude each financial transaction. If he ever did experience concern about the speech pattern, it was not a problem now and anyway he knew about the faculty types. Many years had passed since "jokes" about his height or speech had any effect on him, and if wife Linda detected any lack of respect for Bill, her "shock and awe" retaliation could turn a faculty member's Harvard crimson gown, burnt orange.

At the bank Bill had a heart of gold and seemed to see the best in everyone. As indirect as it might seem that proved to be an asset to the department. For example, his mortgage loan to firefighter Ron Ayers assured that we would have Ron's significant firefighting abilities for years. Having a heart of gold is not always an asset in the banking business, but to my knowledge it was not the thing that eventually led to Bill's leaving his position. The local gossip alluded to his resistance to the entry of computers into the banking world. Bill, it was said, steadfastly refused to learn, or even try to learn, anything about how computers were to be applied to his work. Whether that reason was a matter of principle, the threat of automation to the hometown bank's image of personal service, or the irreversible mind-set that served him so well on the gridiron, isn't clear. What was evident was that Bill remained as resolute about his decision as he had been when "he was going up the middle toward the goal line." In any case he left his job at the bank. I think he just might have engineered it.

Ever since leaving high school, and maybe before, Bill had wanted to drive a sulky and race at the county fairs. That is what he did when he left the bank, and to my knowledge, he never took another job that would interfere with training his horses and hitting the fair circuit. I can almost hear the fans as the sulkies were in the far turn. "Look, there is no driver behind number 7. He must have fallen off." "But look, he is pulling into the lead." So when I tell you that Bill was a volunteer fireman, it is entirely consistent with his heart of gold and hence his willingness to help anyone as best he could. It is also true that the training, inspections of equipment, and of course, emergencies often occurred at hours when the horses needed training, the stable needed cleaning, or a race was about to start in a distant county. But there was never any doubt that when he did respond Bill stood ready to help out at a fire scene in any way one might ask. Nor was there any doubt that he had his eye on the finish line at the fairgrounds just as he had on the goal line. Nothing could divert him from trying to get there first.

In a way that is still true. Even though Bill must reside in an assisted living facility he finds a way to go back out to his Gambier home where son Billy has built a race track and they work together with the horses as intensely as he did to get them ready for the county fair circuit of harness racing. And even though Linda is there only in spirit, they know she is looking down and smiling with every lap that gets one of the equine competitors closer to their goal of a record time at the finish line.

Bill could be counted on to vote for whatever the chief proposed. Or if there was a need for someone to help set up tables for the annual firehouse Christmas Party, he would happily join in to get the job done. If a firefighter needed a home loan Bill tried to assure that the member would remain a resident of the community. There are many different ways to support a volunteer department other than responding to all the emergencies. Those local folks, like Bill, who provide behind the scenes support, are truly invaluable to the culture and morale of the volunteer departments.

6

THE FEEDGRINDER TEACHES THE PROFESSOR: LESSON ONE

When I came on, Robert B. "Bob" Gorsuch, aka "Feedgrinder" and "Grandpa," was Chief Hobe Brown's assistant fire chief. As Dorothy's brother Bob shared many of her traits but kept the unmanly aspects carefully guarded under a gruff veneer. He was, in fact, a grandfather. His daughter's name was Dorothy, too, and she was married to Bill Lahmon, on the department, and so was their son Jim, but family ties did not influence Grandpa's role as assistant chief. At first glance you could see that he was short. What was not revealed was the muscular build well camouflaged under a size-48 belt. His employment history included maintenance work at the college and, before the building burned, a job as feed grinder at the Gambier Farmers Co-op. Legend had it that his fingers became so strong from tying feed bags that once he grabbed you between thumb and forefinger there was no way to get loose. By 1970, his agility had declined but his judgment and his knowledge of engines and pumps made him an indispensable asset at fires. Perhaps as important was that he was respected by everyone at the station as a leader and friend.

The familial lineage, longevity in the community, mechanical skills, and, at one time, the physical strength, combined to establish a legacy consistent with his high rank. The chief, but few others, recognized that Bob was also sensitive and affectionate. Those were traits he seldom dared show in the firehouse kitchen.

His native intelligence was hidden by a limited formal education and a lifetime of work that did not require a spectrum of oral or written communication. Those who are familiar with Cattell's approach to the measurement of intelligence would recognize him as having high "fluid" (innate) intelligence and low "cultural" intelligence (reflecting formal education). Regardless of how people might rate his intellect, his experience and judgment warranted leadership status in the views of the firefighters. (Actually the people around the station did not evaluate people's intelligence except in the context of a pejorative reaction to someone with whom they disagreed.)

In 1970, Bob could still run a pump and teach new firefighters how to do things with unambiguous, if mildly profane, instruction. At least it seemed mildly profane by firehouse standards. For others it depended on how they viewed "Goddamn" in their hierarchy of profane expressions. No matter how it is evaluated, it was heard often. Richness of language was not needed to understand how he assessed one's performance.

Although the guys referred to him as Grandpa and Feedgrinder, I sensed that he did not appreciate either nickname though he never made an issue of it. Most of the time I called him Bob while in his presence. Occasionally I slipped. He was sensitive about his educational poverty and pugnacious about any inference that he lacked sophistication. I learned that the hard way. Bob spent most of the day in the wooden swivel desk chair in front of the fire frequency two-way radio. The chair was rotated a quarter turn so that he could rest his beer bottle beside the radio's microphone and still be able to address those conversing across the oval table and from behind the bar. His station there was not an assertion of privilege but a result of his increased discomfort caused by the open sores on his lower legs and feet. He was a diabetic, but his diet was not compromised by that diagnosis. The disease was advancing, but he kept going on runs until the pain said no. Despite advancing health problems, the chief had confidence that Bob's knowledge and one-on-one affection for his "students" would make him an excellent mentor.

Grandpa was my mentor and tried hard to help me overcome my impassioned aversion to anything mechanical. He was a patient instructor and agreed to give me a passing grade when I bumbled through the final exam. The chief set a small box of sticks on fire in a metal barrel down by the railroad tracks and had me respond driving Tanker #5 with Bob in the passenger's seat. I was to position the truck appropriately, start the pump, pull off a booster line, and extinguish the fire. I performed awkwardly with my muscles rigid with fear of failure and my professorial brain in lock down. Bob said I did okay, but he and the new chief could tell that they had not found a star in that phase of firefighting. I think I was the first guy he ever knew who couldn't learn to double clutch the transmission on a fire truck, but he remained committed to the task.

Bob took me on as a "project" with the aim of making a firefighter in short order. On my first real field fire, he realized the magnitude of that challenge. The fire was next to the state route north of town. A ten-acre field densely filled with four-foot high weeds waving in a stiff breeze had been ignited. By the time I reached the firehouse, Grandpa, who had been resting in his swivel chair in front of the radio transmitter and nursing a Blue Ribbon, was already in old Pumper#1. As I came around the corner of the open bay door into the station, he shouted, "Come on Charlie, hop in." It would be just the two of us in #1 but #5 would be right behind us with a crew of four. From the north edge of the village we could see the smoke. The wind was driving the fire rapidly toward houses in the distance. We rolled to a halt at the very edge of the field.

"Grab the booster line, Charlie, and I'll put the pump in gear."

I pulled about fifty feet of booster hose off the reel and worked my way into the field. Just then the wind shifted. Suddenly the fire was coming right at us. It blazed higher and higher and moved faster and faster. I could already feel the heat and knew it would overrun us in a matter of seconds.

"Grandpa, Grandpa, what should I do?"

"Put water on the goddamn fire."

I did what he suggested, and it went out. Almost immediately, I wished I had thought of that.

I could see from the expression on his face that he realized what a teaching challenge he had taken on with me as his student. That task would be confirmed on several more occasions, but he never wavered in his resolve, or his expletives.

Even though I was one of those "smart-assed" college professors, Grandpa admitted me to his circle of friends. There were, however, interludes when I was not his pal. Once, after I became EMS officer, I presumed to correct him on the proper procedure for answering emergency calls. That made him really angry, and he chased me around the oval table in the FD meeting room. I had twenty years on him and was able to escape his thumb and forefinger. After trotting about four circuits, and winded from jogging while uttering "Goddamns," he finally sat back down. The other guys, especially Harvey, thought that was the funniest thing they had seen in years, but they made it clear to me that Grandpa was in the right because "he had 'been on' longer than you," which was the criterion by which all new guys were evaluated whether they were officers or not. In another ten minutes we were friends again.

The inevitable happened. Bob began to have trouble walking. There was no formal farewell, though there should have been. Maybe people thought it would be too sad for him. Months later we learned that his feet had been amputated and that he was learning to walk with prostheses. One Sunday morning he appeared and we raved at how well he was getting around. It was the last time we talked with him. Not very long after, we listened to his eulogy at the funeral parlor.

When I think of my earliest years in the department the memories always include Bob. His voice is recalled, helping me to bridge the long gap from academic to firefighter with his tireless, if not always patient, coaching. We were from different worlds, but we found warm friendship in the culture of our second home, the firehouse. That relationship developed rapidly as the assistant chief guided his student firefighter through some introductory lessons.

7

HIGH SHOOL MATH AND PHYSICS SAVE THE FIREFIGHTER

By fall, after joining the department, I had learned to distinguish between a booster line, an inch-and-a-half, and a two-and-a-half inch hose. (they are always referred to as "inch and a half" and "two and half") Each is a type of hose carried on a fire truck. In ascending diameter they determined the volume of water that could be delivered to the nozzle. Nozzles are of many types and determine the characteristics of the water stream. A straight stream nozzle is not adjustable and can project water in a narrow, highly pressured stream over a long distance. The most versatile nozzles are adjustable so that the firefighter can vary the output between a straight stream and a spray. Inside a structure it is sometimes more effective to use a dispersed spray. Over the years opinions have varied as to the proper stream to use in specific situations.

The 1½" and 2½" hoses are carefully laid in separate areas of the hose bed atop the truck. They are generally in fifty foot sections and a number of the sections are joined with connectors that screw together. At a significant fire these must be pulled from the hose bed without tangling. As much as a thousand feet or more of hose may be stored in the hose bed. When enough is pulled off to put it in position to fight the fire, one end is attached to the matching size outlet on the pump panel and a nozzle affixed to the other end. Laying the hose in the bed so that it does not tangle when pulled rapidly at a fire is an exacting task that requires teamwork. When a hose is "charged," the pump is sending water through the hose under pressure. If the pump forces water through a 2½" line at one hundred or more pounds of pressure, it may require more than one firefighter to control the water forced from the nozzle.

The booster line is reeled like a garden hose onto a motorized axle mounted on top of the truck. The nozzle for our booster line had a pistol grip. It was grabbed as soon as the truck arrived at the fire and the hose rapidly pulled from the reel. The booster hose has ¾" or 1" inside diameter and is primarily employed at small fires. The pistol grip nozzle allows one to turn a straight stream of water on and off and can be managed by one person. Booster lines are used less often today. A pre-connected 1½" hose is preferred because of its potential to provide a greater volume and versatility of streams of water when equipped with an adjustable nozzle.

In my first few months in the department I had also learned to don the turnout gear. It included a classic black NYFD helmet, a knee-length black rubber-on-fabric coat, and black rubber hip boots. Just in case, there were a few smoke masks that covered the face and challenged one to try to breathe through a charcoal filter. Those were carried on the truck in a compartment, but most firefighters couldn't remember which one.

In those days, no local, state, or national agency was responsible for assuring safe practices in the fire service. No EPA, OSHA, or NFPA (National Fire Protection Association) gathered research statistics to inform the profession about dangers or enforce safety regulations. No one considered suing anyone or sending them to jail for allowing unsafe practices or conditions. On the contrary, the prevailing sentiment was, "If you can't take the heat, get out of the fire service." Manufacturers of firefighting equipment had not realized how much money they could make by encouraging safety and inventing devices to improve survival. Even after they did, it was about twenty years before conglomerates started noticing their bottom line and began to buy them.

Eventually, the NFPA began establishing standards for everything related to fire prevention and firefighting safety. Although it is still working on that task, it is now clear that few rural departments have the financial resources to meet its standards. Liability lawyers know that, too, and believe the thick books filled with the NFPA standards are greater than the books of the Bible.

Firefighting in the 1970s was comparable to riding a motorcycle on gravel in a tee shirt, shorts, and a head band. Firemen were excited by the challenge of pitting their skills against the serial killers fire and smoke. Hazardous materials hadn't been invented yet, as far as the rural fire service was concerned. Lying in bed with lungs burning and night sweats were earned like purple hearts, but no ribbon on the medal was long enough to hold the oak leaf clusters earned during a career as a firefighter.

Most of the volunteer firemen in the department, the inclusive term firefighters had not yet been mandated, lived within "earshot" of the station. That was good because it was before the pager generation, and the siren mounted on a utility pole twenty feet above the station was the principal means to announce the need for members to respond to an emergency. I lived only two blocks from the station, and the siren was loud enough to create sympathetic vibrations through all the timbers in the house. When it sounded, all the members in hearing range of the siren raced to the fire station and waited for someone who knew the nature of the emergency to arrive and start initiating a response. Especially at night when local citizens knew the worst emergencies were likely to happen, a few excited, thrill-seeking villagers, including at least one faculty wife, er spouse, followed the flashing red lights of the engines. They would then provide eye witness accounts of the incident to everyone they met at the post office the next day.

It was late fall of that first year when the siren roused me from bed about midnight or a little after. Dorothy's had closed for the evening, and the "click clack" dispenser of the firehouse beer cooler had rewarded the last hard-

Old #1. Carol R. Gantev's gift served the department for 30 years. Bangor ladder on top, front mount pump at the hood.

earned quarter with a final Blatz. I jumped out of bed and dressed quickly, stepped into my side-zippered plastic boots, and ran the two blocks to the station. The first and only person there was Mayor Baer. Just like me, he had been roused from a deep sleep, and just like me, he seemed to be having difficulty processing the events in his surroundings. He unlocked the side door to the equipment bay. Being a lieutenant (almost all the old-timers and maybe half the department were officers), he ordered me to suit up for a fire. I awkwardly donned my gear and jumped into the passenger side of "old #1." It was Mr. Ganter's very serviceable 1955 Ford pumper with a booster reel behind the cab and a three hundred gallon tank of water.

I had assumed we would wait until more help arrived and other firemen would jump onto the back platform, wrap a hose tool around their waists, attach it to the grab bar and hold on for dear life while enjoying the cool wind of a late fall "convertible ride." We didn't wait. Instead we careened out of the station with lights and siren warning other arriving firefighters to avoid a head-on crash by entering the post office driveway instead of Scott (Firehouse) Lane. We roared around the corner and onto state route 308.

The fire was reported to be a structure fire on a township road off the highway less than a mile north of the village. We screamed toward the village limit and passed the water tower at twenty five or thirty miles an hour. Old # 1 seemed reluctant, almost as if she were fighting a fifty mile-an-hour head wind. By the time we passed the tower, I detected the smell of something hot. It reminded me of times when I had driven my car with the hand brake on. Hesitant to ask the lieutenant whether that was possible I debated the question for a moment but as the smell got stronger, I gave in and asked.

The answer was quick and irritated. "This truck don't have a goddamn hand brake." I had to accept the pronouncement since, as a rookie, I was in no position to question the mayor/lieutenant. The smell continued to mount in intensity, and as a scientist with a Ph.D., I could not resist testing my hypothesis. I knew about where the none-existent hand brake handle would be located between the front seats, just in case, on the slightest chance, the mayor/lieutenant, could have forgotten that there was one, or had confused this truck with another. But, it was pitch black in the cab. We were almost at our turn when my searching hand fell upon a handle and lever that seemed very like a hand brake. Its position suggested that it was indeed in the "on" position. Without saying anything, or really thinking about the consequences, I rejoiced both in confirming my olfactory memory and being able to understand the engine's sluggish performance. I depressed the lock button and released the brake. With the mayor/lieutenant's foot pressing the accelerator to the floor, absolute confirmation was instantaneous. Old #1 exploded forward as if suddenly turbocharged. Unfortunately, the surge occurred as we should have started to decelerate for our turn on to New Gambier Road, which was an unpaved township road to Gambier and the site of the reported blaze. The road's name shot by in a blur before the mayor could reach the brake pedal or utter a single curse. I do recall that a stream of profanity did follow, but I was busy contemplating how to explain the brevity of my membership in CTFD on the "community service" section of the annual report to the provost of the college.

At that point in time, we could have debated which of us was most at fault. However our progress had not gone unnoticed by others. Assistant Chief, Feedgrinder, Grandpa Gorsuch was in pumper/tanker #5, formerly right behind us. Irritation was not suppressed in his voice received on our radio.

"Five to One, Five to One, you missed your turn."

"One to Five, we are turning around."

It took us only a couple of minutes to reverse course, get to the turn we didn't make, and to find the fire. When it came into view I could see that it was in an abandoned house on the south side of the road. It was a property owned by an elderly man, who was in the early stages of what the locals referred to as "old-timer's disease".

As we started down the hill on our approach to the blaze, we could see

Harvey's 100mph Cadillac Ambulance.

#5 parked on the road. Lieutenant/Mayor Baer asserted that there was an old driveway leading to the house about one hundred feet behind Tanker #5. "I think its right here," he opined and turned off the road into a barbed wire fence. The fence did not provide much resistance, and we ended up on solid ground that sloped toward the house. The structure was not fully involved yet, but flames could be seen rising toward the second story at its front. Baer brought #1 to a halt about forty feet from the northeast corner, set the hand brake, and hopped out. I am not sure where he went but I was sure of several other things. There were no longer any hand brakes for him to set, the slope of the land was toward the burning house, and #1 was now coasting toward it. I had a quick answer to that. I reached my left foot over and pressed the foot brake pedal to heroically save number #1, and myself.

It was then that Assistant Chief Grandpa came over to the driver's side window and ordered me out of the truck. I recall saying "but Grandpa" before he said "Get out of the goddamn truck." He repeated that twice, and it became clear that he was acting as asst. chief and I should do what he said regardless of the consequences. He had, of course, already placed a "6 by 6" (six inch by six inch by 12") block of wood under the front tire and effectively stopped the "progress" of #1. I moved over to the driver's side to get out because there were head high-weeds on the passenger's side, plus remnants of the fence.

As I stepped on the running board to jump off I glanced up and saw Chief Brown appear in our headlights. He was just visible below the tops of the weeds and he was tugging a 2 1/2" line parallel to the house opposite the hottest blaze. That hose, when hooked to a gated Y connector, would allow us to supply one or two 1 1/2" lines to fight the fire. The weeds were taller than the chief but we learned exactly where he was. There was the sound of metal crashing on metal coinciding with a clearly audible mixed variety of swear words. I guess when the old fella gave up on the house, he moved some of the plumbing fixtures out into what was then the yard. Among them was the bathtub and the chief had found it. The good news was that it was empty, except for him. One does not laugh at a chief, and I don't recall anyone making light of this potentially dangerous accident--in his presence.

As our initial excitement at having a real fire to fight began to subside, we began to apply our professional competence to extinguishing it. Grandpa brought #1 around to the back of the house, and a ladder was elevated up to just above the second story rear window. I helped with the ladder, applying my first lesson in ladders by placing its feet on the ground one-fourth the height of the ladder's resting point on the house. I was given the booster hose nozzle and ordered to ascend the ladder and play the hose stream on the fire now showing beneath the eaves. Grandpa delegated the pump operation to another firefighter and disappeared. I climbed to the top of the ladder, about twenty feet up, locked my left leg over a rung and back under and over the one below to secure myself. I pointed the nozzle at the fire coming out between the eaves and the roof. "Ah, my first real house fire!" I depressed the trigger, and water burst from the nozzle onto the fire powered by 125 pounds of pressure. Since I was preoccupied with putting the water on the fire, it was a couple of seconds before I realized that the pressure of the stream of water against the house was acting like a solid wooden pole pressing against it and forcing the ladder away from the wall.

My academic background leads me to take an intellectually analytical approach to situations, and it was very interesting that a stream of water under pressure could create sufficient power to cause the ladder to actually move away from the wall of the house. Most water I had experienced had always meekly streamed over a surface or down a drain with little effect other than wetness. There was an element of trigonometry here that led me to consider the angle being inscribed from the ground to the top of the ladder as it moved away from the house. By my almost intuitive calculation, if the angle reached a certain number of degrees, the arc would exceed the point beyond which I would begin to accelerate rapidly, according to the laws of gravity, away from the house in a downward direction and then stop suddenly. My comprehension of those implications caused me to quickly release the trigger. The ladder returned to the side of the house, and fire returned to the eaves. At that point I was somewhat puzzled as to what to do next. My puzzlement did not last long.

When the pump is in gear it pushes the water out of the nozzle, but when the nozzle is turned off the water circulates in the pump. If a valve to the water supply tank is open, things are fine. If the water does not circulate into the cooler water of the tank it stays in the pump and absorbs heat generated there. While thinking through the physics of hose stream on house equals ladder going backwards, and working out the trigonometry problem, the water had been circulating only through the pump because no one had opened the valve to the tank that would have cooled the water. The physics of heat transfer was now being demonstrated.

Meanwhile, additional rapid calculations led me to conclude that I could use an intermittent burst of water on the eaves and prevent the ladder from going too far away from the house. But during those calculations the temperature of the water had continued to increase. When I pulled the trigger for the next burst, what seemed to be boiling water came out of the metal nozzle, and instantly heated my trigger finger and grip hand to a painful level.

I reasoned that I could drop the nozzle and the hose but that would lead to more embarrassment than my self-image could take. Fortunately, as water came out it began to cool and I could hang on to the trigger. So until most of the fire had been controlled in the rest of the house, I choreographed a sequence that squirted the water against the house until I felt the ladder move, shut off the water for a few seconds but not long enough for a big heat buildup, and then squirt again, etc. I got the sequence down to a graceful rhythm.

Almost every minute of my first structure fire, from the alarm to the "fire's out" (today the report would more likely be referred to as "situation contained," which means "I think it's out but I've seen so many rekindles that I do not want to make myself legally responsible for any damage that happens if I'm wrong") was a stream of consciousness. I reflected on each event as it happened and recorded it in memory as visual images. It didn't register with me for several years that my professorial bottom was often in danger or that my ignorance could have been fatal. Most of my fellow volunteers didn't think about danger either. They were very aware of my ineptitude on the ladder and ready to laugh at me for years to come as we stood around the kitchen table. At the same time they had been sober (for the most part) and serious about putting out the fire, and they did.

If TV channel x had been there recording that empty house blaze, it would be a classic comedy featuring at least three stooges, and probably more. The "on the scene reporter" might have concluded that the fellows performed like a "well oiled" machine, and in one sense of that saying he would have been right. The videotape could have been used in every fire school beginner's class on how not to do everything when fighting a fire. But the fire was out, no one got hurt, and best of all I had proven myself as someone who would try, no matter how ineptly, to get the job done. That run meant acceptance, and acceptance meant that I got to work with the guys for many years. I had survived my first structure fire. Grass fires provided yet another kind of challenge.

Another Lesson in Fighting Grass Fires.

There were many, many more grass fires than structure fires in my first few years as a firefighter. That was true mainly because the railroad still went through the township. In the autumn, the engine and a couple of cars loaded with sand from the quarry east of Gambier would creep through on its way to the soon-to-be defunct glass factory in Mount Vernon. As it did, either by accident or intent, it found a way to ignite the brush and dried weeds at several spots along the roadbed. Sometimes there would be fires here and there for several miles. After a while I was pretty good at working the hand-pumped Indian Tank. It held about five gallons of what seemed to be awfully heavy water. It strapped onto one's back and was kind of like a hand-operated bug sprayer. Walking along the fire line squirting the water at the edge of the grass was necessary when the fire was inaccessible to the Scout. I had already learned to use a hand pumped bug sprayer so using the Indian tank proved no problem.

The Scout was International's answer to the Jeep. It was a four-wheel-drive model with a cab and a one hundred-gallon tank of water in the bed. The experienced firefighter stood on the twelve inch wide back platform behind the tank, started the gasoline-fueled pump and directed water at the blaze from a booster nozzle as the driver drove along the line of burning grass and brush. I was not an experienced firefighter.

Old #1 could get off the road a ways to fight grass fires if the ground was not too wet, but usually it and tanker #5 stood by at the road-side to refill the Scout. Mutual-aid Jeeps from other departments were dispatched to help us if the fire was significant. All this seemed pretty simple, but I found there was a learning process with the grass fires, just as I had with the structure fires.

I had felt foolish at my first field fire under the tutelage of Grandpa Gorsuch but not as much as during my first lesson on the back of the Scout. That was because more people witnessed it. The alarm came in for a field fire south of town near some rural residences. I was not yet approved to drive, nor did I know how to find a fire anywhere in the territory if it was outside the village limits. For that reason, it was my job to board the back end of the Scout and ride with the air pulling my fire helmet tightly under my chin. Carroll Dial, a candidate for the chief's job at one time and a veteran of many fires, was in the driver's seat. He was a serious firefighter and not particularly into the training of rookies. His mood was not good when he had to stop the Scout, get out, and start the pump for me when we arrived at the scene.

The pump's noise was extremely loud and drowned out any chance of conversation or exchange between the driver and hose holder in the back, especially with the cab windows closed. When we arrived at the fire we stopped while Carroll shifted into a lower gear. I took that opportunity to jump off and unwind about thirty feet of booster line. What I had not yet learned was that bit about the guy on the back standing on the rear platform and squirting water on the fire as we drove along the fire line. Carroll knew that, but I didn't. So he put the Jeep in four wheel drive and low gear and started driving along parallel to the edge of the fire at a goodly rate. After the full length of the thirty feet of booster line had been extended, I found myself squirting and sprinting trying to keep up with the Scout. I yelled a couple of times, but the pump noise and the closed windows of the cab prevented Carroll from hearing me.

Fortunately, there was no television coverage to present eyewitness tape of the forty-year-old distinguished professor of psychology at Kenyon College, a nationally recognized private college in the Midwest, sprinting at his top speed in a rubber coat and hip boots over a hay field, squirting water on a fire and yelling "wait, wait, wait." In defense of my effort, I did not fall down. I was a bit winded before we had to stop at the edge of the woods. Carroll explained my mistake at that point in a voice loud enough for me to hear over the noise of the pump.

Now I was also a tested veteran of grass fires. I had quickly supplied the kitchen regulars with enough humor to earn their criterion as a new faculty firefighter who did things that were noteworthy.

Having passed the various initiation fires, I established the habit of dropping by the firehouse for a few minutes in the afternoon between four and five p.m. on weekdays, around noon on Saturdays, and then from about 9 a.m. to noon for Sunday inspections. Then of course there were Tuesday evening training nights. A few months later we began the emergency medical training. It was obvious to the most casual observer, or spouse, that being a member of the department entailed much more than responding to the siren when there was an emergency.

One inevitable consequence of this extracurricular was that I became familiar, more aptly, a part of, the social culture of the station. As a result, old timers accepted me into their "club," but only as a silent partner, except when they asked me what I was thinking after each faux pas, but they did not call them that.

8

WHEN THE VILLAGE SIREN WASN'T SOUNDING

We were typical of small departments throughout the country. Although we put out fires, pumped flooded basements, and got cats out of trees, most of the time dedicated to volunteering was spent attending regular training sessions, inspecting vehicles, and servicing equipment. Initially, members met the first and third Tuesday nights of every month from seven p.m. to ten p.m. A couple of years later it was every Tuesday night, and later all those plus special training. The first Tuesday of the month was called business meeting and was dedicated to announcements, planning fund raisers, and establishing wish lists.

At seven p.m. on the first Tuesday evening of every month, twenty to twenty five firefighters crowded around the oval Formica table in the fifteen by twenty five foot room at the back of the firehouse for the monthly business meeting of the College Township Volunteer Fire Association. The meeting room also served several other purposes. It was the kitchen, dining room, radio communication center, locus of the beer machine, gossip center, and site of many pinochle games. The first Tuesday's business was to discuss and decide any issues that had come up since the previous month, vote people in or out, and listen to the chief's comments and plans.

Getting voted out was difficult to accomplish. The bylaws stated that missing too many meetings or inspections in a row was the basis for being ousted. Attendance was taken at every meeting and training session, but no one kept score from week to week. If a chronically missing member had done something to make people angry at him the records might be consulted. Then a letter had to be sent to the sinner, but if he showed up at the next meeting the "clock" was reset. In July 1970, however, one item of the business meeting was a vote on the candidacy for membership of me. I don't ever recall a single candidate who wasn't voted in, so my anxiety wasn't justified.

The Fire Association was the club/organization comprised of the members. The Association was formed as a means to separate the aspects of the department that responded to emergencies and therefore were governed by the township trustees, from the other activities of the members. I suppose it was an important distinction to legal authorities but no one in the department ever discussed the specifics or uttered a "point of order" protest over a conflict of interest.

The Association carried out programs that supported the department, such as fund-raising and parties. It had officers. The president, who could not be the chief, ran the meetings. The vice president did nothing, the secretary took attendance and minutes, and the treasurer kept the bank account and paid the bills. The Association could raise money for its bank account and spend donations for whatever it wished. The largest expenditures supplemented the tax supported budget of the trustees. Some of the funds went for food after training sessions and inspections. The treasury also sent flowers for funerals, newborns, newly-weds, and the infirm who had some benevolent connection to the membership.

The Association's expenditures for firefighting apparatus were based on a priority list created at the business meeting. Fund-raising was also important to sustaining the social culture (meals) that kept volunteers morale high. The beer machine paid for itself and did not require a subsidy. It might have been awkward to sponsor a fund raiser to support it.

The annual checks issued to us by the trustees, fifteen dollars per year, were signed over to the Association the moment they were received. The "salary" assured that we were legal employees of the Trustees and therefore eligible for worker's compensation if injured in the line of duty. The fifteen dollars went into the "kitchen fund" to help pay for the food bought at the local grocery.

The more money the Association could raise on its own, the better equipped the fire department and the better we ate. In the 1970s there were several fund-raising events but only one that did a lot for the department. Years earlier, in 1964 for example, the Association had sponsored the Nolan Carnival Show in the middle of town. Proceeds ($281.48) were used to buy some fire boots and helmets. More lucrative entertainment came later.

The Henry Ade Shows

An item of business on the first Tuesday of each June was an accounting of the proceeds from the annual country and western show. The show was always the first weekend of May and featured entertainers from Nashville who were talented but not featured at the Grand Old Opry. In the eyes of much of Knox County they were even better. The Henry Ade shows were our biggest fund-raiser, even though we only netted 15 percent of the take. In January, three-hundred-pound Henry hired a crew of local women who loved talking on the phone. They called every phone number in the local phone book and asked people to buy one or more tickets to support the great work of the department. Tickets were mailed, and the money came in to the department's Gambier post office box. Local businesses were asked to buy an ad in the show's program, which had little articles by the chief telling of our progress during the year. The telephone sales ladies annually got us into trouble with a few people for their sales tactics, but these problems were always resolved by a phone call to the offended donor. Lieutenant John Ridenbaugh was the liaison with Henry. Johnnie was a technician with the local phone company, and he wired up the bunch of phones used by the callers and started the paper work necessary to pay the phone bill. He lived in a trailer several miles east of town, so he did not get to many fire runs, but when he did he could drive a truck and run pumps with skill. In his left shirt pocket he always carried a couple dozen pens and pencils. I never saw him without them, but I never knew why he needed so many, and he never volunteered that information when asked. He stayed after the show to count the money. Sometimes our share would be six or seven thousand dollars even though members had done almost no work. Most of the department attended the show at the Memorial Theater in Mount Vernon to do the ushering. A couple dozen tickets always were given to the state developmental center to allow handicapped residents to attend.

A cross section of Knox County residents came to the shows. For some, especially those who lived in the remote Appalachia areas, it was the most anticipated event of the year, at least as big as the county fair. So many came, in fact, that it was necessary to have two sessions. The Knox County Memorial Building in the city could seat about a thousand people. The first show was always packed to capacity, and the second show filled all but a few seats.

The morning after the show the emergency phone line at the station would ring all morning with grateful praise for our having sponsored the greatest show the caller had ever attended. The department members who were authorities on country music did not always agree. When a show did not meet expectations, there would be a vote at the June business meeting to decide whether we should sign a contract for the next year. The answer was always affirmative. In part that was because it was the easiest money we could earn for the CTFD Fire Association treasury, but for some it was an event they loved to attend, for free. If the members weren't 100 percent pleased with the performances, Henry would be just as disappointed as we were, and would make sure the next show was a hit.

More than thirty years later, the ladies still arrive to pick up a key and get organized to start their calls again. Johnnie Ridenbaugh died years ago while sitting in his chair in the trailer. Henry Ade died more recently, but the shows went on for a few years under his name. Long-time Firefighter/EMT-I Neal Bower, who runs an auto repair shop in Monroe Township, assumed Johnnie's role as representative to the show's management. In recent years it is a different show in a different month of the year. Neil does the job as well as it has ever been done, and he does it with only one pen in his shirt pocket.

I always volunteered to stay at the station in case there was an emergency during the show. The only one I recall was when lieutenant and professor of economics, Alan Batchelder drove engine number 6 (#6) into the path of a car while responding to a minor accident. Kenyon student volunteers Susan Thompson and Tom Faulkner were riding on the rear platform behind the hose bed and hanging onto the grab bar. They no doubt still recall flying off into space on impact.

There were other fund-raising events. One very modest source of funds was the annual, or sometimes variably annual, chicken barbecue. An old metal barrel was bisected vertically so as to become two charcoal grills. The barbecue committee, appointed at the business meeting, took responsibility for cooking and setting up chairs and tables in the equipment bay after the engines were parked across Scott Lane in the post office driveway. That committee was appointed every year and always included the same people. The cook-out was publicized in the <u>Mount Vernon News,</u> but about the only people from outside the village who came were volunteers from other departments. We, of course, were expected to reciprocate when they cooked something. The chicken feasts were important to public relations and allowed people in the village to mingle with the firefighters and explore their station.

Third Tuesday: Fire Training

The third Tuesday of the month was fire training. The chief planned these sessions to cover the most important topics in firefighting. One month would be on pumps, one on ladders, one on testing the hoses under high pump pressures; one session was on familiarization with the big college buildings and planning where to park the engines in case some building caught fire. There were more topics than Tuesdays.

The most dreaded training night was fire rescue. Putting the Bangor ladder up and climbing to the roof of a college building while carrying heavy equipment was not a problem. But once a year we were asked to jump the twelve feet from the roof of the station onto an eight-foot-diameter canvas fastened with springs to a steel hoop. It was held chest high by a dozen firefighters. I always had to go to the restroom when my turn came. Those brave souls who actually did it later envied my bladder. They limped silently away holding backs, and necks. I guess landing in the "net" would have been better than burning in a dorm room, but I wasn't sure we needed to prove it even once a year.

The "protective" masks we were trained to don before entering a smoky building were of two kinds. One had a charcoal filter that was supposed to prevent the smoke particles from being inhaled. It fastened around the head with rubber straps that had to be pulled tight to seal out the smoke. The other was a chemical mask. When it was activated it produced pure oxygen. The chemicals were stored in a container that hung down in front of the chest and was connected to a mask by a one inch diameter tube. That outfit might have been the inspiration for the Darth Vader costumes a couple of decades later. We were cautioned not to breathe the 100 percent oxygen for too long because it could cause us to pass out.

The guys listened to the chief's explanation on how to use the masks, but for some reason the old-timers were less attentive. I learned why at a fire one hot summer day on Zion Road just outside the village. By the time I climbed to the top of the ladder and onto the porch roof, my respiration rate was elevating. Soon the heat in the house was warming up my long, heavy, rubber fireman's coat and hip boots, which in turn were warming me up even more, especially since I was also pulling a fire hose full of water. The area I entered was hot and very smoky. I donned the filter mask and climbed through a second-story window. Panting now from exertion, it became clear that the only way the mask could allow enough oxygen to reach my lungs was to sit quietly in a chair and inhale slowly. I was gasping for air and getting none. I made a quick cost/benefit analysis as to the merits of breathing smoke and ashes versus getting zero oxygen. I ripped the mask off and took a deep breath of wonderful thick smoke and then knocked out windows to ventilate the attic and douse the fire with water. When I came down, oxygen starvation, heat, and smoked lungs left me pouring sweat and panting. Fortunately, there was a nice maple tree in the yard twenty feet from the house where I opened the rubber coat, sat down, and leaned back for a while.

That night I was miserable. I sat up in my bed supported by pillows, lungs burning and aching, and debating whether I needed to drive to the hospital for help. I was too tired to get out of bed. There had been no emergency squad on standby at the fire, and in fact it was assumed that if you could ride an engine back to the firehouse you were okay or would get help on your own. Besides, I had to teach an 8 a.m. class. Wow, what a gas! We saved most of the house.

I will admit that the mask was more of an asset when our oft-visited diabetic farmer collapsed in the manure pit.

A second reason the old-timers did not use the masks was firefighter pride. Real firefighters ate smoke. Get a line into the building, put out the fire, cough a couple of times, and then strut out laughing at the enemy you had vanquished. That macho image was not limited to volunteers and, if anything, was amplified several times by the career firefighters. There are still some of those types in the firehouses around the country, and a few who are not there anymore but who could have been but for their dedication to macho. Woe be to today's fire chief who does not enforce the order to wear the NFPA mandated self-contained breathing devices of the twenty first century.

The year I was elected, some third Tuesday evening training sessios were added for first-aid classes. A fellow came and told us about the places pressure could be applied to stop arterial bleeding, how to splint broken bones with flat pieces of wood or pillows, and how to do artificial respiration by rhythmically pushing down on the lower posterior rib cage to revive a person who drowned or stopped breathing for any reason.

It did not matter what the training subject was; the chief contended that if the firefighters worked hard at every drill, they would be happy and proud of their teamwork. That was when there was one training night a month. That held true after we assumed emergency medical services. Soon after it was first Tuesday, business meeting; second Tuesday, squad training; third Tuesday, fire training; and then the last Tuesday was officers meeting and rescue training. When there was a fifth Tuesday, something would be added to the training schedule, like hazardous materials or decontamination. At first, firefighters did not seem to mind as long as there was a good meal and a beer at the end of the session. But eventually training for many other types of emergencies were added to the burden. The time commitment and spousal objections began to take its toll on the membership.

Thanks to Chief Brown, we were becoming as well trained as any volunteer department could be. However, there is no substitute for experience. Even though it had been formed in 1961, had a station in 1963, and began the regular training sessions, CTFD was still not an effective fire department. It had responded to some major fires in the community. It did a much better job than the GFD group, but some essentials were lacking. There were a couple of fire engines, but they were old and insufficient for large fires. The water supply system in the village was still inadequate; the "starter set" of firefighters from the bar stools at Dorothy's were getting older; and the new people had not had enough experience working as a team. Until Chief Brown was elected, CTFD had not had a chief who could inspire the pride in competence that motivates firefighters to aspire to professionalism.

To achieve Brown's objective of excellence the department needed a dozen or so dedicated, young, energetic recruits with mechanical aptitudes who would rapidly learn the trade. When he engineered the contract to assume protection of all of Monroe Township and welcomed volunteers from within its boundaries, the department was soon rock solid.

Monroe

One of Chief Hobe Brown's most important strengths was foresight. It was clear to him that if the department was to become truly effective, it needed two more assets: more money and more firefighters. It needed the money for engines and equipment, and it needed strong younger men to replace the aging crew from Dorothy's.

The township immediately north of College Township is Monroe Township. It is trisected by two major highways. In July of 1970 only the southern third of Monroe was covered by CTFD. Chief Brown saw the potential to achieve those much-needed resources if CTFD could achieve a contract to cover all of Monroe Township. As an incentive, Hobe laid out a long-range plan that included locating a substation of CTFD in the middle of Monroe. The result would be superior coverage for the residents in that area.

One Tuesday night, the chief asked the members of CTFD whether they would be willing to serve all of Monroe Township. That would increase the size of our coverage area to forty five square miles. It would include a few miles of state route 3, the "Three C Highway," the pre-freeway connection between Cleveland, Columbus, and Cincinnati. The vote was on the three inch by five inch slips of paper always used to provide anonymity when voting on new members and major issues.

The chief, of course, already knew how the vote would turn out, having had "confidential" conversations with enough members to assure the outcome. He was a master of engineering people to see things his way, and his way was always a carefully analyzed, meticulously documented proposal that resulted in a better department. He already had negotiated a financial deal with the Monroe Township Trustees that would allow the department to acquire much-needed equipment. He may have suggested that at some point a fire station would exist on the 3C in order to decrease the response times in the northern part of their township. The Monroe Township Trustees found the idea especially appealing because that would assure that their residents would likely be staffing that station.

The agreement was reached, and the planning began. The first step was to recruit potential firefighters among the residents of Monroe Township. The results turned out to be an asset to the department beyond expectations. The new members, who as a group became known as "Monroe," had personalities and manual skills that strengthened CTFD. They were mature, hard-working, and strongly motivated.

The Gambier crew was getting older, the local demographics were decreasing the number of potential new members, and the manual skills of new Gambier recruits were not as relevant. Perhaps as important as any of the Monroe men's characteristics was their size. Almost all of them were taller, heavier, and stronger than the College Township crew. In the 1970s there was no physical exam as a condition of membership, either as a new recruit or as a continuing member. There should have been. Three of the apparently big, strong, vigorous recruits from Monroe would die of heart conditions in middle age.

Among the early Monroe volunteers were Bob Barton, Roger Heaton, Rich Yarman, Ron Dupler, Billie VanDyke, Ray Seavolt, Charlie McDonald, Carl Holmes, Roger Heaton, Tom Fish, Stan Anderson, and Dave McCoy. They all started within the first year or so. The effect of adding a dozen men who were strong, talented, and enthusiastic was profound. It meant not only that Monroe Township would be well protected, but that CTFD would almost double the number of firefighters who were physically strong, had the appropriate aptitudes, and were enthusiastic responders. The morale of the group was high, and they eagerly set about to learn the engines and equipment and to create their fire station. Their skills included auto mechanics, carpentry, metal fabrication, electrical wiring, plumbing, and butchering. They were not quite as good at housekeeping.

When they were trained and equipped, CTFD had the capability to attack and extinguish a major fire in any business or college building in their territory. CTFD became recognized, by us, as the best volunteer fire department in the area and voters in both townships overwhelmingly voted in favor of the requested tax support. Fire fighting and rescues were the strengths of the Monroe crew. When the department began emergency medical service, some were less enthusiastic but they tackled that challenge with a professional demeanor.

It was an extraordinary group of Monroe residents who volunteered to join CTFD. Most were approaching or already in their forties, settled in their homes, hard-working, and with the confidence that arose from being self-sufficient. They held jobs that required intuitive mechanical knowledge and well-practiced manual skills. Those skills proved to be the rock-solid foundation for what is still called "Monroe," "Station 2," and, "the Substation." That first group almost literally created a fire station and equipped it using what many would have called junk. The materials included discarded military surplus vehicles and first-aid supplies from the disbanded Civil Defense bomb shelters around the county. For a short time their equipment was "housed" in an unheated ramshackle shed with no heat and gaps between the siding boards. They spent Tuesday evenings learning firefighting and emergency medical care at Gambier and worked other nights and weekends to create the necessities of a substation.

Their substation was just large enough to house a 1957 Pontiac ambulance and a nearly antique engine that had been purchased as the "starter set." In its first winter, because the building was not heated, the sliding doors of the garage sometimes froze or were blocked by snow. Water would have frozen in the pumps, so they had to be drained in November. Victims who had to lie on the ambulance cot in January were candidates for hypothermia in addition to anything else that might ail them.

All in all, the men of Monroe substation quickly became adept at improvising to meet all kinds of emergencies. By 1973, they were ensconced in a strong cement-block building that had been a service station right on the 3C in the middle of their territory. It had two serviceable garage doors, heat, running water, electric lights, flush toilets, and other luxuries not found in that original "station."

Their first miracle began with cutting off the roof and part of the sides of an olive-drab, 1962 military ambulance. It had been secured from the surplus center thanks to Civil Defense head Chuck Imel. It had big wheels, four-wheel drive, bare metal floorboards, and an engine that still had gumption. The result was a grass fire fighting truck that would go anywhere in the rugged terrain of the township. They mounted a small tank, a pump, a generator, and a huge flood light on the top. The light could be raised on a telescoping metal pole to illuminate a fire or rescue scene. She was "Ethel."

Pride is never in short supply in any fire station, and the Monroe guys were justifiably proud of what they did with little help from people at the main station. In the process they became a tightly knit social group. When women were finally admitted to membership, among the first volunteers were spouses Sue Barton and Joan Dupler.

Training and business meetings were held at the main station, and the Monroe crew had to travel to Gambier every week. Inevitably, the one-sidedness of the travel created some resentment, and still does. It was difficult for the chief to affirm that we were all one department and must work that way when the Monroe guys always had to come to Gambier. It never went much further than gripes because the after-drill meals were at Station 1, and therefore the Monroe volunteers got to "eat out" once or twice a week in Harvey's firehouse kitchen. Their complaints were uttered with mouths full.

The addition of the Monroe guys ended the 150-year-long search for competent fire protection in the Gambier community. It also signaled the beginning of the end of the Harvey Mathews, Grandpa Gorsuch, Dorothy's Lunch, beer-cooler FIRE department era. The first signs of the dominance of emergency medical service also appeared. There was new leadership based on the traditional talents of manual skills but founded on the physical strength of younger men. Hobe Brown's concept of a fire department had replaced the last vestiges of the Chuck Imel model, almost. The roster still admitted volunteers on the basis of the elections at the business meetings, and the beer cooler was just as important as ever.

9

MY FINAL EXAM WASN'T ORAL OR WRITTEN

The first years as a firefighter lived up to my expectations and despite several embarrassments, I began to feel as if the chief was right: we have lots of fun. For me it was a complete break from the intensely cerebral activities of teaching several courses, designing research projects, gathering data, going to professional meetings, and attending faculty meetings. The latter were especially frustrating. For example, the entire faculty gathered in a single room to engage in a passionate hours-long debate over the intellectual principles that should influence whether a senior drama major should be allowed to get credit for his experience at a circus school. (He did get credit and later became a famous show-biz producer.)

I began to see that other firefighters did things I could laugh at and to realize I was not the only one who screwed up. Neither did I need to be concerned that long wordy arguments would be held to reach fire department decisions. One or two expletives from the "for" and "against" sides and a vote on the three by five slips of paper settled the issue, and then we could eat and have a beer.

We put out some fires, did not get singed, and got to ride the engine with the siren screaming. Oops, I am wrong about singed. Ray Seavolt lost his eyebrows and some of his precious dwindling hair when he threw gasoline on a training fire and then tossed a match to light it. He forgot that gasoline fumes can follow the designated lighter, and the flash of the fumes left him red-faced. Ray was a great asset to the department, but tragically he would later die of a heart attack during a Tuesday evening training session.

If we filled out forms issued by the state, we could get red lights and a siren and install them on our personal vehicles. Some guys even drilled holes in the roof of their pickups and attached a four-foot wide light bar with enclosed siren. It did not get them to the firehouse any quicker because there wasn't that much traffic or distance to travel. But having the lights and siren was a sure indication of a person committed to being a firefighter.

There were things Grandpa couldn't teach me about the fire service. I had to learn those on my own. There had been plenty to laugh about after my initiation at the grass fires and the structure fire on New Gambier Road. What I had yet to learn was that there are fires that evoke the antithesis of humor. I had to learn whether I could take a different kind of heat. I was still in the learning stage but a tiny bit more competent when I experienced the definitive test of my ability to cope with the other end of the fire service continuum. That came a little later and it also revealed the need for fire, medical, and law enforcement emergency services to work well together. Cooperation between us and the law enforcers was primitive by today's standards but the first experience showed clearly how far it needed to improve. There were, in fact, no standards to guide the overlap of agencies responsibilities at emergencies.

That definitive test came during a Sunday morning inspection, while Grandpa and the others were out checking the oil on the vehicles and I was doing the one thing I was competent to do: checking tire pressures. The fire phone rang and its buzzer on the outside of the building resonated loudly enough to be heard a couple blocks away. Harvey was cooking breakfast, and as soon as the long continuous ring of the phone indicated an emergency call, he was on his way to the dispatcher's desk. "That's a good one," he shouted, as he always did, whether he was right or not. A "good" one was bad for the caller. Harvey ran from the stove to the fire phone. When he was in the building, no one else dared to answer. "Firehouse," he exclaimed, then listened and began to write down the information. The inspection crew hurried into the kitchen/meeting room/radio room/bar. Our anxious anticipation drained if Harvey's voice dropped an octave indicating a nuisance call "cat in a tree," or something else that Harvey didn't consider "good."

"There's a car fire out on [Route] 308 almost to [Route]36." The other veterans shrugged and hurried into the bay to don their gear. A car fire is not very exciting and often turns out to be a radiator problem that sends steam out from under the hood. Usually, it was a woman driver or a professor who does not recognize the important differences between steam and smoke.

Grandpa was the commanding officer on station, and a car fire was something he thought was a perfect way to introduce me to another firefighting experience without much danger to me or the car. He climbed up into old #1 and yelled what he always yelled when I was around. "Come on, Charlie get up in here with me."

We were the lead truck, and Tanker #5 followed just in case we needed more water. Old #1 had the three hundred gallons of water in its tank and the booster reel sat behind the cab and above the hose bed. Grandpa assumed that I still knew too little about running pumps, regulating pressure, or charging the hose. He had taught me to point the nozzle at the fire and squeeze the trigger on my previous grass fire dilemma: an encouraging gauge of my progress.

"When we get out there grab the booster line and run it over to the car, I'll charge the line." Siren whining, we traveled out 308 to my car fire.

As we approached Brown's orchard, we could see smoke, a lot of smoke, up ahead. "Looks like she's in 'full bloom' Charlie, better pull the pre-connected inch and a half off the back." I could hear in Grandpa's voice that this was going to be a bit more complex than he had expected. He radioed engine #5 to "step it up" with the extra thousand gallons of water and manpower.

As we arrived at the scene we observed that the car was fully involved in flames. The reason it had burst into flames was that it had slammed into a large tree. The hood of an auto, when it makes a direct hit against a tree at high speed, stops somewhere deep in the engine, but the rear end continues to move forward and upward and hits the roof with great force, smashing and compressing it downward toward the seats.

When a car hits a tree that is twelve inches in diameter at one hundred miles an hour, the tree often dies within months or weeks. When a vehicle hits a tree that is three feet in diameter at that speed, the tree may not die, or may die ten years later, as was true in this instance. The young man who was driving the car died in a millisecond.

I did not analyze all those consequences at first, because I was trying to make Grandpa proud by following his instructions. I pulled the hose and proceeded to the driver's side of the burning car. Grandpa charged the inch-and-a-half, and I opened the nozzle and began to apply water to the blaze. My protective gear allowed me to get fairly close, although I was a bit concerned that an explosion might occur. Grandpa didn't warn me about that, so I assumed that it was not likely.

Chief Deputy, soon to be sheriff, Paul "P.K." Rowe arrived and stood about twenty feet behind me as I opened the nozzle. Through the flames I saw a lone figure seated behind the steering wheel. The situation was way beyond the radiator steam that Harvey imagined or what Grandpa expected would be good training for me. PK calmly pointed out, "You know there is a person in there don't you?"

Without losing concentration, I responded, "Yes, I'm aware of that."

As the fire began to subside and the chief and number 5 were helping extinguish the blaze, the figure became more clearly visible. He was, ironically, "frozen" in a sitting position as sometimes happens when a person is incinerated. His head above his eyes was gone; severed, I think, by windshield glass or the rearview mirror. The charred remains looked more like a singed Egyptian mummy than a college-age teen. Inside what remained of his skull, the brain matter boiled steadily from the still-hot interior. Intellectually, it reminded me of TV news films of self-immolations being reported from Vietnam. I continued to store the visual and malodorous sensations in memory but walled off the emotional revulsion.

In Knox County, violent-death accident scenes were treated quite differently by law enforcement than they are today. P.K. recruited several bystanders to help remove the corpse after pry bars had opened the doors. The rigid mess was lifted out of the auto and assigned to a hearse. The funeral directors would still provide transport for those beyond our emergency medical skills.

Investigation consisted of P.K., the chief, and the rest of us looking over the characteristics of the accident and trying to deduce what might have happened. There were no skid marks on the highway where the car left the road. It had come over a slight rise of the pavement at a high rate of speed. There was no indication that it had touched the berm or the grass between the road and tree. It had been airborne from the top of the little rise to the tree. The impact likely ignited the car as engine parts disintegrated. That was our hunch. There was no state highway patrol carefully measuring, photographing, interviewing, and calculating the geometry of the scene: just P.K. and us.

Somehow word of the wreck got back to the college, and it was discovered that the victim had been visiting his sister on the weekend. The dean was notified and the sister was brought to the scene. Mercifully, she was prevented from approaching the vehicle and its contents.

I don't think that the sheriff's office had detectives in those days, so it was P.K. and anyone else he trusted to help investigate. Later that evening, Chief Brown called and asked me to meet with him and P.K. at the filling station where the car had been hauled. It sat close to the curb along West High Street in Mount Vernon and had attracted quite a few curiosity seekers earlier, but they had gone. When we arrived, P.K. asked us if we had seen anything of a gun in the car while we were at the scene of the fire. It was a curious question. After we had completed the search, he told us why.

As a matter of routine, the Knox County sheriff's office had teletyped the auto description and license number to the home town of the victim in West Virginia. The reply came back immediately. Law enforcement there was very interested in what had happened. They reported that there had been a double homicide at the home of the victim. Both his parents had been shot to death, and their son was missing. The investigation reached the conclusion that the victim in the flaming car was the killer of his parents and that his death was a suicide.

It was an era of informality in the approach to fires with law enforcement implications. There was no critical incident stress debriefing (CISD) for firefighters and others who could have experienced persistent disruptive emotions due to witnessing and participating in the gory scene. As it turned out, a different acronym, "CSI," would have been relevant, but "Cold Case Files" did not qualify, either thermally or as an unsolved crime.

There were not many deputies in the sheriff's department and since they did all the auto accident investigations in addition to law enforcement they were always busy. They needed more deputies but then, as always, the county could not afford more. Shortly after the incineration incident, P.K. became sheriff and remained so for a couple of decades. After his election, he told me that he had wanted to appoint Chief Brown and me as special deputies to help him with the fire and EMS incidents that had law-enforcement implications, and to help us when we had problems with drunken college students. Fortunately, before he could anoint us, the legislature passed a bill that required all deputies to receive formal education in law enforcement, and the sheriffs lost the privilege of appointing whomever they wished. I still think it would have been a "hoot." I often contemplated being the only deputy sheriff in the whole Kenyon College faculty. I could have arrested and handcuffed some colleague and led him out of the faculty meeting on a charge of aggravated first-degree pedantry. "You have the right to remain silent."

It was obvious that CSI by the Knox County sheriff's office (KCSO) was less formal than the scientific format of the twenty first century. Before those advances arrived, however, more situations required the interaction of CTFD with KCSO. P.K. and I met often in the years after that incident both as friends and professionally.

Harvey Mattews, the Founder of CISD?

It would be years before the field of emergency services addressed the problem faced by many responders who are called to help at horrific incidents. Just as soldiers sometimes exhibit stress related symptoms that prevent them from functioning well in their home lives and jobs, law enforcement, fire and emergency medical personnel can be afflicted with incapacitating emotional distress after responding to incidents that do not turn out well. Once it was realized that those problems resulted in resignations and worse, the field began to experiment with solutions. One form of remedy was Critical Incident Stress Debriefing (CISD). It was similar to group therapy in that those involved met and talked about the incident, sharing their frustration and grief over the bad outcome. Harvey Matthews could have taught the founders of CISD his innovative version without moving from his two square foot station in the firehouse, but it likely would not have been adopted.

Emergency workers did experience severe stress-related maladies long before the CISD remedy publicly addressed the problem. Now it is an openly acknowledged concern. Thirty years ago, most emergency workers did not comprehend that stress could lead to a diagnosed syndrome. When I joined

CTFD getting "shook up" by a run was treated by different techniques than the subsequent official forms of CISD.

In CTFD's early years, volunteer firefighters who experienced emotional stress after an incident didn't say anything about it for fear of decreasing their colleagues' respect for their toughness or manliness. Some just stopped responding to emergencies. They resigned without resigning. A second option was to gross out others with a humorous recitation of the goriest details of the incident. This was, in a way, similar to CISD in its ability to reduce the incapacitating aspects of the emotions by converting the emotions of horror to humor. The humor made every individual in the group aware that others were "grossed out" too. Laughing is incompatible with feelings of horror. In volunteer departments, members who had grown up on the farm, butchered animals, and acquired a host of skills that made them self-sufficient seemed most able to function well when injuries to a victim were severe or fatal. But, the old-time volunteer really preferred to regulate pump pressures, keep engine r.p.m's at the proper levels, or rip the door off an overturned auto.

The emotional implications of "bad" runs at CTFD were subsumed within the normal ethos of the department in ways that would thrill an investigative reporter and evoke outraged oratory from political candidates.

The beer machine was a component of the social glue of the early years at CTFD. It was, therefore, not unusual for some of those responding to emergencies already to be prepared for the worst. Maybe some were sedated at all times and thus always prepared for the most traumatic incidents. However, there were especially bad events that required fire house contemplation and discussion for days afterward. The process of emotional debriefing began upon return of the crew to the firehouse.

Harvey Matthews, czar of the kitchen, brooked no invasion of his domain. That meant that no member dare touch supplies that were intended for the membership at training meals or special occasions. Harvey decided what was special. Toward the end of his reign he and the old Cadillac ambulance/hearse retired from active service and he could no longer jump into the driver's seat and test its top speed. So he assumed command of the department two-way radio and was at the mike to assure coordination of the event from the station. It was from that dispassionate and objective post that Harvey decided which events were sufficiently upsetting to warrant his form of CISD.

The first stage was initiated immediately on the return of the crew. As they entered the kitchen from the equipment bay, Harvey's right hand appeared above the bar holding a fifth of Wild Turkey, and the left hand clutched a number of shot glasses. All who were so inclined took the debriefing medicine and downed it promptly. As this was happening, Harvey was initiating the next step in the process by inviting ("Was he in pretty bad shape?") the telling of every detail of the run. By the time sufficient participation in the debriefing process was complete, those who had acknowledged their need had supplemented their beer machine inoculation measures with Harvey's more thorough post-traumatic prescription and were unlikely to be plagued by a sleepless night of endless replays of the emotionally affecting memories of the incident. Each responder had reported his version with the associated beneficial catharsis. Each member had also rewarded Harvey's altruistic ministrations with the confidential details of the incident, which he could whisper to a close friend, or casual acquaintances encountered at the post office the next day, or even the next week. The rehearsal of Harvey's CISD technique, prevented any epidemic of stress syndrome in the department.

It was a few years before officially sanctioned CISD methods and other forms of treatment for post traumatic stress became formal areas of research and treatment. I am not sure that they work better but I will address some of the latest approaches in another chapter.

Harvey's method seemed to work but by the time members reached a level of relaxed calm that resulted in their being emotionally prepared for the next emergency it should have raised the anxiety level of the whole community.

10

FIREFIGHTERS, CHURCH BELLS, SIRENS, BEEBEEPS, AND RATS

The alarms that call volunteer firefighters to their stations control their behavior 24/7. The technology used to communicate an alarm has progressed rapidly in the past thirty years. Unlike the sudden arrival of EMS at the fire departments, communications evolved by technological steps over several decades. It was rapid evolution, but step by step.

Long ago a pealing church bell in a community might be used to call citizens to the bucket brigade. In my first year as a firefighter, a powerful siren mounted on a utility pole at the side of the station alerted the volunteers who lived within hearing range. The siren could be triggered by either the sheriff's dispatcher in Mount Vernon or from the "fire bar."

The "fire bar" was a set of connections that linked nine telephones in firefighter homes and one at the station. The phones were the pre-touch-tone-era rotary dial model. A person dialing the emergency phone number caused all the phones to ring at once. Each would continue to ring for three minutes or until it was answered. The "bar" was a special link of circuits connected at the telephone company's substation in Gambier. The phones in residences were where a firefighter lived. But they were only placed in homes where whoever answered, firefighter, spouse, or other person would likely be calm enough to pick up the receiver, answer it, take down the information, and then dial zero. The system eliminated having the station staffed at all times. Dialing a 0 closed a contact on the siren and caused it to rev up. Any of the phones could initiate the siren. The sound of that continuous ringing of the phone started the hearts racing in all those homes, and people who lived there held their breath, expecting to hear a report of a disaster in progress.

The siren's wail could penetrate homes and buildings all through the village and was audible for a mile or so. It would awaken everyone in the village at night and assured a standing-room-only group of spectators at fires inside the village and traffic jams on rural roads. (Some firefighters hoped they would get the chance to apply the chief's order about spectator's cars that blocked access to a hydrant: "Bust out the side windows and run the hose through the car.")

The flaw in the fire phone system was that a baby sitter or child might answer it and, just as with today's 911, not everyone understood that the phone number was to be dialed only in an emergency. After the country music show, grateful people from around the county called the emergency number to thank the department for sponsoring it.

Once in a while a person would report an emergency, but one that was not our specialty. "My husband is standing in front of me, and he says he is going to knock me right through the floor." "Yes ma'am, the number you want to call to report that is ### ####, the sheriff's department." I was tempted to add "If he does knock you through the floor, call back on this number and we will bring our ambulance right away."

The next of several advances in alerting technology was a device called a Plectron. It was a radio receiver contained in a metal box about three inches high, twelve inches wide and eight inches deep and it had a handle for easy carrying. It responded to a transmitted radio signal from the station or the sheriff's office by emitting a short burst of "beeps." A voiced message communicated the location and nature of the emergency. The Plectron was relatively expensive, and at first only officers in our department carried them. They provided a significant advantage by allowing an alarm to be received many miles from the station. Officers learned the nature and location of the incident, and it permitted them to decide in advance the best route to the scene and how to staff personnel for the response. The disadvantage of the Plectron was that it was cumbersome to carry around and if it fell off the tractor one had to stand out there in the field until another tone was transmitted in order to find it and dig it up.

The Plectron was succeeded by versions of today's common pager. They are much smaller and cheaper than the Plectron, and are usually worn on the belt. They have a wider range of reception. Then came hand-held two-way radios. They allow officers to communicate with those who are also enroute and allow one person to report directly from the scene of the emergency, and with county dispatching operators. The officers then designate the appropriate equipment and staffing before reaching the station or can request assistance from another department. The radios are expensive and are supplemented by pagers. Direct radio "traffic" between different departments, law-enforcement personnel, medical facilities, and emergency management agencies allows excellent coordination of emergency responses, unless, as on 9/11, too many people are trying to communicate with too many other people, on too many radio channels, all at the same time. When that happens one message "walks on" another preventing either from receiving information. Those situations raise the question "Can those in charge learn to talk and listen to several messages simultaneously, on different wavelengths, under extreme stress, in an unprecedented emergency?" The answer is that an incident command hierarchy can help coordinate operations but cannot eliminate communication problems. Emergency operations at major incidents are going to be vulnerable to errors caused by faulty communications.

Commercial technology firms eventually made listening to emergency radio "traffic" available to everyone. The development of the emergency-frequency radio scanner allowed anyone to buy one and then listen to the radio transmissions of law enforcement, fire, and EMS departments. They are programmable and can select specific agencies to monitor or automatically switch to whichever one is transmitting. For some time after the scanners became available, they were a fad much like the citizens band (CB) radios of the same period. A great many people who were not emergency workers had them in their homes or carried them about.

There is a system of numbered codes and signals used by emergency agencies. Each code number indicates a type of emergency situation so that those responding could anticipate what action might be required. In theory ordinary citizens would not know the codes. A code 28, for example, was a fire. Soon curious listeners had a little card by their scanner with all the code numbers interpreted for them. It was a form of vicarious participation, and of creating "mind witness news."

In our county, when scanners first became available, they led to traffic jams at major emergencies as listeners hopped into their cars and raced to the scene. I would guess that every volunteer department experienced the same phenomenon. Some listeners actually beat the engines or squads to the scene of the emergency. Most, however, were content to follow the lights and sirens at a discrete distance. I do recall one intrepid tow truck driver who monitored radio transmissions with a profit motive. He took the initiative and sped to an overturned car. By the time CTFD units arrived he had hooked on to the vehicle and righted it, with the unbelted injured victim still trapped inside. He profited by being the first tow truck to arrive, but the victim was a bit more "shook up."

If new and untrained volunteers do not already have a scanner before they join the department, they soon buy one that enables vicarious participation in emergencies throughout the whole area. The scanner allows them to enjoy the action of all the departments within range of their radio antenna. When these neighboring stations are responding, they hope fervently that help (mutual aid) may be needed from other departments, particularly "ours." Scanners are always turned on during the day, and for some, day and night.

The most pervasive influence of technology on emergency personnel is still the pager. It has become the electronic leash that threatens to jerk the volunteer back to the station at any moment, 24/7. Because volunteer stations are often vacant it is necessary to have some means to alert personnel wherever they may be so they will rush to respond. It is seldom clear whether enough personnel are available to manage an emergency, and in recent times fewer and fewer volunteers live close enough to the stations to hear a village siren. In most communities today a 911 central dispatch system receives all incoming emergency calls in its jurisdiction and can set off the pager beeps for one or more emergency service. When a pager "beeps," volunteers are expected to stop whatever they are doing and race to the station unless they are too distant, or otherwise unavailable. Availability can be a significant problem for married couples.

When a new member completes some basic training he or she receives a leash (pager). The device is activated by a radio signal transmitted by a 911 dispatcher. The signal "opens" an electronic switch and initiates an audible tone or a vibration that can be felt through clothing. That is, it "gooses" the volunteer. Alert tones are specific to each department and, unless the pager is in "monitor" mode, people in other departments will not be disturbed by a transmission intended for CTFD. Upon "opening", a voice message announcing the nature and location of the emergency is broadcast but its volume can quickly be reduced or muted.

Although the "goose" may result in a reflexive movement or sudden vocalization from the volunteer, the vibration itself does not create a sound that distracts others. The vibrator option assures that even in very loud environments, or in church, there is no excuse for ignorance of the alarm. If in church, however, the sudden reflexive leap elicited by the vibration may be mistaken by others as a spiritual rebirth.

The pager alarm results in a race to the station. There is no flow of saliva like that by Pavlov's dogs in the original conditioning research, but the concept is pretty much the same. Physiologically, and cognitively, the alarm does stimulate emotional arousal and intense speculation about the nature and severity of the emergency. Through the pager, the department controls the behavior of the volunteer for as far as the transmitted radio signal reaches.

Pagers are worn every waking moment. At night, it is at the head of the bed. More than one marriage has been stressed by a pager that forces the volunteer to choose between rewards. Interruptions of this sort are modeled in animal studies. They have shown that withdrawal of the reward results in aggressive behavior on the part of the person whose potential payoff has been terminated unless there is an equally attractive alternative. Spouses of volunteers often underestimate the strength of the attachment between their mate and the fire department. A firefighter making the "wrong" choice can threaten the marriage. Chronic interruptions of family routines have resulted in resignations from the department.

For a few it is likely that the department is more important to their own needs than vice versa. One is reminded of an old tune slightly modified, "Oh father, dear father, come home from the firehouse." The most effective accommodation of family/firehouse relations has been the involvement of the whole family in the activities of the department. Social events, bringing the kids to Sunday morning inspection, auxiliary clubs, and husband/wife memberships have all been effective. But the demands of today's fire service have now undermined the social and cultural opportunities that used to make membership fun and are in part the reason for the decline in volunteerism.

As for me, I never considered that my responses to alarms were analogous to pushing a lever to get a reward. That kind of explanation is for psychologists to speculate about. I never think about why I did it for more than thirty years. Uncovering motives is a mystical task best pursued on a therapist's couch. No volunteer is going to be that curious, but maybe it is worth considering the lever-pushing notion.

Rats, Monkeys, Gamblers, and Firefighters

The chief of a fire department is the preemptive authority, but I was puzzled when Hobe's first words to me after I was elected to membership, were "Congratulations; you'll enjoy it. We have lots of fun."

What did he mean, we have lots of fun? I hesitated to question an assertion by the chief in the first minute of membership. He is the fire chief, so it must be true.

I went home puzzled. Did he mean we have lots of fires and it is fun putting them out? We play games and get rowdy in between fires? Isn't heroically battling flames to save lives and property serious business? How could I, with a wife and four kids, three courses to teach, and a big research grant, justify joining something that was fun? The answer to all my speculative questions turned out to be yes. The chief was right. It was fun but not always the way I would have anticipated.

My Ph.D. persona was hoisted on its own backdraft almost immediately. Classroom rationalism gave way to survival-of-the-fittest empiricism at the top of a ladder with water under high pressure coming out of a heavy nozzle into flames that would like to taste my professorial butt.

I learned too, that fire fighters did more than squirt water. "What do you mean, put the engine in fifth, ease the pump into gear, draw suction, and draft from the creek, but be sure to put the end of the hard suction in a bucket?" What's fifth? What's hard suction? What is a pike pole, pick head axe, Kelley tool, Hux bar, Halligan bar, plaster hook, roof ladder, chafing block, water hammer, minuteman load, ball valve, class B foam, air bag, A post, and so on. I already knew what a bucket was.

Few rookies anticipate how much has to be learned, or the time and energy required to become a useful volunteer firefighter. If responding to the siren and squirting water on a fire from a safe distance once every month or so was all that was entailed, that would be a nice thing to do as a civic-minded citizen. In reality, it is a part-time job with no pay and lots of health hazards.

If others' expectations were as wrong as mine, why do people stay volunteers for years after they realize the full implications of serving? The answer is sometimes they do, sometimes they don't, and sometimes they do and don't. For some, it becomes a passion that impacts all aspects of their lives, even to a fault. Some quickly find they cannot or do not want to do the things required of fire fighters. Others fail to achieve the personal satisfactions they sought in membership. Some volunteers love the work and training but find that they cannot get to the station quickly enough to hop on an engine and are often left behind, so they quit.

Asking volunteers why they become firefighters will evoke a variety of reasons. Whatever the answer, I would be tempted to respond with "Yeah, but what is the real reason?" Uncovering motivations is a mystical task, you will recall, and I do not know any firefighter that is interested in learning why.

I do have some theories about why some of the most dedicated volunteer firefighters join. But I think I know what controls much of their lives minute by minute, hour by hour, day by day, once they are committed to an emergency service. In my first years the behavior of the most committed volunteers was controlled by a unique ring of a phone and by the town siren. Today their lives are controlled by a "bebebeep" or a goosing vibration. I will elaborate on that, but first, some speculation about why they join and stay

Genetics, Physiology, Motivation, Self-Esteem, and Sometimes Guilt

Was it something in their childhood? There is nothing more fundamental to a baby's accommodation to the world than sensory stimulation. Tactile, visual, auditory, olfactory, gustatory sensations are the basis for coming to know what is "out there in the world" and how to learn to live with it. We all seek and respond to the energy forms that mediate our relationship to the world. Almost as soon as they are born, babies actively begin to explore their surroundings. First by looking, listening, smelling, tasting, and touching, then by reaching, crawling, and walking, and then, by teen-age years, the explorations get worrisome. As in most human attributes there are significant individual differences.

Each of the modalities becomes calibrated in such a way that we react physiologically and behaviorally to a greater or lesser extent, depending on the intensity and relevance of the stimulation. The more intense the stimulation the greater the response. Very high level intensities can be aversive. Extremes in exploratory behavior can be dangerous.

Some people, however, seem to crave the extremes. They welcome and even create strongly arousing events in their lives, even to the extent of testing their ability to cope with physical forces that threaten their survival. Some of these stimulation seekers become fighter pilots, or mercenary soldiers. Some become firefighters, and some of them become fire starters.

It has been argued by theorists that such extreme stimulus seeking behavior is akin to an addiction. They must seek the risks and escalate their need for bigger fires, greater danger, more and more frequently. When there is a lull, when there are few emergencies, when they are not in the midst of the symbols of the trade, they long for them and become irritable and depressed at the inaction. Morale in volunteer fire departments declines when there are no emergencies for long periods and zooms to their apex when the lull is followed by a few "good ones" over a short period.

People have noted the risk taking, stimulus seeking of firefighters for a long time. Ernest B. Furgurson in his book <u>Freedom Rising: Washington in the Civil War</u> describes the antics of New York City firefighters who were serving in Washington, D.C., during the Civil War. He tells of one fireman who held another by the ankles so he could hang down and direct water onto the flames. He writes about their heroism but also alludes to their often rowdy behavior. His description would be valid for some career firefighters and some volunteers of every generation, including the present. They become firefighters to seek the stimulation of danger and the satisfaction of defeating the devil appearing as fire, and they can't get enough.

Some individuals are driven by a personal sense of insignificance. They are fearful, but they will risk their lives to achieve the approval and recognition of others and thus a better sense of self worth. Being a volunteer does not require competing for membership or having the extraordinary physical strength that is asked of the career firefighter in urban communities. Age limits are linked more to physical health than to chronological years. Being a volunteer provides opportunities to achieve recognition they otherwise would never realize. They will take risks, too, though perhaps not as skillfully or wisely as the rowdies do. They are loyal volunteers, but even some of them start fires. Neither the firefighters who are stimulus junkies nor those who are praise seekers are likely to satisfy their needs.

Among volunteers, there are those who crave the blaze. Some, who join for the thrills and don't get any, quit. Some get the training as volunteers and then leave for a full-time career at a department where they are assured of "runs" every day. Former CTFD student volunteer Dave Digdon graduated from Kenyon, went to law school, and opened a law office near Seattle. He returned to Gambier for the first CTFD student firefighter reunion in 2000, went home, closed his office, and became a career firefighter.

There are other factors that sustain long-term commitment to the fire service. For some, the teamwork and camaraderie with other volunteers is their principal social life. It provides status important to their self-esteem, and status among their peers that is not likely to come in other contexts. Some have not been successful academically, socially, or athletically. But they have mechanical skills that are recognized as assets to the department. They earn self esteem through demonstrations of that talent.

Stimulus seeking and social approval are supplemented by many other satisfactions around the firehouse, but they remain basic. Without opportunities to express those drives, volunteer firefighters do not last. What the most dedicated members may not realize is that their behavior is so under the control of the fire service that it can endanger personal relationships outside the department.

Firefighters are Like Rats.

In graduate school, I learned that rats, pigeons, and monkeys didn't need to receive a food reward that was delivered every time they went over and pressed the lever in the Skinner box. Once they learned that pressing led to a little drop of liquid to slake their thirst, or a tiny food pellet to quiet their growling tummies, they would keep on hitting the lever even if their efforts were not successful on every press. Initially there was not much else to do in the box. When a certain sound sometimes occurred with the arrival of a bit of sustenance, they would hang around the lever and push it even if the only reward was the sound of a "click" of the lever. Once in a while, one of the bar presses would deliver a food pellet. How much bar pressing a test animal would do for little or no reward was amazing. They kept on pressing the bar even if the reward wasn't adequate to sustain their nutritional needs. The lab animals would do an enormous amount of work over a long period of time if a final lever press delivered a huge reward. Their behavior was controlled by the reward schedule. If the reward came irregularly and unpredictably, the tenacity of the lever pressing was awesome.

To avoid being anthropomorphic, I wouldn't say that rats and monkeys looked forward to getting into the old Skinner box, but as soon as you put them in there they surely keep pressing the lever day and night. If you substitute the words "casino," "slot machine," and "jackpot" for the words "Skinner Box," "lever," and "food pellets" it may be easier to grasp the principles involved here. The gambler may keep pulling the lever till he or she goes bankrupt. Firefighting has the kind of attraction that the crap table does at Las Vegas, except if you crap out while fighting a fire, any winnings go to your next of kin.

As a psychologist biased toward empirically validated explanations for behavior, it was obvious to me that the behavior of volunteer firefighter/EMTs is subject to the same kinds of influences that affect rats and gamblers. Think of the fire station as a Skinner Box. Think of excitement as a rewarding pellet. Not everyone finds the stimulation of firefighting rewarding, but not every animal will work for rat food pellets either. For those who are reinforced by the intense adrenaline rush of the sights and sounds of the fire service, the analogy is valid. A volunteer doesn't get paid for his labors, but who needs to be paid if you can drive a fire truck with siren screaming? Just as with the animals, once the firefighter comes to the station, gets a "taste" of what goes on there, and finds it "cool," more and more time will be spent there. The analogous sound of the bar-press clicks for the fire fighters are numerous. The color red; hearing the whoop, yelp, and wail of the siren; or even listening to the two-way radio transmissions of other departments, all become signals like the click of a lever. They sustain being at the station (Skinner Box), even if a real pellet, 'er emergency', isn't available at the moment. With an emergency radio pager one does not have to be at the station and can even be home in bed.

Then, completely unpredictably, and only after many of these pseudo rewards, an alarm signals a real emergency. The firefighters' behaviors become accelerated, their hearts speed up and pound, they don the turn-out gear for self-protection, shout, and jump on an engine (all of those are like bar presses). Sounds of big diesel engine noises, amplified radio communications, sirens, the sensations of speed; the flashing red lights, white strobe lights, smoke, and tangled wreckage become the cues (clicks of the lever) that are connected to the reward. Those few minutes are like seeing three lemons appear on the slot machine and hearing the clatter of coins fall into the bin and the bells and whistles that announce your jackpot to everyone. Even if the emergency turns out to be a false alarm, almost all the sensory components of a big payoff are there and all the behaviors that bind the volunteer to the department (Skinner Box) minute by minute, hour by hour, day by day are strengthened. Putting out the fire or rescuing a person from pain or death is the firefighter's jackpot.

Add to all this the fact that the CTFD firehouse meeting room contained a red Coca Cola machine with a coin slot. If you fed a quarter into it and pulled up on the top of a bottle, it would "click clack" and supply one Pabst Blue Ribbon or its equal. I wouldn't suggest that the beer machine explained why some members were loyal volunteers. It is a fact, however, that since the machine is gone, it is harder to find firefighters who are at the station most of the day. Rats would work for a drink, too.

There is also a negative correlate to the process. What if the volunteer fire fighter/EMT lives too far from the station and seldom arrives in time to participate but loses lots of sleep anyway? What happens if the rat never gets another pellet after pressing the lever dozens or hundreds of times? It stops pressing, and the firefighter stops responding to alarms if never in time to help. What if the time invested in training puts a stress on a marriage? What if the experience of witnessing a gory accident is so horrific that it is punishing? What if the rat is shocked when it presses the lever? Those circumstances also affect some members of the department and lead them to avoid the environment where they happened.

I never considered myself to be pushing a lever to get a reward at the fire station, but I was.

PART THREE

THE MUTATION OF THE FIRE SERVICE AND THE RELATED CHANGES IN LAW ENFORCEMENT AND MEDICINE

When most fire departments in Knox County also became emergency medical services (EMSs) it set off a chain reaction that affected the local hospitals and the practice of medicine by physicians. At the same time there were major changes in the field of law enforcement and in emergency communications. It is understandable that the dramatic differences in function did not occur without problems. This section elaborates on how fire, law enforcement, and the medical services struggled to reach the level of excellence now available to the citizens of Knox County. Similar efforts were going on across the country.

At first we did not anticipate how our responsibilities would instantly change when the funeral directors stopped ambulance service. For example, the extent of our obligation to the residents of our territory was ambiguous. Nowhere was the word <u>emergency</u> defined and at first it was interpreted to be equivalent to any need for ambulance transport. Bringing a mom home with a new baby was okay, as was picking up an ill township resident a hundred miles from Gambier and transporting her or him home. It soon became apparent that volunteers were being asked to do too much.

Some, but not all, volunteers who still saw themselves exclusively as firefighters enjoyed shifting their manual skills to becoming experts in rescue. Every vehicle crash meant a chance to use the engines and tools for extricating victims. In some ways it invigorated them because there were sometimes more crashes in a month than fires in a year. Tearing a car apart was a "blast."

In part 3 the undertakers caused some perplexing situations to arise and they changed the dynamics of the fire house kitchen.

11

THE EVOLUTION AND THEN THE MUTATION OF THE FIRE SERVICE

The term "evolution" is used by biologists to describe a gradual transformation of the characteristics of a species over many generations. The changes equip an organism better to meet challenges to its survival within its habitat. In that sense the history of firefighting is analogous to evolution. The fire service had changed gradually over decades and centuries. It adapted its methods and technology, improved its performance, and as a result more people and property survived dangerous fires.

The science of genetics gave us the concept of mutation. It is a sudden altering of the genetic code resulting in an organism that has different characteristics than the original. The mutation may or may not result in a form that survives. Metaphorically the term is applicable to what has happened to the fire service. In a period shorter than the careers of most firefighters it became a new species. In that short time putting water on fires no longer was its principal activity. Instead of experiencing the gradual advancements in firefighting equipment and techniques of previous eras, a sudden change, much like a mutation, created a significantly different "organism" whose human component is largely comprised of firefighter/EMTs. It took about thirty years to determine its viability.

Those who joined volunteer fire departments around 1970 and stayed for a couple of decades were faced with unforeseen challenges to sustaining their participation, and new threats to their personal survival. Traditionally, firefighters responded to a damaging fire and used water and tools to put it out. Now, that is only one of many types of emergencies they are expected to resolve. The proliferation of expectations has volunteers today saying, "I am asked to do more than my family and job allow." When enough individuals say that, the funeral pyre of traditional volunteer fire departments is ready for the match. But means still had to be found to meet the emergencies.

The first volunteers at CTFD needed to acquire a limited number of basic skills. They learned how to drive and service fire engines; operate the pumps; select and connect the appropriate hose, man a nozzle; climb a ladder; use a pike pole and axe; don a rubber coat, a helmet, and rubber boots; operate a gasoline-powered saw; draft water from a pond or creek with a portable pump; carry a five gallon tank of water on their backs to fight grass fires; and use some crude rescue tools. Most of them already knew the roads and streets of their community. The volunteers of that period had no problem setting aside an evening a month to review those topics and service the equipment.

If advances in firefighting technology and procedures were the only issues facing volunteer fire fighters today, little would have changed in most departments. In recent years they added rescue equipment such as the jaws-of-life and then air bag "jacks" to their list of tools. Firefighting today also requires donning a self contained breathing apparatus, wearing engineered protective gear, and carrying personal alarm devices in case of injury or entrapment. Infrared heat detectors and other technical improvements augment their resources. There are new training courses on identifying and responding to hazardous materials, special gear to protect firefighters from dangerous chemicals, and training on decontamination of those exposed to them. The volunteers could have accommodated the burden of those changes.

Many departments were suddenly required to adopt emergency medical service (EMS) beginning in 1971. The impact of emergency medical responsibilities has exceeded the limits of participation for many volunteers. The EMS gene immediately transformed the definition of the volunteer's duties. Small volunteer departments that formerly had ten to twenty fire calls per year may now average one or more emergency medical calls per day.

The addition of EMS required volunteers to become emergency medical technicians (EMTs). Their early successes with the basic training led to more advanced training. The first course created an EMT-B (basic), next an EMT-I (intermediate), and finally EMT-P (paramedic). At first only written and practical EMS exams were required for certification. Then mandatory continuing education and refresher courses were instituted. Standard operating guidelines (SOGs) and medical protocols were written to direct medical procedures. Expensive ambulances, defibrillators, endotracheal tubes, intravenous fluids, and drug pharmacology were added to the department budgets. Many departments now require members to be certified both as firefighters and as EMTs. Liability issues required governing bodies to reexamine their role in supervision and increase their insurance expenses.

The effect of the mutation on activity level caused by the EMS was immediately evident in fire departments across the country, but comprehending the implications of the change took decades. Now the mutation threatens the existence of volunteerism. In volunteer departments the addition of EMS was often greeted with enthusiasm. It meant more action, more adventure, and new, exciting experiences. We did not recognize that EMS could kill the traditional volunteer fire department culture.

Each of the added responsibilities and the governmental regulations that accompanied them reduced the number of volunteers who were willing or able to participate. The improvements in equipment and procedure did increase the likelihood of survival for firefighters and victims, but they also added to the time and energy required of firefighter/EMTs. The new governmental policies and regulations were based on the assumption that those providing the service would be full-time employees of urban fire departments. The political and organizational influence of the volunteer departments were not effective in asserting that the new requirements were too burdensome and might result in too few volunteers to staff their stations. The counterargument is that more advanced training saves more lives. Awareness of the technical progress led citizens of every community to expect the most advanced level of emergency service.

To recruit and keep qualified personnel, the traditional meaning of the word "volunteer" has changed, and the notion of service without pay has eroded. Departments tried to find ways to hold members with monetary rewards. That has not always been effective in small-budget communities, and so they must now question their ability to staff or afford their emergency service. The question that must be answered by each department is "How much is the public willing to pay?"

The differences in assumptions about what is expected of rural versus urban fire services are now barely detectable. Catastrophes such as 9/11, Katrina, and Ike demonstrate that mobilization and training of all emergency services must now share a common foundation and include integration of multiple agencies that extend far beyond metropolitan boundaries. The implications of that became clear as Drew Kalnow, Oliver Benes, and James Breece, young volunteers from tiny College Township Fire Department, appeared in the ruins of the World Trade Center passing buckets of rubble. Those young men and many others from around the country arrived in New York City as volunteers. They shared nationally recognized certification of basic training that was comparable to all those who came there to work, and they shared a motivation to use their training to help in any way they could.

Few of those volunteers at the World Trade Center were aware of the enormous differences that have occurred in their fire departments. Less than a generation ago there were some volunteers at CTFD that seldom had traveled more than fifty miles from their homes. They had no interest in doing more than putting water on a fire. The people and culture of that station are gone. The new generation bears little resemblance to those who volunteered back then. They are a new "mutant species."

There is no question that the public is better served by present-day emergency services. The chances of a catastrophic fire are diminished by effective prevention measures and multiple jurisdiction cooperation among departments. The chances of surviving critical illness or injury are immensely greater. That is true in small communities if there are enough "volunteers" who respond in time.

Fire department EMS led to changes that would be mirrored by the revolution in hospital emergency departments and the creation of a medical school specialty in emergency medicine. The period also saw the gradual awareness of the need for fire, medical, and law enforcement agencies to cooperate in their convergent interests.

The next few chapters find members of the department discovering how different medical situations are from what they had done as firefighters. Their fires were largely impersonal events. Medical emergencies are always personal. After a fire it was usually easy to go to sleep. Some medical runs could ruin one's sleep for many days. There were still very few fires, but medical runs could occur several times a day. There seemed to be an infinite number of different kinds of medical emergencies, and some were unpleasant surprises.

The day EMS was added, life at the station had to change. Many of the "old guys" who staffed the firehouse could not have passed the mandatory physical exams that are now required. They didn't even want the skills required of EMTs. A sample of incidents from the early days of transition at CTFD demonstrates how this new responsibility opened our eyes to a whole new category of experiences and some jaw-dropping surprises. CTFD has transitioned to its mutated form. How far it can leave its traditional volunteer roots and survive remains to be seen.

12

EMS IS BORN: IT WAS A HIGH RISK PREGNANCY

Several components of emergency medical care had to be developed before an effective <u>system</u> could serve the citizens of Knox County. In the end there would be a seamless merging of communication technology, treatment of victims in the field by EMTs, transportation to the appropriate health facility, and medical expertise that would assure the patient the best possible outcome. In 1971 each of those variables existed in embryonic form but it took a decade or so of pregnancy and some pretty harsh labor pains for a true system of emergency care to emerge from its Knox County uterus.

Knox County and CTFD came through the ordeal in their typically stormy way of achieving progress. That is why the words <u>civil war</u> and <u>revolution</u>, also seem as apt as the birthing metaphor in describing how difficult it was to achieve an integration of all the components of an emergency medical <u>system</u>. A short history of the era may help one appreciate the obstacles that had to be overcome.

Who Wants To Be An EMT?

Even before our first course in victim care Doctor John Drake, local surgeon and former Kenyon College physician, lectured us about the value of first aid. We were in awe that the most prominent surgeon in the county would take time to come to our village and assert that we could save lives by learning to provide some treatment of victims before they arrived at the hospital. He told us of a man who had been raced to the hospital in an ambulance, based in the eastern part of the county. When the driver and his assistant opened the back door of the ambulance all four wheels of the cot were standing in a pool of blood. The victim was dead. His point was that if someone had been able to stop or slow the bleeding at the scene of the accident, the man would have been saved. His tale aroused in some of us visions of life-saving actions by the CTFD emergency squad. Inspired by Doc's lecture, we imagined administering heroic procedures to save a life, or maybe two, or perhaps of a whole bunch of people, all at one time.

When the morticians declared that they would stop providing ambulance service everywhere on the same day, communities were unprepared. Who would provide this potentially life-saving service? There were several considerations that affected the answer. It seemed logical to some that the duties would be assumed by the local fire departments. Logical to some perhaps, but not to all firemen, CTFD included. The only similarity between fire fighting and emergency medical service was that you got to drive fast and yelp the siren. For some that was enough. But for many old-timers the idea of running an EMS was a violation of the traditions of the fire service, and besides the mechanical aptitude challenges just weren't there. The resistance was somewhat ironic at CTFD since the department had housed the 1959 Cadillac ambulance for a number of years. Picking up a victim, loading him or her into the back, and slamming the rear door, was something that you had to do if you wanted the thrill of driving one hundred miles per hour on Mt. Vernon's East High Street. Harvey Matthews made sure the '59 Cadillac would go that fast, and since his auto repair garage was fifty feet from the station, he always arrived in time to get behind the wheel and demonstrate that "it wasn't bragging if you could back it up."

Bedside manner was an alien concept to old-time volunteer firefighters. Among the strongest opponents to EMS were many of the czars of fire departments all over the country, the chiefs. Some didn't know anything about EMS, didn't plan to learn, and had no interest in managing anything you couldn't extinguish. Extinguishing victims was understood to be unprofessional, though the idea was humorous. Of course when EMS became a source of big money for fire departments, a lot of those convictions melted in the flames of greed.

Knox County reflected all sides of the ambulance issue. There was resistance to the idea of fire department/EMS. Many of the old-timers in the Mount Vernon Fire Department, the chief included, refused. In a historical first, the firefighters union agreed with their Chief. In the rest of the county, volunteer departments had mixed opinions. Fredericktown's volunteers said no and an excellent independent EMS still prevails there.

College Township already had the 1959 Cadillac. Long standing disputes with the Mount Vernon fire department had led to a militant attitude toward that near neighbor and had accentuated local pride in the volunteer organization. Chief Brown was certain that no matter what Mount Vernon decided about ambulance service CTFD would have its own. He placed the question before the members. My life-long interest in things medical made me an immediate supporter and most of the members went along too.

When undertakers started the revolution in emergency medical care the immediate result was a nation-wide proliferation of emergency squads, some based in fire departments, some in hospitals, and some under other sponsorship. Outside the big cities it was not immediately recognized that the number of sick and injured people arriving at hospital emergency room doors would quickly exceed the ability of the medical profession to provide competent care. There were not doctors and nurses trained and waiting to treat the full range of ailments in the emergency rooms, and the hospital facilities were not equipped to manage the influx. It did not take long for the medical community to recognize the potential for saving many lives by becoming prepared to meet the most urgent emergencies arriving in ambulances. Neither did it take long for hospitals to recognize the potential income that could be derived from welcoming those patients. It soon became obvious to people that if they took their medical problems to an emergency room they could get same-day treatment, and it became equally clear to family doctors that they could get more sleep. People flocked to the emergency rooms, and the hospital emergency departments expanded exponentially.

Citizens began to call the emergency squads for the insignificant problems, as well as the serious ones. Initially there was resistance from many medical professionals to the notion that the rough-and-ready volunteer firefighters could be trusted to provide even basic care to patients. However, as they demonstrated they were competent to provide life-saving care, more and more advanced procedures were added to the EMT's skills, and more people lived to reach the emergency rooms.

The undertakers had tipped over the first domino. Emergency squads became the top of a giant funnel that emptied out patients at the emergency rooms. As the emergency medical picture began to develop in Knox County, a larger issue came into focus, and some of what occurred was ugly.

Intelligent, Skillful, Benevolent, Professionals Can Be Nasty

In Mount Vernon in 1971, there was an emergency medical service vacuum. The city's firefighters were not interested in becoming "sissy" EMTs. Some kind of EMS would have to be developed either as a city enterprise or by a private provider. It appeared to one group that the need for an EMS provided a huge opportunity to save a hospital from bankruptcy.

At that time Mount Vernon was served by two hospitals. There were two hospitals because of an outbreak of religious hostility in the 1960s. Mercy Hospital, which had been the only hospital in town, was operated by the Catholic Sisters of Nazareth. Communion carts still rattled down the halls early each morning. That was fine, and no one complained much because all local doctors admitted their patients there. Besides, when you were in the hospital, it doesn't hurt to have a little spiritual presence audible in the hall at any time of day, no matter its allegiance.

The story goes that a benevolent local industrialist, a Protestant, set aside his religious bias, and, as a generous member of the hospital Board of Directors, gave a valuable Oriental rug for use in the lobby of the hospital. Not long after, the gift rug was shipped to the Sisters' headquarters in Kentucky. From that unconscionable act arose a campaign to erect an alternative to

Catholic health care, Bert W. Martin Memorial (Protestant) Hospital. Donations for its construction were asked of all those who worked at the plant where the industrialist was boss. It was understood that each employee would voluntarily contribute. The community took sides. Those who had contributed their own money to build Memorial Hospital, or felt strongly about the religious issue established a fierce allegiance to it. Catholics and those favoring Mercy were equally firm in their commitment. The competition between the two soon included hostile rivalries among doctors, nurses, administrators, staff personnel, and Boards of Directors. At the "bottom line" of the disputes was the bottom line of their respective balance sheets.

The economics of health care, however, were changing rapidly in the wrong direction. The community was not large enough, nor the hospitals efficient enough, for both to survive. Before their eventual consolidation, the board of directors of the smaller Memorial Hospital came up with the idea that starting its own emergency medical service was a possible life-saver for the hospital. What if the hospital bought a couple of emergency squads, trained a few emergency medical technicians, and sent them into the city and county to bring the injured and ill citizens to Memorial Hospital? Some of them would, in theory, be the sickest, worst-injured folks. They would need the most expensive care for the longest period. The ambulances were purchased and the technicians hired and trained. Publicity made the community aware that it was the best-equipped and best-trained EMS in the county.

With financial motivation at its heart and religious hostility at its soul, the new EMS began to operate throughout the county, and thereby initiated one more area of nastiness among benevolent providers of emergency care to the sick and injured.

A gossipy cynicism among locals was that the only emergencies that created a sense of urgency for the mortuary vehicles were those in which a death was highly likely. If the hearse/ambulance could get there before the competitor's and lay first claim to the corpse, the bottom line would be improved. Competition among the funeral services for this source of revenue was said to lead to high-speed races to rescue the dead. I doubt that such a state of affairs actually existed, here or elsewhere, but the story sparked some humor in an otherwise dismal topic. It is a fact that the competitive practices of the Memorial-based emergency squad inflamed the antagonism between the two hospitals and aroused antipathies among some county volunteer EMS squads. In retrospect it can be argued that it hastened the advancement of life-saving changes in emergency care.

Fierce pride in one's local fire department is ubiquitous. Anything perceived as a threat to the honor of the department will be met with aggression. In

Knox County, the same could be said of the two hospitals. When a hospital established an emergency squad that began to invade the territory of the volunteer departments, it was almost inevitable that the competition would become "personal" and ethical standards would be compromised. The war spread beyond the walls of the hospitals and into the emergency medical services of the entire county.

It was the practice of the hospital-based squad to respond to emergency calls anywhere in the county even though a volunteer EMS was miles closer to the victim. On one occasion it came into Gambier village a block or two from the College Township fire station. The ambulance roared past a volunteer EMS station on the way to a cardiac emergency. The minutes lost by not calling for the closer source of aid could have endangered the victim. In their defense they cited the fact that they had a higher level of training, would be in their squad quicker, and could provide essential experience in patient care not available from the volunteers. Those assets were indispensable in optimizing treatment for victims but only for those who were viable when they arrived.

The volunteer services believed that the "go anywhere" hospital policy was robbing some of their residents of the chance to survive. When both the hospital group and a volunteer group arrived at the same incident, tensions were high. On one occasion the chief of a volunteer group and the chief of the hospital service faced off inside an ambulance. That somewhat dismayed the victim looking up at them from the cot.

The Memorial Hospital squad likely tried to avoid taking victims to Mercy Hospital, and county volunteer squads took sides by developing an allegiance to one hospital or the other, as had the doctors. In the early days of the conflict, however, it had become evident that the welfare of the victim depended much more on which doctor staffed which emergency room when he or she arrived. Some physicians were better than others in the practice of emergency medicine. One could win or lose at either hospital. Losing was a bummer.

I never learned the specifics of the financial impact of the emergency service on Memorial Hospital. I doubt that it was favorable. The costs of ambulances, their maintenance, the employee salaries, supplies, communications equipment, and insurance had to be significant. The emergency service may have acquired some patients for the hospital that would otherwise not have been admitted to it. The tendency of some other squads to avoid taking patients to Memorial Hospital lost some patients who would have been admitted. The rival, Mercy Hospital, was placed in the position of having to duplicate the staffing of the Memorial emergency department, so its bottom line continued to be troubling. At the time there were no local doctors who specialized in emergency medicine, and those physicians who staffed the ERs were sometimes hazardous to one's health.

The costs and complexities of medical care eventually made it clear that the merger of the two hospitals was the only hope of gaining a level of financial security capable of sustaining hospital care for local citizens. The fundamental altruistic motives of the EMTs finally produced the insight necessary to cooperation. An organization was created to provide a forum for airing turf problems and establishing enlightened policies. It included emergency room doctors and nurses and led to something much closer to an emergency medical system. Next came the problem of merging two hospital organizations that hated one another, loved their buildings, and were both going broke.

How Medical Care in Knox County Gets Dragged, Kicking and Screaming, Into the Twenty First Century

The members of the two hospital boards of directors were good people. Good people can disagree and feel strongly in their beliefs and that their convictions are worth fighting for against other equally good people with whom they differ. Sometimes dignity and reason are sacrificed. The directors of the Mercy and Memorial hospital boards realized that a merger was the only possible way of assuring hospital care for the community. The legal and financial merging proved much simpler than the amelioration of the underlying passions. It seemed that merging just meant that the fighting would be more intimate with the members of each board now meeting in the same room. Then an unconscionable proposal was made by some enlightened members of the new Knox Community Hospital (merged) Board of Directors. Based upon their analysis of the deficiencies of the Mercy and Memorial buildings they proposed to build a new modern hospital.

The whole community took sides on the issue and it seemed that the only thing they agreed on was that there would be no new hospital. Conflict raged. Not only were local citizens opposed but a new federal government program appeared at the same time and it was an obstacle to proposals for any new medical facilities or equipment.

Across the United States medical costs were threatening to exceed citizens' ability to pay for their own care. Technological advances were promising to save thousands of lives and every medical facility wanted every one of them. The new devices diagnosed and cured people and they promised to bring in lots of money to those medical providers who could use them to treat their patients. If they did not have them they could lose lots of income. The government decided to create a system to try to control the costs. Federally funded health planning federations were formed comprised of citizens who were not employed in health care and their counterparts, the providers of care. Their mission was to decide how many CAT scanners, nursing home beds, hospital beds, and even whole hospitals could be justified in each geographic region of the country. The government argued that if every provider bought every medical device or built every new facility they wanted, the cost of paying for too many facilities would be divided among too few patients, and the expense of care would skyrocket. They were right. In Mount Vernon both hospitals would have sought to duplicate each others resources lest the other have a competitive edge. That had already happened when both Mercy and Memorial had created round the clock emergency care in each hospital.

The federally motivated plan was intended to limit the cost of health care and thus make it more affordable. States were divided into geographic regions. There were local planning groups within each of them. I served as a member of the Mid-Ohio Health Planning Federation at a crucial time for Knox County. Our committee met and voted on how many of everything was enough for any given community in our whole region of the state. We were to keep anyone from getting more than enough, according to us. It was democratic in both connotations of the word, and in the final analysis it didn't work.

In Mount Vernon and Knox County the government's health planning system became immersed in a white-hot conflict. The opponents in the partly religious war between the two old hospitals were the emotional combatants. There were two hospital buildings housing two sets of patient rooms, two operating room facilities, two emergency rooms, and two professional staffs for a town of fifteen thousand citizens plus the folks in the surrounding rural areas.

When their financial and governing merger happened, every member of the board of each hospital became a member of the board of new Knox Community Hospital. Then the real hostilities began. There were still two different buildings in two different locations and the same groups of rival doctors, workers, and patients who detested their rivals at the other building. The merger in no way eased the hostile moods. The two continued to operate as if nothing had happened. When it was proposed that the two flawed and out-of-date hospital structures be replaced with one new modern hospital building, uncivil war broke out. The allegiances of Protestants to the bricks and mortar of Memorial hospital were equaled by the traditional devotees and doctors of the Catholic Mercy bricks and mortar. Each side was opposed to any new hospital but adamant that if something were to be built, it would have to be an addition to its own cherished building and envisioned the demolition of the hated rival structure. Under the leadership of respected and dedicated leaders such as Samuel S. Lord of Kenyon College and banker William Stroud, of Mount Vernon a plan developed to erect a modern new facility. But the plan had yet another obstacle. It could not proceed without approval of the Health Planning Federation.

The process of convincing the community of the wisdom of building a modern facility did not go smoothly. It had never been so divided and contentious. The Mount Vernon News printed scores of letters to the editor from each faction, maligning the idea of a new hospital. The letters were angry and some were irrational. One opponent asserted that the architect's plan of the proposed new hospital would allow bedpan smells to permeate all the patient rooms on a floor. Another, written by an engineer, claimed that the site selected for the new building was on quicksand and the new hospital would sink into a quagmire. After several tension filled months of listening to the, for and against debate, the Mid-Ohio Health Planning Federation gave its blessing to the construction of the new Knox Community Hospital.

The plan, to build a new hospital was still however, being cursed and damned by many business owners, doctors, and religious leaders. Local citizens who had contributed their personal dollars to either the Catholic or Protestant buildings were particularly outraged. If a store owner publicly favored adding to one old building or the other, some customers would stop shopping there. If the owner favored a new modern hospital, almost everyone would stop shopping there.

Today, there is one modern hospital, staffed by competent doctors and nurses, a few of whom were "enemies" during the "troubles."

Equally volatile battles were fought in health planning federations across the country. Most agree that cost containment was not achieved. On the other hand, the market forces that won the battle enabled the widespread availability of technology that potentially benefits everyone (who can afford it). That steamroller, for example, brought "intelligent" defibrillators to every emergency squad, then to fire trucks, then to law enforcement vehicles and shopping malls, and now you can get your own personal version, sometimes implanted in your chest.

The "heart" of this life-saving progress was not (in my opinion) purely technological. The greatest advancement has been in the rise of an emergency medical care system that now can flow seamlessly from where the victim drops to the most advanced care necessary, sometimes in less than an hour. No matter whether the victim is suffering a potentially fatal heart rhythm or pinned to the floor of his car by its roof, there is a vastly greater chance of survival than in 1971. It came about by various scenarios all across the country. The evolution of emergency medical care may have benefited more people than any other medical advancement in the past three decades. It has also dealt a near fatal blow to some of the traditions of the fire service: which is a good thing.

A couple of decades after a new Knox Community Hospital replaced the hallowed halls of the two warring factions, those old conflicts have finally been laid to rest, in part that is because many of the principal contestants have, too. Throughout this period, the evolution of emergency medicine was continuing. The enormous progress in the whole emergency medical system has made those early days seem humorous, ironic, and tragic.

The Mount Vernon Fire Department eventually assumed the City's emergency medical service, though some of the early hospital-based personnel still staff it. It confines its coverage to the city and the townships it has contracted to serve but will respond with "mutual aid" anywhere, anytime, they can be of assistance. Volunteer departments still serve their townships, but some have a few full-time paid members who are paramedic/firefighters able to administer life-saving drugs.

The rise of the emergency medicine field in the U.S. led to a new curriculum of technical education that in turn has produced thousands of well-trained EMTs at each level of certification. The revelation that emergency medicine is a legitimate specialty of physician training has resulted in emergency room physicians and staffs that maximize the chances of survival in even the most critical cases. Many victims that formerly ended up in the funeral parlor now take flights to a trauma center and then ride home in the family car. All that progress came within one generation.

Nearly as important is that serious complications have been prevented by proper prehospital care in non-life-threatening situations. The progress that has been achieved is perhaps best communicated by stories about victims who are not around to greet, or create, the next generation.

After almost thirty years an integrated emergency management system composed of firefighters, EMTs, doctors, hospitals, law-enforcement agencies, and governmental agencies cooperate in the public interest.

No one should cite those early years as "the good old days." Pioneers often explore many trails before they arrive at their "land of plenty" and some of them are dead ends. The full meaning of that assertion will become apparent in the next few chapters.

13

AT CTFD: SQUAD RUNS 90, FIRE RUNS 10, SQUAD RUNS WIN

The mutation that changed a FIRE department to a service that responds to medical and other kinds of emergencies came about overnight when the funeral directors announced that they were out of the ambulance business. The result was a sudden, dramatic expansion of their responsibilities.

The most important long-term implication was to move the initial treatment of the seriously ill and injured from the doctor's offices and hospitals to wherever the patient lay. It forced the medical community to revolutionize its approach to emergency medicine. Once the process was started the pace of change accelerated for three decades. Thousands of people who would have died during that time are still here to appreciate the morticians' decision.

The Mutation Hits CTFD.

Abruptly in January 1971, we at CTFD were charged with caring for sick and injured people. There were no training manuals, no instructors to teach us how to administer proper care, and few ambulances. Some of the guys at CTFD were excited about taking on the responsibility, some were not interested. None of us recognized that the department would never be the same. In the first year or so some victims paid the price for our lack of preparation.

It took quite a while for the states to legislate EMT certification programs. When it finally did the immediate effect of the new laws on us was two-fold. Our Red Cross first-aid class was no longer approved, so we had to take Red Cross patches off our slightly stained "doctor's white coat" squad jackets. Second, one could only be an EMT by taking a formal course from a state-certified instructor and by passing both a written and a practical exam. Before that could happen, there had to be courses of instruction and textbooks, and qualified instructors had to be created.

We had become emergency medical technicians (EMTs) by default, not through education or training. To help us assume responsibility for EMS Chief Brown arranged for Ed Dick, of Centerburg Fire Department in the southern part of the county, to come teach us some techniques and principles. Ed had the maturity and personal qualities essential for instructing volunteers in victim care and was one of the most important Knox County EMS pioneers.

Most of us at CTFD were excited about the prospect of having more runs and maybe even saving some lives. What we did not know about emergency medical care was almost everything. Before Ed Dick laid a foundation of useful training, the first-aid course was our only preparation. Our most important asset was the 1959 Cadillac hearse that had been painted red and white and whose engine had been so souped-up by Harvey that it could win any "stock ambulance" race in the country. There was a brief period before we graduated from the first state-certified class when we were as dangerous as the funeral directors. Imagine having an emergency medical crew on duty at the station just sitting around sipping beers from the department's own beer dispenser.

Even the ambulance could be lethal. The old Cadillac was constructed like a hearse, because that is what it was. One characteristic of the interior was that the space between the floor and ceiling required the care giver to sit with head slightly bent over the head of the victim. When it had been a hearse, accessibility to the victim was not a priority. As an ambulance, however, it required that the victim lie flat while being loaded or suffer a possible concussion. Bumping the victim's head when being loaded into the ambulance was sometimes not the worst thing that could happen.

The road to Heaven is Paved with Good Intentions.

We had taken old Bill to the hospital a few times because he was having trouble breathing. The diagnosis we were given in the hospital was congestive heart failure (CHF). It is a condition in which the heart is not functioning effectively. As a result, fluid accumulates in the lungs, making respiration difficult. CHF was a really nice new medical term for us. We could impress laymen by using the acronym.

Bill was the first of our "frequent flyers" (patients who were transported to the hospital many times). On each occasion, he was sitting up in bed when we arrived. Even though he complained about difficulty breathing, we knew that he wasn't that bad off because he was sitting up. We did not listen to his heart, count his respirations or take his blood pressure because we did not have a stethoscope or a blood pressure cuff, nor would we have known how to use them.

When once again we were called to pay a visit to Bill, we coasted down the hill to where he stayed with a relative. He was sitting with a pillow for support as usual. We loaded him on the cot with the head of it elevated for his comfort. We rolled the cot to the door, picked it up and carried it over the bumpy walk to the back of the Cadillac and sat it on the driveway till we opened the back door. "Okay, Bill we will have to lay you flat for a minute till we get you into the squad." The head of the cot was lowered, and the four of us took our positions and lifted it into the back. When we got in, Bill was dead.

I learned more about CHF. In a sitting position the patient may have labored breathing but may remain awake and conversant. In the advanced stage, if the patient is laid supine the lungs can immediately fill with fluid, and that's it. When an old friend is killed by one's ignorance, it provides strong motivation to learn how to avoid making the same mistake again. Now, no ambulance door requires the cot to be flat when loading it. Today, a paramedic would assess Bill's heart and lung function, apply electrocardiograph leads to monitor his heart rhythm, and administer appropriate drugs and high volume one hundred percent oxygen while he sat up in his bed. That might have enabled Bill to live a while longer. As far as I know, Bill was the only person who ever died because we were ignorant.

Our friend Bill's death was a tragic lesson, but it was only one of thousands of lessons being learned throughout the country. As inept as we pre-emergency medical technicians were, the state of hospital emergency medicine was just as archaic and could be just as tragic. We discovered that very quickly as our squad runs accumulated. That is the downside to the story. The upside is that the beginning of EMS initiated the revolution in health care that saves thousands of lives that would have been lost in the year of Bill's death and before.

Everyone knew that formal courses in victim care were needed right away. People began working on the development of training courses but progress was not smooth. Political and turf issues were predictable. Would EMS be governed by the state fire marshal's office, medical authorities, or a new organization? The National Registry of Emergency Medical Technicians arose to set standards for training, testing, and certifying the preparation of EMS personnel. States, however, wanted to set their own standards and some rejected the National Registry initiative. The objective of the National Registry was to assure uniformity of standards throughout the country. It was decades before that came to pass. Each state and each community knew what was "best" for its own jurisdiction. Predictably, therefore, there were years of competition, political maneuvering, and legislative wrangling before relatively clear procedures and practices prevailed.

In Ohio, the state fire bureaucracy decided that it really wanted to rule EMS. The teacher education lobby and the medical establishment were competitors. The fire service already had instructors organized to teach firefighting, so they jumped into the training vacuum and quickly asserted that fire instructors would double-dip as EMT instructors. After all, it was mostly fire departments that would be responsible for responding to the emergencies. There was a significant time lapse before instructor training programs and standards for teaching EMS would be established with the welfare of victims as the first priority.

With their inherent head start, the state-certified fire instructors could acquire the first textbook on emergency medical aid and teach the courses.

The fact that there is very little relationship between expertise in teaching how to put out fires and teaching medical knowledge was irrelevant. It was a quick way to produce some standardization in training for EMTs and it gave the fire service a head start on ruling EMS. The qualifications of the instructor could be addressed later.

At the outset, many career firefighters did not want to be trained in both areas, and some refused. It also became apparent that many individuals who are excellent firefighters are not talented in victim care, and vice versa.

It took several decades for dual-trained firefighter/EMTs to become the norm and EMS training to be standardized and taught by carefully screened instructors and health care professionals. In recent years candidates for full-time employment in the fire service often are required to be certified in both fire and EMS, but not all communities have placed EMS in the fire department. At first, dual training in volunteer departments was a special challenge. Many volunteers came to the fire departments with life skills that transferred easily to firefighting. A goodly proportion came from farming families and the construction and manufacturing trades. They were skilled with mechanical tools and motorized equipment. Delivering a baby, managing an overdose, or talking a person out of committing suicide were not types of things they joined to do. The subsequent exponential growth in time required by training and service as both EMTs and firefighters discouraged more and more volunteers from joining or remaining.

In the first few years, some instructors who were certified to teach firefighting courses did not necessarily have the background for teaching emergency medical technology. The assumption was made that if one is an adequate teacher in one area, then the teaching skills will readily transfer to the other. CTFD quickly learned otherwise.

Can John Say Cardiopulmonary Resuscitation?

Chief Brown was able to locate a state-approved fire instructor for our first formal EMT course. He hailed from nearby New Albany, a short distance down state route 62 from Knox County. New Albany at that time was a two-traffic-light junction at the intersection of state routes 62 and 161 near Columbus. The feed mill and the pizza parlor were the distinctive landmarks. Later, in the 1990s, The Limited clothing conglomerate CEO Lesley Wexner formed a company that bought hundreds of acres of land in and around the village. It created a "way upscale" community with million-dollar homes, a performing arts center, and golf courses. Long before it became home to millionaires, New Albany was already famous, but for only one thing.

John Spellman was a New Albany volunteer firefighter and certified fire instructor, but his profession was town cop. John and his associates in the police department had, figuratively, put New Albany on every AAA map in the state and possibly in the country. They ran the most effective speed trap in all of Ohio. Twenty-five miles an hour, not twenty six, was the limit, and the boundaries extended from the center of town out beyond where one could even see the village.

But John was a good old boy and understood pumps, engines, hose pressures and the like, as a member of the New Albany Volunteer Fire Department. He became a fire instructor in the eyes of the state of Ohio Trade and Industrial Commission, which had jurisdiction over fire fighter education. One obvious flaw in his transition to teaching of the emergency medical curriculum was his difficulty with the English language.

John got along fine with the vocabularies of the fire service and speed traps, but when he was required to go beyond the topics he had grown up to know, words baffled him. His transfer from fire instructor to EMT instructor was, therefore, a bit ragged. He courageously persevered in teaching emergency medical knowledge, as was his right. He arrived on time for every session and faithfully read the text to us, one word at a time. But terms related to medical technology were strangers to his vocabulary, and "hooked on phonics" was not yet available to rescue him. As we followed along his recitation, we could usually help him. When words like pneumothorax or epiglottis suddenly appeared in mid-sentence, his utterances faltered. They would cause his mouth, lips, and breath to get out of synch resulting in a vocalized randomization of vowels and consonants. Maybe that was for the best. His teaching method made it mandatory to read the text ourselves and to emulate the illustrations in order to pass the written and practical exams. John's sincerity and ability to laugh at himself endeared him to us, and we loved having him teach at CTFD.

To those of us who were truly interested in this new emergency medical responsibility, learning about all the things that can happen to people and what to do to help them was exciting. The rest of the department endured the training and stood ready to do their part but were quite happy to let the enthusiasts do victim care. After all, it meant many more opportunities for the adrenalin rush of driving fast with flashing red lights and wailing siren.

Chief Brown had been in the U.S. Navy Reserve, training to be a corpsman, but by nature and preference he was an engines, pump, and nozzle man. His profession engaged him in the manufacture of huge jet engines, and his avocation was farming. He loved fire trucks and eventually had one or two of his own. Administering the department, maintaining relations with neighboring departments, and leading regular fire training sessions dominated his evening and weekend free time. At the same time, he believed fervently that our community would be best served by an autonomous local EMS. The added responsibility of creating and managing EMS required some additional assistance.

Sometime after John Spellman taught our first course and we were certified EMTs by the Trade and Industrial Commission of Ohio, the chief approached me with the idea that I take responsibility as his assistant in charge of EMS. I was flattered by the invitation. I didn't feel confident at first and was not comfortable with people confusing a doctor who is a Ph.D. with the ones who are M.D.s. If you are addressed as "doctor," people make assumptions about what and how much you know. Some attributed status to me that was not warranted by my expertise in human, whale, and bat hearing.

There is a big distinction between a Ph.D. and an M.D., and knowledgeable observers know who to trust in medical matters, but in this instance the confusion was to my advantage. I was, however, uneasy about my elevation in rank because, up to that point, when you "came on" seemed to preempt other qualifications for authority.

If we followed the department's traditional seniority bias the other Ph.D. firefighter should have been delegated the role. He was the professor of religious studies, and that would seem to make him closer to issues of life and death than to infernos, though I guess some would want to debate that. However, even the old-timers had come to question his judgment after his canine-tooth brushing incident, and they raised no objections to my appointment as "assistant to the chief for squad."

I guess that Hobe, not having seen me do anything really foolish or, more truthfully, not having been around when I did, assumed I was worth the gamble. It worked out well enough that I continued to serve under him for twenty five years.

One reason for my endurance was that the department had expanded membership to include more Kenyon students. They were as dedicated to EMS as the old-timers were to the fire service. Kenyon students began to play an important role in the department and are now essential. Almost unnoticed was that fewer and fewer volunteers from the community lived in the village. The students were always in the village and therefore quickly received lots of valuable experience.

The department, the community, the college, and the nation have benefited from the subsequent careers of some of those students after their graduation. They have continued significant roles in public service as volunteers, professionals, and citizens.

Learning Neat Stuff That Saves Lives

Of all the subject matter in the EMT curriculum, the area that generated the most dramatic visions of heroic intervention by EMTs was the new cardiopulmonary resuscitation (CPR). The idea that one could learn a skill that could bring someone back to life and who had stopped breathing and had no pulse, was a revelation. Dare we think that we could become the mediators of resurrections?

The technique was not difficult to learn and is still saving lives even though every few years the American Heart Association changes the exact procedures required to be certified, and even when their procedure is different from the method taught by the American Red Cross. Fortunately, if one uses last year's method, people do not automatically die from out-of-date CPR.

If one examines the "save" data showing what percentage of people receiving CPR survive, the numbers vary but 5 percent is probably the average. (Today significantly more can be saved. The development of defibrillator technology and the proliferation of paramedics who can promptly administer appropriate drugs have increased the survival rate. That is true only if aid is delivered to the victim very quickly after onset of cardiac arrest. Under those ideal circumstances maybe as many as 20 percent of arrest victims will survive the incident.)

Many variables affect the likelihood of survival from cardiac arrest. The first crucial factor is how quickly CPR is initiated. If it is within the first moment, the chances of survival are enhanced but by no means certain. If CPR is initiated immediately and defibrillation occurs within five minutes, and a paramedic can administer appropriate drugs within around seven minutes, survival rate is encouraging enough to make EMS people feel good and the survivors feel alive. It is when all those measures are carried out within moments of cardiac arrest that the save rate reaches as high as 20 percent. Those optimal conditions are most likely to occur for a monitored hospital patient. It is not common elsewhere.

In a rural volunteer EMS department at the time we started, and even now, a save is rare. Few "arrests" are witnessed, so there is a delay in starting CPR. Of those that are witnessed, they are often not witnessed by people who are trained in CPR. When witnessed, and CPR is initiated, the window of opportunity is open for some but not all, and if open, other aid must be administered very soon. The defibrillator is the first great hope. If a shock to the heart occurs within five minutes of arrest, it is more likely to reestablish a heartbeat that will supply circulation to vital organs. If, after restarting the heart, oxygen and appropriate drug therapy can be administered, the chances of sustaining the heartbeat are enhanced, but survival still remains less likely than you would hope if the victim is you. People who can do CPR, administer oxygen, use a defibrillator, start an IV, and administer appropriate amounts of the correct drug need to be at the victim's side rapidly. In the early days only the first two assets were possible. We did not know about the others, and even if we had, the medical community would have been horrified by the thought of EMTs being permitted to do the last three.

The farther the victim is from a hospital or EMS, the less likely it is that aid can be administered in time. Urban areas now provide a reasonably quick response with all the necessary elements.

In rural areas, survival from cardiac arrest is still rare. The primary reason is the distance/time relationship. The distance from the EMS to the victim is, on average, greater than in urban locations. Hence, travel time from the station to the victim is likely to be longer than the survivability of the heart, even with CPR started immediately. Small communities do not have the tax base necessary to pay personnel to staff an EMS station 24/7. In many volunteer departments, that means that once EMTs are notified of an emergency there will be two or more minutes before a full crew is assembled and ready to respond. Often that will be five minutes or even longer. That time must be added to the time necessary to drive from the station to the scene of the emergency. At CTFD it may be three to six minutes before the crew will be on station (during the day), and travel time from station to a victim may be as long as ten minutes. Survivability declines with each minute of delay. In recent years defibrillators have been placed on emergency squads, persons trained to start an IV are part of a crew, and training has included the insertion of endotracheal tubes to assist administration of oxygen. But many rural departments do not have paramedics trained to start the required heart medications. Fortunately, mutual aid policies of urban departments often permit paramedics to come quickly to aid the rural EMS heart victim. If you have an arrest and survive, you should be amazed as well as grateful. Remember, if you have chest pains call for help early. There is no record of any 911 call from someone who is already in cardiac arrest.

That fatalistic perspective was not presented to us when we were taught CPR. In fact, we pretty much saw ourselves as high-probability heroes who couldn't wait for our first victim's heart to stop. It happened in a good place: a football game.

An emergency squad is required to be in attendance at the Kenyon College football games. The NCAA rule is a sign of our advanced civilization. Certainly it has been recognized that sports can lead to serious injury since the days of the Roman Coliseum.

Taking the ambulance to the football games of early fall are usually delightful opportunities to hang around the squad, soak up some sun, read a book, or on rare occasions watch the team enjoy a brief lead in the score. The guys play hard, but not dangerously hard. There are numerous certified athletic trainers and a team physician on the benches ready to pounce on the strains, ligament tears, and boo-boos for which normal people might call an emergency squad. But football types fear the label "wimp" more than death itself. Occasionally, about once every two or three years, there is a significant problem, usually a head or neck "ding" or a collapse from heat exhaustion that begets EMS involvement.

More often it is the fans who are visited by EMS. Most common are the stings from the yellow jackets that convene at the stadium on football Saturdays for a taste of soft drink or mustard-splattered hot dog. The fan fails to notice that the yellow jacket is dining or drinking at the very point where refreshment and oral cavity meet. Responding to the rudeness of the selfish human, the yellow jacket resorts to a venomous attack on lips, tongue, or whatever is accessible. If the unfortunate stingee has a severe allergic reaction to the stingor's weapon, it could rapidly be a life-threatening insult. A massive systemic reaction can close the breathing passages and result in death in minutes. An emergency squad had better be close.

Fantasy Becomes Reality: Once

After our training from John Spellman and some more thorough courses, we envisioned ourselves as able to render a directed verdict of "life" for those fortunate enough to have us respond to their crisis.

In the first quarter of a game with a neighboring college, while fans were still arriving, the public address announcer suddenly broadcast "Is there a doctor in the stadium? Please report to the area next to the press box." Seated in the squad fifty yards away, I wondered aloud what was going on. First of all, didn't that yahoo on the p.a. system know we are here? If there is a medical emergency, we, not a doctor, ought to be called. I decided to go up to see what was going on.

Just outside the gate next to the press box, I could see a number of people looking down. Following their example, I followed their gaze and saw a man lying face up on the ground. Kneeling beside him was another man, who it turns out, was a doctor. When I reached them I advised them that I was an EMT. They seemed to accept that, probably because in those early days we wore those white doctor's office coats. When I asked what was wrong and proceeded to go through the ABCs (airway, breathing, circulation, the first steps in victim evaluation procedure), the doctor looked up and said, "This man is in cardiac arrest!" in a tone that implied but did not articulate the coda "dummy."

My reply was "Yes, sir," followed with the initiation of CPR and a call for the squad to be brought to the location. Student EMTs Jay Andress and Homer Richards took turns doing CPR as the man was loaded onto the cot and into the squad. His wife, who was standing by in shock and concern, got into the back of the squad with us, and we started for the hospital. As we hooked up the oxygen and continued compressions, we learned that the man's name was Whitesy. It was an unusual name.

A minute into our race to the hospital, Mr. Whitesy suddenly took a breath. We stopped compressions and continued to give him oxygen. This is the way it is supposed to happen. The reason for optimism and elation quickly disappeared. Mr. Whitesy once again stopped breathing and had no pulse. We restarted CPR the rest of the way to the hospital, but there were no more hopeful signs. Fortunately, a doctor was in the ER. It was anesthesiologist Dr. Cassady whose turn it was to be doctor in the ER that day.

Given the age and specialties of those on the hospital staff, patients experienced a gamble that most never knew. I had learned that not all doctors know how to manage all medical emergencies. Some of the victims we transported to the hospital didn't live to achieve that insight, or achieved the insight and didn't live.

Dr. Cassady did know what to do for Mr. Whitesy. He and a nurse quickly hooked up the EKG to see whether there was any sign of activity in Mr. Whitesy's ailing heart. They saw ventricular fibrillation. That indicates that the heart is still trying to beat but that the heart muscle is not able to act in a coordinated pump-like sequence necessary to circulate blood. The defibrillator applies to the heart muscle an electric shock of sufficient intensity to stop its chaotic activity. That seems counterproductive, but it actually gives the heart a chance to reset its usual neuroelectrical sequence. Then, with good fortune, the part of the heart that is supposed to contract first does so, the next part follows, et cetera. until voila, a heartbeat. It doesn't always work.

Dr. Cassady shocked Mr. Whitsey's heart. It stopped but did not reset itself. He shocked it again: same result. He shocked it again. The EKG suddenly showed electrical activity of the heart that indicated it may be beating. Feeling for a pulse, he found one. Mr. Whitesy began breathing.

Meanwhile, Mrs. Whitesy was seated out in the hall beyond the ER door. We tried, as our text said we should, to assure her that everything was being done that could be done. I also told her that he was in serious condition "as you certainly know."

Dr. Cassady came out. He told us that Mr. Whitesy not only had recovered a heart beat but that he was awake. A week later he walked out of the hospital and went home.

Aren't we something else? Isn't being a volunteer emergency medical technician just about the neatest thing one could ever do? Letters of commendation came from many sources. The president of the college sent a personal note. Even some doctors who had been skeptical of this new system sent notes, surprised that volunteers could make the difference between life and death.

Now thirty years later, I realize what an exceptional case this was. Several things worked in Mr. Whitesy's favor and all of them combined to his benefit. First, his arrest was witnessed and CPR begun quickly; second, an emergency squad and crew were present where he collapsed; third, supplemental oxygen was administered with CPR; forth he was transported to the hospital in less than 10 minutes; fifth, Dr. Cassady, one of the few physicians in the community who could defibrillate him, was waiting at the hospital upon his arrival.

From that day on to this, more than thirty years, I never participated in another successful save through CPR. The biggest reason is likely that those first two variables never prevailed again. The time from arrest to effective CPR has been too long. The revolution going on now in which defibrillators will be available and used promptly may result in a significant ability to save more people in arrest, but not all. The ability to use drugs to prevent its onset is also more common and can sometimes prevent cardiac arrest until definitive care is available.

One variable not recited above is the most deadly factor in coronary attacks. People, especially men, deny the symptoms until it is too late. Chest pains and other symptoms of a heart problem are unwanted sensations. "My chest pain is not a heart attack. I have too much I need to get done right now." "I have to finish this task before I think about whether the pain is worth considering." I point this out because even if the reader is aware that people do deny the cause of their symptoms until it is too late, it does not mean that the reader will be instructed by that knowledge. I can say this with authority because a local EMS medical director and I denied our symptoms and got away with it. If I hadn't lucked out, my grandchildren would never have been able to read this book. If the doctor hadn't wised up to the truth when his pain persisted for hours after he used his chain saw to cut up a tree, many lives, in addition to his own, could have been lost. He was the physician who taught advanced cardiac life support to paramedics and other physicians of the community. My advice is do what the economist would do, that is, a cost/benefit analysis. Decide ahead of time what decision you will make. There is no excuse for gambling that your pain is indigestion and dying of a heart attack due to your ignorance or negligence. If you are not having a heart attack no doctor or nurse will yell at you for bothering them. They do not get paid by the save.

There is a postscript to our success with Mr. Whitesy. For years after he walked out of the hospital I wondered how long he survived. Given the knowledge and experience since that day in 1974, I guessed it would not have been very long. One morning in 2007 I was reading the <u>Columbus Dispatch</u> newspaper and scanned the obituaries. As one grows older it becomes a new habit. You start with the local paper. If you are not listed in it there is a sigh of relief. After a while, you start reading the regional obits, just in case the local paper missed yours or decided it wasn't noteworthy.

In the middle of the page, the name Whitesy popped out at me. It was the announcement of the death of Mrs. Whitesy. It noted that she had been preceded in death by her husband in <u>1979</u>. We had spent fifteen minutes together in 1974. That little interlude gave him five years of life.

CTFD received a giant endorsement of its new role as an EMS. That one life-saving incident, however, was minuscule when compared with the nationwide revolution that was spawned by the decision of the morticians to stop providing ambulance service. It affected not only the fire departments but all the care-giving professions and industries. That there were problems and tragedies due to mistakes at all levels of emergency health care should not have been surprising. People in the medical community are not exempt from human error. That fact had a direct effect on another growth industry, medical liability litigation.

14

IS THERE A DOCTOR IN THE HOSPITAL?

In its early years, emergency medical care of victims was primitive, and the situation at the two local hospital emergency rooms was archaic. If we arrived unannounced at Mercy Hospital with a victim and it was after midnight, we rang a doorbell at the emergency room entrance. The lights were out, and the door was locked. The bell rang at the second floor nursing station. After a couple of rings, a light came on up there and a nurse's aide appeared at a second-story window and looked down. She stared down at us, made sure we looked legit, and then disappeared. Then she walked half the width of the hospital, waited for the elevator to arrive, got on, pushed the button for the first floor, waited for the elevator to creep down its shaft, opened the elevator door, reversed the walk to one floor below her upstairs lookout, turned on a hall light, came to the door, turned on an outdoor light, opened the door a crack, and asked "What is the problem?"

It seemed to us that the same aide was always on duty. She wore a black-trimmed uniform, her hair looked as if it had been dyed black, and she had only two facial expressions, scowl and arrogant. Given how we must have appeared in our tee shirts, jeans, work shoes, and scruffy two a.m. beards, I cannot blame her.

Once we were admitted, a second hall light was turned on to show the way to a treatment room. That room was lighted, but no others. After assessing symptoms, she had to decide whether the situation required that a physician be called in the middle of the night, aroused from his sleep, and asked, with great reluctance, whether he could come to treat the patient. The physician asked questions that might allow him to give an order over the phone and go back to sleep.

Those early experiences quickly shattered one of my long-held assumptions. I believed that every doctor knew how to treat every illness and injury. I learned that they don't. That conclusion became more evident with every month we delivered patients to the ERs. In Mount Vernon the assumption of the all knowing physician was reinforced by hospital policies and led to the death of some victims.

As our training in how to help victims of illness and injury advanced, the local hospitals were suddenly being delivered large numbers of patients who formerly did not seek help at a hospital, and some who would have been dead because they were not transported by EMT staffed ambulances. The hospitals were not ready.

In a fairly short period, small community ERs went from being dark and lifeless at night to being busy sites of a new and promising field called emergency medicine. To capitalize on the economic potential of the revolution, both local hospitals had to provide rapid access to physicians around the clock.

In those first few years after the ER's were staffed day and night, there was still no direct radio connection to the hospital from the emergency squads. The information that CTFD was bringing a victim to the hospital and the nature of his or her complaint, were relayed by our "fire band" (radio frequency) to the sheriff's office dispatcher or to our station; then it was relayed by telephone to the hospital ER.

Because there were two hospitals a decision had to be made as to which one was appropriate. Mercy Hospital was closer to us than Memorial Hospital, but the two hospitals were at war with one another and the doctors had taken sides. The pediatricians in town would treat children only at Memorial. Other patients were loyal to their doctors, who would only treat their patients at the facility where they had chosen to be on the staff. If victims were conscious, we tried to comply; if not they went to the nearest one. For us that meant Mercy Hospital.

Then Memorial Hospital started its own ambulance service and hired medical staff to cover its ER day and night. That was a good marketing tool and a victory in the competition for patients during the war between the hospitals. Rival Mercy Hospital managers and physicians had to counter it, since both hospitals were going belly up and neither could afford to lose patients. The best response to Memorial's strategy was to get some Mercy Hospital family doctors and medical staff volunteers to serve in the emergency department around the clock. Unlike Memorial which had to import doctors, the Mercy medical staff had a larger inventory of physicians from which they could recruit doc's to meet the staffing challenge. The competition between the hospitals began to improve care for many victims but not all.

The assumption that a doc was a doc was a doc was not true, and the physicians who staffed Mercy ER knew it, but could not admit it publicly. Some of the first who served in the ER were long-time family physicians who had retired. One of the best had given up his practice after suffering a stroke but had recovered unimpaired. One or two may have had a lagging practice and wanted some extra income. Those up to date in family practice medicine were not adequately prepared for the spectrum of patient complaints that came through the ER doors, especially the treatment of trauma. They relearned suturing, prescribed the usual antibiotics, and could call in a surgeon to set the bones and take out the appendix. What they were not prepared to do was respond to the needs of the critical patient. A few, like anesthesiologists, had some relevant experience. They were able to intubate patients to help them breathe by ventilating them with an oxygen-inflated bag valve mask, and/or to defibrillate a spasming heart. They and the surgeons were best equipped to handle the critical patient. Experienced nurses often were, and still are, more competent with the immediate hands-on care of victims than the doctors and many patients benefited from their skills.

The most obvious deficiency of the early ER doctors at Mercy Hospital was in the treatment of those critical trauma patients. If the situation was assessed as a life-threatening injury, a surgeon was to be called from his office or home to come to the ER as soon as possible. The time lag was sometimes fatal.

Doctors Smythe, Risko, and Westerheide were general surgeons and shared the on-call responsibility for trauma at both hospitals. Smythe was especially well equipped after his experiences during the Korean conflict. All three were eager to help train the county's emergency medical squads and they allowed us to witness some of the procedures used to aid victims we delivered to the hospital.

Smythe's conviction that EMTs could save lives was supported by his action. He and a couple of other doctors came to my kitchen table one evening and taught several of us how and when to start certain IV solutions from old-fashioned glass containers. Soon the ambulance was stocked with the solutions and the bottles were carefully placed under the bench beside the cot. We were told to use the solutions to treat patients threatened by shock from trauma. That training and the doctor's endorsement resulted in me being classified as an "EMT-Advanced" only by virtue of their authority as physicians. It would be several years before a state certifying curriculum was established to anoint the EMT-Intermediate (EMT-I) who was permitted to start intravenous fluids and administer even more risky treatments. I was "grandfathered" because of the recipe learned in my kitchen. After all, there was no law against it. Later, when an approved curriculum was in place, a mandatory refresher course greatly expanded the occasions when the IV was appropriate and that course kept me "legal."

Dr. Cassady, the anesthesiologist, worked well with all the surgeons and enjoyed his shifts in the ER. He was an early ER doc who recognized true life threatening signs and symptoms and, even better, knew what to do, as Mr. Whitesy certainly appreciated. Whether the patient lived or died often depended on the skills of the on-duty doc or how fast the surgeon could get to the ER.

Born thirty Years Too Soon

In the 1950s the VI (Village Inn) in Gambier was a family restaurant run by Mr. Trittipo and his wife. It was highly regarded, even written up in the Ford Motor Company travel magazine. When the Trittipos called it quits, the VI endured a series of resurrections, the latest in 2007. It has been a restaurant on several occasions, but whether it opens again depends on whether it can offer legally sedating liquids to the customers.

It was during the second or third post-Trittipo era that the VI was most prosperous, thanks to the Ohio legislature. It was successfully argued that if eighteen year-olds could be called to fight and die for their country, they should be able to buy a drink in a bar. The drinking law corrected that injustice, and the VI profits sky-rocketed on bottles of beer and shot glasses of booze. Students were extremely happy with the change, though in that period less willing to die for their country. The CTFD emergency squad "benefited" by increased activity.

The beer and booze sales were so good, that one manager decided that the food aspect of the business was superfluous to the real purpose of the customers. He shortened the menu to hamburgers and increased the stock of chips. We went to the VI for a beer one night and ordered a pizza delivered from the Pirate's Cove down the street. "Not a problem."

First-year students at Kenyon College often learn to drink alcoholic beverages shortly after they arrive on campus. Calibrating how much one can safely drink requires practice. The first rule is that it is important to out-drink your peers. What some do not know is that a few of the peers have tested the limits in high school and have improved their tolerance. Some already have drinking problems. If the naive and the veteran party together, the amateur may get into trouble.

I estimate that over half of the squad runs for "alcohol poisoning" on campus are for first year students. One memorable emergency run to the VI was for a "freshman" woman who had, with the urging of her peers, demonstrated that she could down twenty two shots of tequila. When the squad arrived she was not breathing. She survived because CTFD had learned how to breathe for her. The ER and the hospital were also ready to sustain her until she was able to endure a memorable hangover.

Other students have not been fortunate enough to fall down drunk with others available to call for help for them. One especially frigid morning Mayor Baer, with help from CTFD volunteers, tried to build a skating rink with sheet plastic and wooden two-by-fours near the college's athletic building. Our attention was diverted to a fuss over by the college tennis courts. We wandered over and got there as the sheriff and a deputy arrived. Lying in a fetal position was a student who had drunk too much at his fraternity, strayed outside, and down the hill, and sat down on a log. The temperature that night had been 17 degrees below zero. Now he was a waxen yellow statue, and no trip to the ER was required. Of course the community was shocked, saddened, and outraged that such a thing could happen. As we have learned to expect, however, the same fate was met by another student in this new century. Again there was shock and outrage about student drinking. Less than a student generation after the latest incident there is serious discussion at Kenyon about allowing eighteen-year-olds to drink on campus. After all, they can fight and die for their country.

Word spread quickly that the Village Inn was a fine place to drink, and some locals from Mount Vernon and vicinity began to sit at the bar and maybe try their luck with a coed. Occasionally they would strike up a conversation with a student on a subject of common interest, like cars. By chance, a couple of guys from town learned about a student who was trying to sell his Porsche. After a bit of negotiation, a deal was made, and the Porsche went to the city, and then came back a couple of days later. The purchasers really had not had time to see what the car could "do," and in the context of sitting at the bar at the VI its maneuverability was debated. They decided on a systematic empirical test, but they did not call it that.

There seemed no better place to do the experiment in the early a.m. than Chase Street at the S curve between Bexley Hall, at the northern edge of Gambier, and the VI. The strategy was to take "her" out to the village limit and then head back into town, increasing speed through the curve on each lap. It did quite well at forty, fifty, and even sixty miles per hour. On the next run they found the car's limit, or at least the limit of the driver to maintain control of the car at high speed while under the influence of alcohol.

The accident was only a block or so from the fire station and we arrived relatively quickly for that hour of the night. A small crowd, some from the VI, had gathered around the Porsche. One Gambier native, came up to us on our arrival and pronounced the driver dead and the passenger still alive. He was correct on both counts.

Even the most casual observer would likely have agreed with his diagnosis of the driver. The car was mangled against a tree and was no longer low and rectangular. It was more similar to a parallelogram. The driver's head had smashed against the front door "A" post at the windshield and had been split to resemble Pac Man. No seat belts were visible.

The passenger was a large fellow probably in his twenties but his age was not clear as he was packaged into the space between the seat and underside of the dashboard of the Porsche. That is a pretty small cavity. He was moaning but not responsive to questions. The first requirement after determining that he was still alive was to extricate him without doing more damage to his broken body. Sometimes it is necessary to take a chance and move an injured person at the risk of making things worse. Until they are out, they have no chance to get better. There was no jaws of life device yet and few other rescue tools. A metal saw, a crowbar, a spud bar, and bolt cutters were the standard.

The young man moaned and was in pain, but it was not clear what hurt most. He was eventually freed and loaded into the squad as quickly as possible. Oxygen was administered, and we began to explore for injuries. His respirations were labored, he did not respond to questions and he cried out when we moved him or when the squad hit a bump in the road.

We arrived at Mercy Hospital ER fast. A "hospital war" doctor was in the building. The cot was removed from the squad and we were directed to the large room that was used for the patients in critical condition. There was one nurse, and she had already aroused the physician on duty. We were already acquainted with him. He was a kind man, quiet, somewhat remote, and, from my past interactions, did not seem comfortable with his ER role. That conclusion was soon verified.

As we began to unclothe the victim, he moaned with pain and said his first words: "You bitch, you bitch, quit it." As we moved him to the hospital gurney, he continued his complaints. As we helped ready him for treatment his respirations became more difficult, and frothy red fluid began to impede each breath. The doctor, however, was immobilized. He obviously did not know what to do. The nurse began to assemble an endotracheal tube, which when placed in the patient's airway would enable his respirations to be assisted. Before she intubated him and began to squeeze the bag, the young man whispered, "I'm sorry, I'm sorry."

If timed properly, squeezing the oxygen-filled bag would supply oxygen to his lungs. The nurse enlisted my aid in "bagging" him. I had never done it before. My training was on the job and consisted of a couple of sentences from over her shoulder as she hurried off to call a surgeon. It was good experience for me and a new skill that would benefit other victims over the years. The most important instruction is "don't stop till I tell you to." I carefully concentrated on the task of coordinating the increasingly stressed inspirations with squeezes of the bag. It seemed like a simple enough task but required disciplined concentration

The doctor went to the far corner of the room. I could just make out his voice "I wish Robert [the surgeon on call] would get here." He never strayed from the corner.

Then the voluntary breathing stopped. I asked what to do. The nurse instructed "Continue to bag him." The endotracheal tube filled with frothy blood and with each squeeze, the bag became more resistant. Everyone in the room knew the patient was now dead.

If there is blame to be attached, I would attach it to that era in medicine. We did not realize that at the time (certainly not while watching the doctor cower in the corner). He had been asked to do something he was not trained to do. No doctor knows everything about all aspects of medicine. He helped, in part, because the hospital needed to compete with Memorial Hospital for emergency room dollars. He was fine dispensing medicine as a family practice physician does in his office. He was not prepared for immediately life threatening trauma. For most people who walked into the ER with ailments and minor injuries he could provide good care with the aid of the nurses and staff.

I am sure there was talk about the incident at the hospital. The experience underscored that emergency medicine is very different from what some doctors had anticipated when they accepted the responsibility to serve in the ER. The occurrence of similar unfortunate experiences brought into focus the need for a revolution in emergency care. That insight was not limited to the ER.

The more patients who came to the ER, and the variety of problems they brought with them called attention to a national health issue. The question was, "How many people have been dying because there was no established mode of care for them when they needed it?" When a system was eventually created to pick up the victims, do basic first-aid procedures, and deliver them to a health care facility, new questions evolved. How much could those EMTs who staffed the ambulances do to improve victim's chances of survival and recovery? How many more people in small communities would be saved if there were physicians, nurses, technicians, EMTs, and hospitals prepared to treat critically ill or injured patients as soon as they arrived. What if victims could be stabilized until they could be transported to specialists who would increase their chance of survival and recovery? How dangerous to the victims could EMTs be if they did "this" or "that?" Is it worth the risk?

Nothing could have saved the driver of the Porsche back then except not getting into the car after drinking too much. Today the passenger would have been extricated from the car with state-of-the-art rescue tools manned by firefighters trained to cut the car away from the victim so as to avoid making his injuries worse. While that was happening he would have been receiving oxygen through an endotracheal tube inserted by an EMT and intravenous fluid in his vein in order to fend off shock. As soon as he arrived at the scene the commander of the rescue would have ordered a helicopter to land behind the grade school one block away. In fifteen minutes, while the young man was being extricated and loaded into the squad, the helicopter would be landing with a trauma nurse and paramedic on board with all the appropriate drugs and instruments. When the victim was loaded into the helicopter it would take off and the victim would undergo assessment by the flight crew. The information they gathered would be transmitted to a hospital classified as a level one trauma center. There, a team of physicians, nurses, and technicians would be assembled to sustain life and diagnose the immediate needs of the victim. Given what we saw in the ER, it is likely that a chest tube would quickly be shoved between his ribs, into his chest cavity, to relieve the pressure of blood and air from punctured lungs that were impeding his respiration. A surgery room would be readied and the appropriate surgeons prepared to begin repair of the life-threatening damage. All this could have transpired in about an hour after the Porsche hit the tree.

The young man was born too soon, and it was tragic that the revolution in emergency medicine had only just begun.

This case and numerous less tragic ones pointed to the fact that the whole field of emergency room care had been ignored and underdeveloped by the medical profession. Once fire department personnel and others began to apply their training and bring victims to ERs staffed with people and technology specialized for treating them, the population of the country began to grow.

At CTFD it was the beginning of a revolution, too. The vast majority of its work became responses to medical emergencies. One long-term consequence was that the department started a number of its Kenyon premed/CTFD volunteers on the path to becoming emergency physicians with a head start on experience. A couple of them have gained international reputations in that specialty. Those Kenyon-bred emergency physicians still come back to visit the firehouse, and absorb the same verbal abuse laid on them by the old timers at the fire house who "kept them in their place" as "goddamn students." The mutation from fire department to primarily an EMS was irreversible. It changed the whole ethos of the department. The old guys who were the original firefighters were no longer the heart of the department. Eventually even the beer cooler was gone.

Ironically, the advances in victim care in Knox County were accelerated by passionate, sometimes petty disputes among the two Mount Vernon hospitals, their doctors, and partisan local citizens. They in turn contributed to bitter battles among those providing emergency medical care throughout the county. The end result was a victory for the ill and injured.

15

EMTs LEARN THINGS THEY DID NOT WANT TO KNOW

One problem for our department and many other small-town volunteer fire departments was that they were too democratic. A lot of the locals were related to one another by blood or by marriage, and so it was important not to do or say anything that might unknowingly be seen as an insult to a kin of a firefighter. Caution in such matters led to all candidates for membership being elected, but results of the votes were never revealed. Sometimes the department paid a price for that by acquiring people who contributed nothing to its mission or who did things that neutralized their positive contributions.

The local men who joined the department in the sixties and early seventies were usually older than today's group by quite a margin, and married. The membership was all male. The original members tried to create a well-organized department. Their objective was to prevent the kinds of disasters recorded in the community's history.

Eventually that focused objective waned, and we began to see a few new members who were motivated to join for reasons other than idealistic public interest. Some just liked to work on and drive the trucks fast. That was fine, and some were skilled and valuable volunteers. For a few others it was their only social life. The private club social atmosphere bonded them to the firehouse kitchen. In that sense CTFD was the same as many small volunteer departments, and tolerating the "social members" provided occasional comic relief.

A small number of volunteers sought one rather unique advantage offered by CTFD membership, that is, the beer cooler. Most members consumed one or two bottles a week. A few spent their leisure time at the station, and their quarters in the modified Coke machine that dispensed Black Label, Burger, Blatz, and Pabst Blue Ribbon beers with every "click clack" that released a bottle from cold storage. A little steel-blue metal box under the bar was stocked with quarters to make change for the very thirsty. The honor system was in effect, and the box never came up short. Harvey and Davey had keys to the dispenser and would gladly cash larger bills. Income realized from the "Coke" machine was reinvested in inventory.

A lot of beer was drunk in the firehouse. The amount was inflated by the fact that members could buy a six-percent beer there on Sunday. At the time, state law required that there be two legal levels of alcohol content in beer, but none in Gambier on Sunday. Six percent was high-test, and 3.2 percent deemed low enough that ordinary consumption would be less likely to cause inebriation. In my experience, 3.2 percent could do the job if you were persistent. The CTFD never ventured into an exploratory experiment on the subject, because it only stocked the 6 percent. Since quarters worked in the cooler just as well on Sunday as any other day, it permitted some to have a few beers on the Sabbath while fulfilling a public service to the community. Sunday was also inspection day when all the vehicles had to be gassed and serviced, so attendance for one reason or the other was assured.

The beer cooler was there for the refreshment of members only. No alcohol incident was so evident to the public that a persuasive argument for removing it was ever presented in the monthly business meeting. Even if there had been a motion to abolish the beer cooler, a strong majority valued the perk and would have defeated any attempt to enact prohibition into the association's bylaws.

I do recall one occasion when a member's readiness to respond to any emergency had been buoyed, but his judgment drowned, by a day near the cooler. He swaggered into the equipment bay and climbed into the driver's seat of the squad and raced off with a crew of students to aid an injured citizen who lived out in the township. The siren yelped and wailed as locals jumped out of the way of the speeding squad. It headed down the hill to the state highway. The siren grew faint with distance until it was barely audible. Minutes passed and still the siren waxed and waned through the county roads. It became obvious to us at the firehouse that it was now well beyond the time necessary to reach the unfortunate victim. Our curiosity and anxiety escalated when the siren began to get louder again, and louder still, and then the squad came screaming down Scott Lane to the firehouse. With the driver's window rolled down and the siren still blaring, we could just make out the urgent shout. "What was that address?" Fortunately, no one died or was in serious condition, and the driver did not breathe into the victim's face. The latitude of acceptable behavior, however, was gauged by how long you've been on the department. The driver had been "on" a long time, so humor, not disciplinary action, was assigned the tale. The incident aroused in me a passing thought about how well this emergency medical stuff was going to mix with the beer cooler. No one had heard of liability suits back then. When the chief appointed me his assistant in charge of EMS I immediately ordered that a box of Certs breath mints be placed in the ambulance.

Occasionally a guy would join because he could get a cold beer on Sunday and also find someone to talk to. Those who drank and helped with the tasks were tolerated without complaint. Randy was one of those. He spent many hours at the station, in part because he was not welcome at home, which, in part, was because he was always at the firehouse. He always did his work on the engines, did it well, and loved to "horse around" with the guys. He was instrumental in the appearance of a mouse in someone's post training chili. He was a loyal member for several years. It was his refuge from the stormy home life. We all loved him at the firehouse and enjoyed his antics and buffoonery.

It was our emergency medical responsibilities, however that eventually exposed one flaw of Randy's that we could not laugh off. Whatever the cause, it was likely alcohol, his relationship with his spouse deteriorated. One evening we were called to their house on the report of an assault on a woman. It was not a serious injury, and Randy was gone. That was a good thing because his stepdaughter came charging in the door ready to do him grave bodily harm. That may sound-semi threatening, except she was a world-class athlete and could have done a job on him or us, if we had tried to stop her. The incident happened in the days before law enforcement automatically would have been dispatched to temper emotions and, more important, to protect us. As far as I know the deputies never knew about the problem. We, however, did know what happened and it put Randy's firehouse antics in a different perspective. He soon had to move into the city to find a place to stay, and his availability to CTFD became less reliable. The guys at the firehouse understood that such things happen, but we did not want to witness or be drawn into such incidents involving a fellow volunteer. Randy did remain a popular member. When he could get to Gambier he still made us laugh, just not as loudly. Then he stopped coming.

The last I knew of Randy was printed in the local newspaper. It was a note in the accident reports. Randy was driving on West Gambier Street in Mount Vernon. At the railroad crossing, he failed to observe the B&O engine that had been parked in the crossing for a half hour. He drove into it. No one was injured. He always drove slowly when he had been drinking.

Those who drank and didn't contribute useful service eventually missed enough meetings and training sessions that they were eased out by the bylaws "for missing too many training and business meetings in a row." One was a "short-termer", Andy. He was a pretty good worker at the college but an habitué of Dorothy's Lunch, as well as more remote bars. His physical appearance and his demeanor caused a few of us to be biased against him. He appeared shifty-eyed, snaggle-toothed, and slothful. Looks are sometimes deceiving but they led us not to expect too much from him from the outset. He fulfilled that expectation.

His kids seemed okay. I know one who, as an adult, is energetic, ambitious, and conscientious. In any case, credit for the children's socialization could have resided with his spouse, or maybe he was fine as a parent; I just never knew about that. Andy's election to membership in the department was attributable to the custom of the fire association to elect everyone who volunteered.

Many of Andy's after-work hours were spent at Dorothy's Lunch, but there were two other places to which he could retreat and preserve some doubt, or at least claim in absence of proof to the contrary, that he wasn't exclusively seeking the suds. He couldn't make that case when on a bar stool at Dorothy's, so he varied his schedule among a bar close to the village and the fire station.

When at the firehouse, Andy could claim both the necessity and nobility of showing up at 9 a.m. Sunday for the inspection of emergency vehicles. He would be at CTFD, as religious in his attendance as others were to their own houses of worship. As a result of his early arrival, his seat at the firehouse kitchen table was assured, and more important, he was within two or three steps of the cooler. Unfortunately, the Tuesday evening training sessions and the department business meetings did not fit into his "tight" schedule. Within a few months, Andy stopped coming to the fire station.

Other than to wave to him on campus, I don't recall how long it was after he was dropped by the department that I saw Andy face to face, but I recall the occasion vividly. It was dusk on a summer evening when the fire phone rang.

The audibly shaken voice reported that there had been a serious accident. It was less than a mile from the station. As we approached I could see a badly damaged auto. It became clear that the car had struck a huge old tree and spun around. We pulled to a halt and I spotted a huddled figure in the gutter across the road from the car. Andy was curled up in a fetal position on his side. The seriousness of his injuries was not immediately obvious. No blood was visible, but neither was he moving. Kneeling beside him, I called his name. There was no response. He was breathing, and that was obvious both by the ominous sounds made by fluids in his airway and by the odor of alcoholic beverage. Carefully, we examined and immobilized him for transport, assisted him with his respirations, and prepared to transport him rapidly to the local emergency room. Based on Andy's unresponsiveness and respirations and the status of emergency care at the local hospitals in those days, I predicted a short stay at the emergency room and a fast trip to a big-city hospital an hour away. A firefighter was dispatched to notify his wife about the accident.

My prediction about the emergency room was confirmed. An initial examination confirmed Andy's critical condition, and arrangements were made to transfer him as soon as possible. No helicopter service was available, so our squad was responsible for racing him down the freeway to a Columbus hospital prepared for major trauma. Andy was placed on the ambulance cot, and we proceeded through the hall toward the door. Just before we reached it, his wife hurried up to the stretcher, her face reflecting powerful emotion. She leaned down to his ear as we moved along the hall and in a clear voice that she hoped would penetrate his coma, she said

"You son of a bitch, I hope you die."

And for once, Andy granted his wife's wish.

We were stunned by what we had heard and witnessed. We were ignorant of the family history and wished we had remained so. Andy had not been a respected member of the department but we did not have any sense of how his private life might have influenced his behavior.

The incidents with Randy and Andy shocked us into an insight about being a volunteer in a local emergency medical service. We will be drawn into the intimate lives of people we thought we knew, but did not really know. It was like receiving an electric shock for trying to do something nice.

16

FOOLS RUSH IN

As first generation EMTs we should have asked certain questions, but they never occurred to us. One would be, "Do we wait to make sure someone is shot before calling for the sheriff or should the sheriff see the blood first and then call us"? It took a few years to sort out the issues posed by such questions. Before experience pointed to commonsense rules, there were some interesting moments.

"Bang!" is loud and sudden and causes immediate, reflexive orientation toward its origin. It activates the "fight or flight" reflexes. It can be a signal of danger. Sometimes it is. In Knox County, people react to them pretty much the same way that most creatures do. There are occasions when they cause relatively little alarm. On the Fourth of July, the number of bangs skyrockets. In Knox County their presence on Fourth of July mornings are about equal to those on the first day of deer season.

On "first day," bangs are heard most often in ones and twos. Legally, they are to be confined to the period from around dawn to dusk and at a lawful distance from inhabited areas. In fact, however, hunter's watches, senses of direction, and ability to see "No Hunting" signs vary with the visibility of an antlered buck. On "first day" one knows what created the bang and its purpose. However, there is enough uncertainty about the personalities of those initiating them that they elicit the turtle reflex, a high velocity spasm by which ones head is pulled down as far as possible beneath the clavicle. It is correlated with the proximity of a bang. Wearing bright orange clothing is supposed to be an effective means to avoid being a mistaken target. It is best if dogs, cows, horses, llamas, and sheep also wear orange. Groundhogs have not been informed of its protective potential.

One might think that over a period of thirty five years, those two days each year would produce "ammunition" for a book by an EMT. Strangely neither day required CTFD to respond to significant trauma due to the discharge of firearms or fireworks. There have been no tragic gunshot wounds on "first day" or serious fireworks injuries on the Fourth.

Several hunting accidents have occurred on days outside the deer season. Once a gun went off as a squirrel hunter climbed over a fence. Another non-deer-related injury occurred when a fellow shot himself in the thigh when doing a quick draw on a ground hog while balancing a Bud Light in his other hand. It would seem unlikely that there would be the sound of a deer gun near the Fourth of July, but it did happen.

It was a couple of weeks after the Independence Day parade in Gambier, which of course, was led by all the engines and squads of CTFD. My white-trimmed officer's hat and navy blue dress uniform were back in the closet until the next Fourth of July, photo op, or next firefighter funeral, whichever came first. The tone alert of the Plectron signaled an emergency of some sort. The dispatcher broadcast a "code 52 on county road 17", a shooting on Hopewell Road. Shootings do occur about every year even in our small territory. Most are accidental. Non-accidental shootings here are usually suicide attempts. From my limited number of observations I do not recommend shooting oneself in the head with a handgun. There is too much chance that a nonfatal wound will leave the victim with permanent incapacities that are very depressing.

On that July day, Bob and Sue Barton were still at Station 1, having stayed around to socialize after inspection of the vehicles. Bob and Sue were husband, and wife, members of CTFD. Bob was a leader among those Monroe guys who created and staffed their substation. He was the principal architect of "Ethel," the army ambulance converted into a grass fire truck. Sue was one of the charter female firefighter/EMTs when the department made the decision to have spousal members. They, Bill Baer, and Kenyon student EMT and future trauma surgeon Jay Johanigman hopped into the squad and picked me up at the end of my driveway.

I recently saw Jay on the Discovery Channel's Life in the ER. As a trauma surgeon he saved the life of a police officer who had been shot. He got his first exposure to those sorts of injuries at five minutes before two p.m. on that July day.

Hopewell road is not in our coverage area. Depending on the address, it was either Danville's run or in the no-man's-land that was coveted by our competitor, the Memorial Hospital Life Support Team.

In the competition for patients between the unpaid "volunteer" squads and the city based "paid" Life Support Team, Knox County Sheriff P. K. Rowe made sure the rural volunteer departments were "toned out" (were sent alarms and radio messages) anytime there was an emergency outside the city limits even if the hospital based squad was already enroute. The advantage we had this time was that we knew the area and house-numbering sequence on Hopewell Road. As it turned out, the hospital group had either missed the lane leading to the house, or were smarter than we were. The address was not easy to find. No house was visible from the road, and only a mailbox at the end of a rutted dirt lane marked the location. We turned into that driveway and ascended a long gradual slope that had no obvious destination.

In the new millennium, no emergency medical squad would approach a shooting scene before law enforcement personnel were there and advised the crew that it is safe to approach. But this was before that wisdom guided our decisions and we were in competition with the Life Support Team to get there first. There was the excitement and anticipation of venturing into potential danger to make a heroic save, and the pioneer EMS policies had not evolved the common sense that arises from experiences with shootings.

Our emergency squad had raced down the country roads with siren blaring and lights flashing just like on TV. After we turned into the lane at the roadside mailbox, there was no need for either. Bob drove at a snail's pace up a grade, trying to avoid some of the potholes that randomly grabbed each wheel. They were filled with water of unknown depth from rain the previous day. We slowed to a near stop, allowing the front tires to tentatively probe with their treads to feel for the depth of each muddy gouge. Racing to aid a victim became a maddening oxymoron. The intense sense of urgency became agonizing as our foot-by-foot progress frustrated our need to know what was up ahead. There were images of blood pumping out with each heartbeat, while we sat helpless in the creeping squad.

The slowness of our progress finally allowed a thought I had suppressed to blast through to awareness. "Oh my, is this wise to do?" "What am I getting my crew into?" "What am I getting into?"

Anxiety led to action. The air conditioner in the squad was turned off and the windows rolled down so every sense could be scanned to search for our objective. Everyone became silent as we bumped along looking and listening for some hint. The silence of the crew, the absence of any sign of life ahead, and the rising unease melded into "eerie." A wall of heat and humidity poured in through the windows. The spring rains had helped the weeds to grow head high and trap the moisture. By the early afternoon the temperature had charged through the 80s into the 90s. There was no hint of a breeze. The humidity, like an octopus, grasped us in its tentacles and squeezed. Every pore spewed a salty stream that made navy-colored splotches on our royal blue jump suits.

It was a day when all the bovines in the fields stood under shade trees, hounds slumbered on porches, and humans disappeared. Insects loved it. They buzzed eagerly around every corporeal entity seeking food, a nest in which to start the next generation, or some viable soul to torment.

We looked ahead, searching. Fear was now straining to be recognized among the topics under consideration by the nervous homunculus giving the orders inside my brain. We were there looking and listening, as if we were actors drawn into a surround-sound, wide-screen opening scene of a Peckinpaugh movie. To get maximal effect, the "director" had even turned off the air conditioning in the theater. The unweeded fields and the long dirt lane going to no visible destination required a sound track orchestrated in Nashville, sung by a remorse-filled country music sinner.

As we rose to the top of the grade, a line of fifteen foot tall willow trees came into view. Their long, wispy switches and skinny leaves drooped almost to the surface of a vegetation-clogged farm pond adjacent to the lane. A hundred yards or so beyond the pond a farmhouse appeared: a front porch, a shed, old farm machinery, but no signs of life. Then, tiny in the ominous vista but slowly coming into focus as through a zoom lens, was the image of a man, sitting on the ground, legs bent at the knees. He was between the rutted tire tracks, five feet from water's edge. At first, no one else was visible. His head was bowed as if looking into his lap. As we reached a point about fifty feet from him, I could see that he was looking down into the face of woman. She was lying on her back, almost hidden by his torso, her legs extended toward the house.

Finally I jerked my attention back to our job. This was an incident when, in addition to rushing to the aid of the victim, it would be our responsibility to record mental images of every detail. This was reported as a shooting. Remember the position of each person and object, remember the path we took when approaching, avoid disturbing evidence while tending to the victim. Oh, and don't forget to follow procedure in assessing the victim. Those lessons from our training manual and my newly acquired sense of caution led me to have Bob halt the squad at a distance from the man and to suggest that the rest of the crew stay in it while Jay and I approached the couple. Jay brought the "jump bag" containing basic needs for medical emergencies. I approached the man, not running but in a strong steady pace. I went around his back and looked over his right shoulder. He did not look up. He was not frantically pleading for us to hurry to her side.

In his lap lay the head of an attractive young woman who appeared to be in her twenties or early thirties. Her eyes were wide open and directly exposed to the intense hot sun. The corneas looked like semi opaque plastic already desiccating from the loss of tearing and the failure of eyelids to shelter them. She was clothed in a halter top and shorts.

While I seized this first snapshot vision of the victim and the scene, I could now barely make out the man softly repeating a single phrase: "She's dead." "She's dead."

It was very obvious that he was correct. Both her eyes were open, both pupils were fully dilated behind the clouded corneas, her chest did not rise and fall, a gentle palpation of her neck found no carotid pulse. The likely cause was a round almost three-quarter-inch hole visible just below and lateral to her left breast. A little blood showed around the opening, and it had trailed down her side to the ground. From beneath her had come a river that flowed down the bank and into the pond. No blood was pulsing or flowing from the wounds now and had not been for some time. The coagulated dark maroon stream was now defying gravity's pull toward the pond.

The news of the event had spread with great speed among the population of indigenous flies. They were ecstatic and arrived from every direction. The sound of their buzzing amplified the surreal visual images. Those images would soon have to be transcribed into a deposition or oral testimony.

<u>ABC</u> is the acronym for check for an open <u>airway</u> (the breathing passage), check for any evidence of <u>breathing</u>, and feel for a pulse that would indicate blood <u>circulation.</u> ABC is the golden trio for EMTs. If they are all present, it is okay to proceed to other concerns. If one or more is not present, every effort must immediately be dedicated to restoring any that are missing. If the EMT is unsuccessful in regaining any one of them the victim is or soon will be dead. A quick check of AB and C made it clear that she was DRT (dead right there).

What was I supposed to do next? Suddenly, thoughts about threats to my own survival evicted those looking for the answer.

"I'm sorry, sir, there is nothing we can do."

I saw no gun. A nudge from my sense of self-preservation urged me to learn where it was. It seemed highly likely that the man knew, and although he seemed to be in control of himself at the moment, the woman lying there with a bullet hole through her chest indicated that self control might not be his strong point. Or if he always was in control, that might be even worse, for me. I looked around us and into the weeds next to the driveway: no gun. How could I ask the man where the gun was when the question might turn his attention to what might happen to him next? Asking him whether he shot her did not seem like a good idea either. Both of those questions had potential implications for survival; mine, that is. If the weapon was a handgun, it could still be in his reach and not visible.

I tried a different approach: pointing to the hole in her chest and not looking at him.

"How did this hole get here?"

Not looking at me, "It's a bullet hole."

Still looking at the hole and pointing to it, "Yeah, but how did it get there?"

He answered as if he were talking to a fool who couldn't add one and one.

"I shot her." He didn't add "you idiot," but that was implied by his tone of voice, just before he summed the 1+1, got an answer, and an insightful "uh-oh, what did I just say?" expression spread across his face.

I did not want to exchange a meaningful glance with him and returned my eyes to the hole in the chest, again feigning puzzlement with "But, where is the gun?" Implying but not saying aloud "If you shot her there must be a gun right here."

I exhaled, trying not to make it audible, when I heard "It's at the house."

I knew, and I think he did, too, that he had just said something that could cause him trouble. His confession to me meant that a defense of "someone else did it" was likely not going to work. I, on the other hand, knew that trying to save lives can sometimes get you involved in things you hadn't given enough consideration to. I tried to act like this was something I did every day and it was no big deal to me. Jay claims he never heard the man admit guilt and maybe he didn't, but I wished he had. Every time I have seen Jay since then, I accuse him of being smart enough to lie about it.

"You understand that in situations like this we have to notify law enforcement, don't you?" That was my next line. I really, really, really wanted to jump up and run to the squad after I said that, but I also knew that his reaction to the question likely determined how much danger we were in. He nodded.

That exchange allowed me, for the first time, to look directly at him and begin to form impressions of this killer. I guessed that he was in his late thirties or early forties. His face was lean and handsome in a rugged sort of way. Rather than detracting from his appearance, long-healed pock marks, maybe from teenage acne, underlined his earthy good looks. His facial expression revealed no anguish, no distress. As we talked, someone at a distance could have assumed that we were having a normal conversation about a topic of mutual interest, except there was a good-looking dead woman whose head rested in his lap.

"Just wait there with her, and I'll be back in a moment."

"Preserve the scene" was the subject of a couple of paragraphs in the EMT textbook. It is important at any crime that evidence not be moved or destroyed. There was this new section in the latest text about Miranda rights. I hadn't read them to him and was still vague about whether EMTs had that obligation. Given my aroused sense of self-preservation, I likely wouldn't have done that anyway. There is nothing like reading the Miranda sentences to call attention to your naive, unarmed role in sending someone up the river. I did think that if I could get him to stay where he was with her head in his lap, P.K. would be proud of me.

I went back to the squad where the crew waited, ready to tell Bob to put her in reverse and get out of there if things turned nasty. I asked Bob to hand me the microphone.

"Squad 41 to KQH 940" (The latter were the call letters of the sheriff's office radio.) "Signal 1, code 52, possible code 32." (Notify the sheriff, a shooting, a possible homicide.) Then I recalled the normally routine obligation to fill out a "run" report for each victim we tried to help. I had to do it, and that meant that more conversation with the killer was needed. I wondered if the man's legs were getting cramped from sitting in the same position for so long. Maybe getting the information for the report would get his mind off his physical discomfort.

"I need some information for my report form."

He nodded and asked for a cigarette. Doing that for him would give P.K. a couple more minutes of travel time. I went back to the squad and bummed a Camel and a lighter from Bob Barton. The "perp" lit up.

"Uh, what is her name?"

"Warren."

"First name?"

"Janice."

"Her age?"

"Twenty-nine, I think."

"Does she live here?"

"Yes."

"What is your name?"

"Warren."

"First name?"

"Richard."

"Are you related?"

Pause. "Yes."

"How are you related?"

"Wife."

"Can you tell me what happened?"

"I don't think I'll say anything about that."

He could have said it was an accident. He didn't.

What struck me at that point was his incongruous calm. His whole demeanor was grossly abnormal for a man who had just shot and killed his wife. Where it had been a fuzzy little hypothesis along with several other possible explanations, the word "HOMICIDE" popped into my thoughts. I now believed Richard killed Janice on purpose.

Of course he had no obligation to tell me about what happened, and I had no right to know. Maybe he had been told at some time in his life that silence is best when you are pulled over for a traffic violation. But he had already violated that principle. There was a long silence.

Janice, pale, waxen blue eyes, hair showing a bit of blondness from the summers' sun, was dead, but still pretty. Alive, I was sure she would have attracted the attention of men, and they would want to know her. Now, flies buzzed around the sticky coagulant on her ribs and on the ground beneath her. They darted around the hole under her breast, and on the thin trickle that escaped from the left side of her mouth, down her cheek, onto her neck. Periodically, Richard shooed them away, but they quickly returned to march in quick steps across her flesh. I began to imagine how this scene could have come to be.

He was near forty; she was thirty. She wore a halter top and short shorts. Her stomach was flat, her hair wispy brown, her face pretty. He was wearing a tee shirt and jeans. He was tanned, slender, and wiry. His face was that of a man who had "been around," who might have been fun to joke with at the country music night clubs. Nowadays, he would have had a number of tattoos on his arms. How he looked and how people appraised him were important to him. Janice was the exclamation point on his self image and the confirmation of what he wanted everyone to recognize about him.

Janice could tell that guys were fond of looking at her and discovered how easy it was to get to know them. But the only time she saw any other people was at work. Living in the house way back off the county highway, she may have found nothing exciting there. Dreary house work after getting home from the job definitely was not as lively as the workplace. True, she had a husband who valued her but as a trophy to admire and a toy to play with when he felt like it. What if there was a cute guy at work who was fun and liked to joke around?

That was speculation on my part, but they were stories that made the scenario plausible. What isn't speculative is the fact that her body was three hundred feet from the house and the screen door of the house was knocked out as if someone had charged through it. The weapon that killed her was a twelve gauge shot gun that fired deer slugs. An expended shell was found near the house, and a couple more down the lane a hundred feet from the body.

Later when the coroner turned the body over, a second hole was visible at a midthoracic vertebra. The bullet had traveled through her. The second hole suggested why there was a lot of blood under her and not much from the one at the front. The slug had severed the spinal cord and followed a path through the descending aorta, lung, and heart. She could not have taken a single step after the spinal cord was severed, and after a couple of fibrillated beats the blood from the severed arteries left her by gravity alone. No powder burns were visible.

P.K. had been sitting at his desk at the S.O. (sheriff's Office) when the "code 32" jumped out from the constant background of radio traffic that echoed through the building. I would guess that he leapt out of his chair and was in his unmarked car within seconds. About ten minutes later he arrived in the lane behind the squad, and soon after, a deputy also arrived. We talked about the events up to that point, and I told him about the confession. He went over and had his conversation with the man, but it was one-sided. Warren, I learned later, clammed up about the events and never admitted to killing his wife except to me. The good news was that the incident was now under the control of the sheriff, and I could assume that we need not be fearful anymore. The bad news was that I was the only one who could testify to his confession. The significance of that didn't really hit me till later.

After P. K. had his conversation with Richard, he called over his deputy and instructed him to escort the suspect to the S.O. car and take him to jail. The young deputy beckoned Warren to follow him. About thirty feet along the way, P.K., in a tone of voice that reflected bemused sternness, offered a suggestion to his fledgling deputy.

"I suggest you might want to put handcuffs on him; he has already killed one person."

The deputy fumbled around for the cuffs while Warren waited patiently with his hands outstretched.

Finally it was time to respect territorial protocol. The shooting occurred in Danville territory, but much closer to our station, and they had not even been notified of the emergency. P.K. ordered that the body be taken to the crime lab in London, Ohio, but said that we would have to stay at the scene until a Danville crew came to transport Janice. There had to be witnesses who could testify that she and the evidence at the scene were not disturbed by inappropriate individuals. We stayed until Danville arrived and gave us the sideways glances that always meant, "What the hell you doing stealing our run?" And "You take our run and then expect us to do a four hour transport to the crime lab." We always worked well with that group and the "irk" did not last long.

As was our custom when there is a bloody incident, the grass truck with its hundred gallon tank of water was eventually brought to the scene and used to wash the gore from the driveway and into the pond.

I knew I would be called to testify and was somewhat anxious about it. It seemed clear that Warren's "I shot her" was going to have to be reported to a jury at some point, and I had not testified in court before. A homicide was sort of starting at the top.

I went back to the daily routine of teaching my three courses and attending the reliably pedantic faculty meetings. I never liked being called from the classroom to respond to an emergency. On the other hand I wished someone would set a fire or fall and crack a skull during faculty meetings: just kidding.

A few days later, when I was back being a mild-mannered professor, I discovered that I had used up all my notebook paper and needed to get some quickly. I had to update my lecture notes on the sonar system of the bat <u>Eptesicus fuscus</u> to include new material from a recent publication by my friend Don Griffin at Rockefeller University.

The Kenyon Bookstore was the most expensive place to buy the paper, but it was also across from the post office where I could get the mail from my box if, and only if, it was after eleven a.m. So I picked up my mail and walked over to the bookstore. A coed preceded me and politely held the door open for me. I grabbed the door handle and noticed out the corner of my eye that a customer was headed out with an armload of merchandise.

I looked up from the packages into the eyes of Richard Warren. When I recognized him, my pupils dilated, and I could feel my heart accelerate. It was clear that he also recognized me. I inhibited my usual "Hi, how are you?" and likely wouldn't have been able to make my tongue form the words anyway. He couldn't find the right words to greet me either, and so we passed one another. As per Satchel Paige, I didn't look back to see what might be gaining on me. Curiosity did, however, get the best of me, and when I returned to the office I called P.K. to tell him of my experience and ask whether it was common practice to let a killer loose to run into the guy who was probably going to put him in a cell for a long time. P.K. admitted that he saw the potential problem, but as far as I know, Warren was free on bail until after the trial.

He was convicted, largely on my testimony. I didn't hear all that was said at the trial, so I don't know why he was convicted of voluntary manslaughter and given seven years. There was something about him testifying that they were wrestling with the gun when it went off, but why was the gun at the house, far from where she lay? As I understand it, she was shot with a single deer slug through the back. I think she had been running away and was dead before she hit the ground. Maybe there was other evidence to support his story, but I won't change my mind.

I speculate. He loved her. He hated to kill her, but it was a case of life or death for his ego. If she was going to stray and flaunt it to him, there was only one way to handle the situation, just like they do in the country music songs.

I think that house on County 17 is gone now. There is no mailbox and I can't even see the long driveway, at least not where I remember it. Warren would be out of prison if he lived through that experience. I hope he isn't around here, at least not hanging out at the bookstore.

17

PK THE LAST OF THE OLD TIME SHERIFFS

It is just as true about law enforcement as it is about the fire service. There has been a revolution during the past three decades. The old traditions dating back to the Wild West were overwhelmed by the science and technology of forensics. The old-timers in the fire service resented the intrusion of EMS and other responsibilities. The old-timers in law enforcement resisted the adoption of intellectual advancements offered by educational programs in technology, forensics, psychology, and tactics.

The death of Janice Warren in 1979 was an example of the primitive stage of the emergency services at that time. There was very little coordination among agencies. Standard operating procedures, medical protocols, and crime scene investigation were ideas whose time was about to come, but not yet. Radio communications were not coordinated by a 911 system. Once in a while little kids who visited their dad at a firehouse would key the microphone and broadcast a grade school sillyism.

The sheriff could do pretty much what he wanted to do. Some, like Paul "P.K." Rowe, were regarded as "good old boys." They had their own moral code. It instructed them in how people should treat each other, but like P.K., they might be a little less concerned about the Saturday night cock fights at some remote farm off the main roads. The sheriff could hire anyone he wanted as a deputy, whether or not the person had any training. Occasionally, P.K. appointed deputies who caused him embarrassment. He blamed alcohol for much of the county's crime, and back then he was right about that. He exercised a sheriff's discretion. If a man arrested for driving while intoxicated belonged to a Masonic Lodge, deputies might be instructed to take him home. If he was not a Mason, he went to jail.

But P.K. also set up an Alcoholics Anonymous chapter for prisoners. If the offender attended the meetings, showed progress, and mended his ways, P.K. might even offer the former drunk a job at the sheriff's office (SO). He believed that there was not only a lot of good in people but also some mischief. In P.K.'s Knox County, almost any sinner could be salvaged.

P.K. was a huge man, and that fact affected the way others responded to him (i.e., with obedience and respect). I do not think he ever had to pull out his gun to get an offender to comply. The "or else" was implicit. During his terms as sheriff, there were very few dangerous bad guys in the county. The present-day criminal commuters from large urban areas were just beginning to discover his jurisdiction. Until the drug market arrived, there wasn't much in Knox County that was worth a crook's hour long drive from the big city.

P.K. was a farm boy born and raised in a long-respected Knox County family. The Rowe's were "good people" church-going, hard working, good-humored, and honest. The boys probably were a bit rowdy, played football and baseball, got into mischief, and wrestled with each other. When P.K. and Helen got married and started their own family, they bought their farm from the Blackburns down in the Brandon area, where most of the Rowe family clan lived. P.K. was fond of the Blackburns' young son Eddie and felt Eddie might make a good doctor. Years later, Dr. Edward Blackburn Knox County Coroner; P.K., and I met at a number of incidents of mutual responsibility.

P.K. was very intelligent but not a book learner. He had great respect, almost reverence, for those who were highly educated and regretted that he had stopped short of getting more formal education. He ruled from a nineteenth century sheriff's office and jail, just east of the Knox County Courthouse.

In that classic old brick edifice, P.K. had an open-door policy. As one came in the front door, his office was the first door on the left, and it was open. If he knew you, he would hail you in right away and motion you to sit down across from his desk. If the topic was football, fine, if it was a law-enforcement matter, the office door closed. Evidence from some recent crime might be found leaning against a wall or on a table across the room. In an adjoining room Helen could be observed preparing the next meal for the inmates. The detectives were upstairs. A classic, long, wooden staircase stretched from the entry hall to the second floor. The detectives were in a front room, where their desks almost abutted. Bill Furness occupied one of the desks and represented the "old school". David Barber sat at another. Dave's growing library of law enforcement texts from his current courses at college shared desk space with his caseload files.

The nineteenth century was slow to leave the county. P.K. knew a great many Knox County people from all walks of life, and that knowledge served him as a frame of reference essential to being a good sheriff. Reelection was certain. That warehouse full of knowledge about the people of his community preempted the need for higher education in the 1970s, but he still somehow felt lacking.

He had a sense of local people's interests, occupations, and range of behaviors; good and bad. After years in law enforcement he was sure that every local citizen was capable of doing something bad but that each was good most of the time. If you did something bad enough to warrant jail time he would be icy firm in interrogations, letting you know that he expected you to confess. Most of the time, people who made a mistake wanted to tell him. Often, however, he had already made up his mind, and no amount of reasoning changed his belief. That was just as true when there was an issue with a deputy, or me. But like a stern parent he would eventually love you again, at least till the next time he thought you sinned.

P.K. and I had responded to a number of incidents in which EMS and law enforcement needed to cooperate even before he ran for sheriff. After he became sheriff, I testified against some offenders who had hurt people. We met at accident scenes on many occasions, and we both volunteered at the Knox County Fair, he as sheriff and I as firefighter and EMT.

He was aware of my label "psychologist." I had transferred my professional interests to animal research but continued to be licensed to practice as a management consultant. I had no interest in regressing to "people" work but was "grandfathered" and kept up my license, just in case someone asked me for an opinion and then sued me because I gave the wrong answer. But P.K. knew exactly what a psychologist was, regardless of what I tried to explain to him.

He approached me with the idea of becoming the S.O. psychologist. More out of respect and fondness for him than a desire to practice that profession, I agreed to help the department if I could. I interviewed all his deputies and some of his staff. Helen was not on the list, but her position and status were never in question since she prepared the best food of any jailhouse cook anywhere. I really enjoyed working with all the people in the department and trying to find ways to bridge the worlds of old sheriff and progressive deputies. In the process I had a chance to gain insights into their work: not a lot, but enough for my timid soul.

There was growing concern that the drug market was expanding in the ripe Kenyon College student culture. One afternoon I met P.K. at a motel in a nearby city. There we talked with a young woman who would be acting under cover in Gambier in an effort to identify sellers of drugs to students. I told her about the college and the village and where some of the rumored trafficking was supposedly based. I never learned whether anything came out of the ploy, but there were no headlines about drug busts in the village, so probably not. I was not comfortable getting that close to P.K's. profession, but when he looked me in the eye and asked me for help I couldn't refuse. I was concerned about the potential conflict of interest between my roles as citizen, faculty member, and psychologist. As far as I know, no one learned of my risky trip along that ethical cliff.

I got to know the "road deputies," the detectives, and the jailers. I was impressed with their personal qualities. Soon I grew to understand their concerns about working under P.K. and was able to counsel some about personal issues that affected their work. One theme that was clear was the clash between P.K.'s old-fashioned ways and the opportunity to bring the county into the revolution in law enforcement procedures.

The contrast is clearly evident in that case of "voluntary manslaughter" on County 17. Today, EMS would not have approached the scene until well-trained deputies had assured it was safe. Any interaction with the killer would have been unlikely, the crime scene would have been undisturbed, and detectives would have been there for hours, photos would have been taken, and it would have been a lot longer before the CTFD grass truck washed the blood into the pond. Radio communications would have been mediated by a 911 staff trained in coordination of fire, EMS, and law enforcement. The handcuffs would have gone on a bit quicker, too. The jail sentence might have been longer with an iron-clad case based on carefully collected evidence.

The embryo of progress was in gestation at P.K.'s department. It was, although he likely did not recognize it, a threat to his version of law enforcement in Knox County. More important, it was based in higher education, something he respected greatly. But he was very sensitive about his comparatively archaic preparation and conflicted by its implications for his way of managing the department.

Some of the bright young guys were impatient with the old ways and eager to start the modernization. The end result was good but painful. P.K. did not run for reelection but identified a person more akin to his ways. The candidate he favored was opposed by the young detective David Barber, who won. P.K. was hurt by the loss and mad at his successor. They reconciled before P.K. died in 1993, shortly after the election. Law enforcement in the county prepared itself for the twenty first century. Symbolically, the demolition of the nineteenth century sheriff's department and jailhouse building coincided with the construction of the 21st century facility outside the city. It combines the functions of law enforcement, emergency management office, and 911 communications quarters. The sheriff's office door is behind several layers of security precautions. Now that there is coordination of all emergency services, operating guidelines are either explicit or understood among all agencies. EMS has the support of SWAT teams, hostage negotiators, and arson specialists, and thousands of hours of education and training are the foundation of each agency's functions.

The old days were more exciting, dangerous, naïve, and fun for us, and PK was just the kind of sheriff the county needed back then. Now it needs all the sophisticated attributes of big city law enforcement.

PART FOUR
SCARS NO ONE ELSE CAN SEE

The volunteer fire department of Grandpa, Harvey, and Davey is dead. There have been only a couple of serious fires in the past decade. CTFD is now responding to about 400 emergency medical calls per year. NFPA regulations and medical protocols determine what is done by the members. There are fewer local natives on the roster and more who are career professionals.

Urban EMTs work their 24 hour shifts and then commute home. They seldom have met the people they help nor have further interaction with them after an incident. The volunteer firefighter/EMTs of a generation ago knew the families they helped, and they still interact with them years after their service to the department is over. Today's CTFD is more like the urban emergency services.

Each of us who served as volunteers in the transition years sometimes felt that being an EMT forced us to witness all the bad things that happened to people we knew. An inventory of emotion evoking images was created. Part Four presents examples of experiences whose images will echo there as long as we live. All volunteers who resided in their community had such experiences. Some of the people they helped are still met in their village. So are the family members of people they could not help and seeing them awakens feelings of regret. The regrets are like scars no one else can see.

The people of the villages are losing the reassuring sense that they will be helped by the altruistic local folks who they know by name or recognize from seeing them annually in the engines and squads at the 4th of July parade, but they are more likely to survive in the hands of the new volunteer professionals.

18

CRITICAL INCIDENT STRESS DEBRIEFING (CISD) REDISCOVERED

The car fire/suicide on route 308 was a crucial test for me as a firefighter and EMT. I realized that I could participate in incidents that were disturbing without a persisting emotional effect. Emergency workers must be able to approach such situations and focus their attention on what needs to be done for victims if the best possible outcome is to be achieved. The ability to cope with those scenes is essential. Some who successfully pass the training courses to prepare themselves for such incidents discover they cannot endure the stress. Some do it for years and then become overwhelmed and have to quit.

During the past twenty years, the emotional effects of EMS work on those who provide it have become a concern to emergency organizations. Some incidents resulted in long-term disruption of the emotional and behavioral health of workers who were involved in them. Sleep disorders, irritability, and sometimes resignations from the profession occurred. Investigations revealed that depression and even suicides were being attributed to participation in horrific incidents. The public learns of these symptoms after well-publicized major disasters such as 9/11, plane crashes, building collapses, school shootings, and hurricanes. They occur, however, in virtually all emergency service departments at some time and are not contingent on the number of victims.

Stress-related emotional dysfunctions are not new. The "shell shock" diagnosis of World War I may have been the first time they were identified in a formal way by the psychological professions. In WW I the term "shell shock" was applied to describe the symptoms of soldiers incapacitated by emotional reactions to battle experiences. Many of those so labeled had not been close to an exploding shell. There was a pressing need to treat the soldiers and get them back to battle. Psychiatry, then in its infancy, recommended the revolutionary new Freudian psychoanalysis as treatment. It was a stretch of logic to argue that the Oedipus complex was the best explanation for why some soldiers were incapacitated by fear and revulsion after weeks of seeing friends blown apart and having the enemy try to kill them every minute for days on end. The seemingly interminable process of psychoanalysis came into conflict with the generals who needed the soldiers back in the trenches for the next suicidal charge into a barrage of gunfire. In a military at war, the prescription issued by a general took precedence.

There is a similar urgency to get emergency workers back on the job if they develop stress-related problems. A citizen may be affected by exposure to a horrifying experience once in a lifetime. Emergency workers may be required to respond to many during their careers and their knowledge, experience, and skills affect the survivability of victims every day. It is important to sustain them in their daily task of saving lives.

Nearly a hundred years after World War I, modern-day technology has multiplied the number of ways mass casualties can be created. It seems that almost everyone is a potential victim of emotional dysfunction after traumatic experiences. One can even be "infected" by watching real-time live television coverage of disaster.

Recognition of the similarities in symptoms of people exposed to traumatic events has led to a formal diagnostic category used by psychological professions. Post traumatic stress disorder (PTSD) is now an active field of research. Experts on the physiological responses to stress, cognitive behavior during and after stress, and the psychology of conditioning and learning are studying the problem and developing approaches to treating the disorder. The current focus of attention is on treatment of the troops who have served in Iraq and Afghanistan, but as effective treatments are identified they will be equally applicable to stress syndrome patients in the emergency services and in the general public.

There is one paradoxical way that emergency workers have long used to help ameliorate the unpleasant realities of their jobs. "Sick" humor is part of the culture of every fire and EMS department. Listeners who hear an example might be horrified that these people who are charged with saving lives also initiate exchanges of morbid humor about tragic incidents. In fact the humor serves as a penetrable shield that sometimes prevents the inevitable bad outcomes from triggering disruptive emotions that could interfere with focused expertise on the very next medical emergency. One can't let emotional stress from past runs result in poor or improper care during the subsequent emergency that may come any second.

The humor works as sublimation. It is a socially acceptable (only within the department) way to share the fact that everyone who often responds to human tragedy needs a way to manage its emotional consequences. The sick humor is one way of diluting personal revulsion by sharing it with others who have experienced similar incidents and who know that there is no way to avoid some really unpleasant situations.

Immediately after they occur, the details of awful things that happen to victims should not be revealed to the public. Where I cite some details of incidents in this volume, I do so as a way of helping readers comprehend why emergency workers can also become victims because of their exposure to personally affecting scenes. The principle employed is that one can't cry while laughing. Sick humor is one semi-acceptable way a crew can avoid disruptive emotions. Because it works to alleviate unpleasantness, it becomes preventive as well. Sick humor becomes a vehicle for empathetic understanding that is communicated among the members of the fraternity of veteran emergency workers.

Question: "How was your victim?" Answer: "CTD" (circling the drain).

Question: "How was your victim? Answer: "DRT" (dead right there)

Such an exchange is in no way disrespectful to the victim. It will not be heard by outsiders. It is a way of expressing frustration with a failure of one's skills and acceptance that sometimes nothing can be done to save a victim.

Words like sublimation, depression, and stress are not high in the word count of firehouse conversation. The term Oedipus Complex was not uttered in Harvey's kitchen. The notion that psychotherapy would be recommended as treatment of PTSD might be greeted with hostility. In recent years it may be mandated by some departments.

An initial acronym for the treatment of emergency workers for symptoms of PTSD was CISD. It arose from the need to help a wide range of emergency responders, both individuals and groups, who are continuing to be bothered by what they experienced. Some incidents can't be laughed off.

Although it is often said not to be a form of counseling, CISD is. I suspect that that denial may be attributed to the resistance some workers would have to the idea that they need counseling. What differentiates it from formal counseling is that it is often conducted by nonprofessionals. Those who lead a session are experienced emergency workers who themselves have responded to many serious situations. In CISD those who responded to the incident are encouraged to recall and describe their participation in the operations. They discuss their role during the event and describe their emotional reactions to specific and overall aspects of it. Openly reliving their own role, listening to others tell of the effect of the incident on themselves, and comprehending the complexity of the situation sometimes increases the ability of workers to cope with their own emotions. The goal is for them to regain their sense of competence and willingness to return to normal duty. In contrast to reviewing a traumatic scene with a stranger or therapist, one knows that a colleague in an emergency service understands exactly what it is like to be faced with shocking sights and sounds. When it is shared with those who have had similar experiences and who have dealt with them successfully, there is no concern that one's revulsion or emotional expressions will be misinterpreted as weakness, nor will they be disturbing to the listener. CISD does not always work and it may be counterproductive for some participants.

In contemporary culture the reflexive reaction of the media and the public seems to be to assign blame when emergency personnel do not produce happy endings. What they fail to understand is that there is no such thing as a generic train wreck, plane crash, or tornado. Each is unique and demands adaptation of emergency worker's skills and innovative problem solving. In some instances the required resources are not available, nor of sufficient power, to accomplish what is required by the situation. The outcome is devastating, but planning for it would have preempted preparation for much more likely disasters and would have needed advance specifications of the nature and magnitude of the incident. No two emergencies are alike. It is always a matter of adapting the resources, training, and experience accumulated by individuals and organizations to each new situation. There will always be situations for which there is no precedent or relevant experience, and things will go badly. People know and recognize hurricanes and earthquakes as emergencies, but how can one respond effectively to the thousand unique emergencies they create all at once? Should the people stranded on a bridge after Katrina receive immediate aid because there is a TV camera there? Why, if the situation was desperate, didn't the TV network send its helicopters to help instead of allowing its reporter to harangue undermanned emergency workers?

For each person, whether a 911 operator who takes the originating call, a law-enforcement officer, a firefighter, or an EMT, the degree of emotional response is distinctive to the individual. Once recorded in memory, it can be recalled and verbally described. Sometimes the memories operate as if they are in a closed loop of videotape that cannot be turned off. With each replay of visual images, sounds and odors reverberate with nearly the emotional intensity of the original. The cognitive tape loop of reruns might focus on the choice required when a conscious but terminally injured six year old child had to be abandoned in order to help a ninety-year-old person who has some chance to survive.

CISD is intended to enable emergency personnel to articulate and consider their own role and that of others in the incident in a blame-free environment. Often insights can be achieved that interrupt and stop negative ruminations and enable the person to be prepared to focus life-saving skills on the next emergency.

The EMT who keeps responding year after year has confidence that skills learned in training can result in the best possible outcome for the victim or victims. Usually death is averted and it is possible to prevent the victim's condition from getting worse. Then the person can be transported to a medical facility where recovery odds are increased. Becoming competent to do the right thing, whether removing a splinter, splinting a bone, or doing effective CPR is very satisfying. There are many more rewarding outcomes than those that are not. Even when learned skills prove fruitless, it is gratifying to know that one could offer experience and instruments that provided the victim the best opportunity to survive. Veteran emergency workers have accumulated years of exposure to trauma and each instance provides them with experience useful in future events. Extensive experience is likely the most important assurance of quality care.

There is no assurance that years of responding to incidents resulting in trauma and death inoculates the emergency worker from their emotional effects. Some experiences will continue to echo into awareness. The crucial question is whether those become incapacitating or disruptive to their daily lives. There are individual differences and some veteran responders do resign as a result of the cumulative memories of horrific events. Others complete their entire career without being handicapped by the stresses. That does not mean that they are unaffected. Reviewing a sample of incidents that continue to reverberate in the memories of CTFD veterans may illustrate why that is true even among those who are long retired.

19
THE BEST VOLUNTEER OF ALL

Who was CTFD's all time best volunteer? It would have to be someone with breadth of experience, demonstrated competence in a wide range of emergencies, and who had proven tough enough to tolerate adversity. Maybe someone who started with basic aptitudes and with hard work and dedication became a respected leader in our department and among peers elsewhere. As a rookie, the person had to jovially accept being teased for mistakes and be resilient after the emotional pain of tragic outcomes. The nominee would have rapidly mastered the training to become both a firefighter and an EMT, and then demonstrated the ability to transfer those new skills to emergencies. After accumulating a breadth of experience fellow volunteers would trust that leader to lead them into a burning building or care for them if they were ill or injured.

Having just two or three members like that would be predictive of a pretty strong volunteer department. By the 1980s CTFD had more than a half dozen and was respected throughout the county and beyond.

One minor problem had yet to be solved to solidify the organization. When the group of residents who lived in Monroe Township joined CTFD and created their substation several miles north of Gambier, they quickly formed a close knit-group. Working smoothly with the Gambier veterans came more slowly. The chief emphasized over and over that we were all one department and the Monroe guys were in every way equal to the members who had long been serving College Township. However, all the best equipment was at the station in Gambier, almost all the training took place there, radio communications were based there, and the officers in command were initially all at "Station 1." The meals and beer machine were also in Gambier. The Monroe guys were equal, but the Gambier group was more equal.

It took special people not to allow resentment about the inequities to interfere with their participation. The Monroe volunteers did not let pettiness prevent them from working for the good of the department. They were all special in that sense. The best volunteer CTFD ever had came from among the Monroe volunteers.

Out of Work, and Doing Good

I don't recall how long the window glass factory had been operating in the city of Mount Vernon but it may have been since the 19th century. It was one of those industries that is an employment bedrock of the community. Son followed father into jobs that assured financial security and enabled the workers to raise the next generation of glass cutters. In 1976 it closed.

A number of the-soon-to-be-jobless workers were CTFD volunteers and lived north of the city on an acre or so in Monroe Township. Some had more than a decade of service with the glass company, were married, and had children. Losing what should have been a job that would see them through to a comfortable retirement was devastating. Some employees were given the opportunity to move to plants in other states. The department lost one of its key officers, Carroll Dial, who had been an assistant chief under Chuck Imel. He moved to a factory in another state. There was concern that the department would lose more. The Monroe Township station had developed into a dependable unit and was providing rapid responses to emergencies in the northern part of CTFD's coverage area. Losing leaders from among that group would be a significant blow to the whole department.

The Monroe guys loved the fire training and used the beer cooler sparingly, except at the annual Christmas party. Most strongly preferred firefighting to squad runs. Rich Yarman was the exception. He liked firefighting, but he also developed an early and intense interest in EMS. He, perhaps more than anyone up there, was eager to accept the challenge of becoming doubly valuable as both a firefighter and an EMT. Rich earned a leadership role and managed many of the Monroe Township medical runs without backup from Gambier. His stock soared with me every squad run he led after midnight because I could go back to sleep knowing the victim would be in good hands. He lost his job at the glass factory. We feared that we would lose him.

After the department assumed responsibility for EMS, squad runs became almost ninety percent of the department's calls. The shift in activity created problems for the department. The preferences of Monroe Township and College Township members were not even. There were more people who enjoyed being EMTs in the Gambier station, but most Monroe guys preferred the engines and killing flames. Some even felt they had not joined the fire department to mess with sick people. They would do their duty and respond for squad runs but maybe not quite quickly enough to catch the squad before it left the bay. Exposure to blood and guts was not the problem. Most, like Rich, were long-time deer hunters and may have helped with the butchering on the family farm.

Early on, Rich and his squad crews demonstrated their ability to improvise to meet a challenge, but their sense of the priorities needed a bit of fine tuning. The morning Earl Jones hit the deer while riding his motorcycle to work is a good example. The sheriff's office dispatcher set off the Plectrons (first-generation pagers) for a Code 4 (accident with injury) east of the village on the state route. A code 4 required that emergency squads from both stations respond in case there were multiple victims, rescue problems, or a need for traffic control.

If the second squad was not needed, policy dictated that the crew on the scene of the incident is to radio orders for it to stand by at the Gambier station. In this instance the College Township based crew arrived on the scene and found Earl in pretty good shape, but they forgot to divert the Monroe squad. It was a cold morning and the five or six layers of clothing Earl was wearing provided good insulation from both "road rash" and the cold. (Road rash refers to extensive abrasions typically acquired by sliding on pavement when unexpectedly exiting a moving vehicle). By the time the clothing was removed to examine Earl, the Monroe squad was nearing the scene.

The deer was not so fortunate and was DRT (dead right there). Since no one had cancelled the Monroe squad, it came racing up to the scene, siren screaming. Rich, Charlie McDonald, and Billie Van Dyke jumped out of it, eager to assist, only to be told they were not needed. They, however, observed a functional imperative lying before them. Within seconds they had the still-warm deer strapped to a backboard and in the back of the old Pontiac ambulance. There was nothing they could do to revive the buck, so they transported it, nonemergency status, to Monroe station for an appropriate disposition, namely the firehouse freezer.

In all emergencies, it is important to be alert to one's surroundings and to be innovative in achieving the best possible outcome. The Monroe squad's ingenuity at Merle's accident and their pragmatic awareness was soon celebrated by most of the department. For the next few Sunday morning inspections, everyone enjoyed the venison omelets for breakfast, then the Tuesday post-training venison chili, and finally venison "Sloppy Joes."

It is true that no one had told Rich and his crew not to use the squad to pick up a dead dear. But it is also true that at that stage of their training they did not anticipate the "what ifs." What if they had suddenly been dispatched to transport a new victim who was suffering from the stomach flu, or schizophrenia. Fortunately, they soon assumed a more conventional level of professionalism.

Rich Learned That Being an EMT Can Destroy a Belief in Life's Fairness

Volunteers usually serve a small community and know many of the residents as friends and acquaintances. It is inevitable that there will be occasions when they are challenged to remain composed and competent while helping someone they value greatly. Rich would discover that fact shortly after becoming EMS officer at Monroe substation. Knowing a little about Rich will help understand the impact of the incident on him.

The term "robust" would come to the mind of anyone who first met him. About five feet eight inches is not tall, but when the chest looks to be about forty six inches, it has a marked taper to the waist, the biceps are proportional to the chest, and the face is hidden by a full, coal-black beard, "robust" seems like the right label. A twinkle in his eyes, a boyish grin, and an almost naive gregariousness quickly communicated "good guy." These qualities combined to make him the ideal Boy Scout leader. He spent many hours with his scouts. He was physically strong and moral, a model of self-sufficiency, and a teacher whom young males wanted to please. His scouts gladly learned from him and grew in their own self-confidence. Before the term became a somewhat trite attribution, he was an excellent role model. In turn, he became fond of each member of his troop and followed their lives as they grew through their teen years.

He and Vi had a good marriage, and their kids were growing and getting interested in extracurricular activities at school. In many ways, the closing of the glass factory placed similar "good guys" in Monroe in the same situation. For a while they had more time for the fire department, which became a way of doing something to bolster self-respect until they could find another job. For Rich it meant more time for scouting, more time for CTFD, and more time to pursue his hobby of hunting with muzzle loaders, and creating pioneer period handcrafts. Describe those qualities to any volunteer fire department chief in the country, and he would be happy to stick the guy's name label on an FD helmet.

Monroe Township has rolling hills left by the glacier thousands of years ago. It was rugged enough that mostly small farms preserved the agricultural traditions. In recent years it has become an area in which building sites pop up that allow nice views from lots of one to five acres. Still, back then, some of the township roads were paved, and some were still gravel. Once in a while, therefore, cars would slide in the gravel or miss a curve and go off the road. Most accidents were minor, unless two or more cars came together. On a sunny weekday afternoon when the Plectron "beebeeped" and a one-car code 4 was broadcast, it was not particularly alarming. Anyone who serves in an emergency service, however, quickly learns that what will actually be found at the scene is not predictable. One learns never to assume.

On this occasion, getting a crew together at Monroe station took a while. The College Township squad and engine were quickly out the doors, and we were first on the scene. As I arrived I saw that the vehicle involved was an older model Jeep, the World War II type. There were two injuries. One was not serious, and one was fatal. A young man, who appeared to be in his teens, had been thrown from the passenger seat as the jeep rolled, and as the Jeep came down, the rear bumper landed on his forehead.

Rich arrived with the Monroe squad. As a lifelong hunter he was familiar with exposed internal viscera before he became an EMT. Since then, he had experienced the parallels in human victims. When he walked up to the Jeep and looked down at the victim his initial reaction was that of one inured to such matters: saddened and affected, but hardened enough to wall off any rising emotional disruption of his job. Then he paled, and his facial expression changed from stoic acceptance to puzzlement and then disbelief and useless denial.

Prior to the instant of his death, the young man had been one of Rich's most promising Boy Scouts. Just days previously, he and Rich had spent the evening working on a project they had started months earlier. Now, the investment in that young life, and the implicit rewards gained by knowing that he had played an important role in enabling a young person to achieve his potential, were lying dead before him. Of all the possible options envisioned for the boy's future, Rich never considered this one. He was profoundly affected.

The need for CISD may have been intuitively understood by people in every branch of emergency service, but it did not exist. Certainly, Rich could have benefited from that form of "debriefing." His facial expression, more than his words, showed us that. We could see his anguish and shock, but we didn't know the lad. Our job was to finish completing our report. For us the experience was just another one of that type that must be endured. We knew Rich was distressed, but we did not know how to help him, or whether we should even try.

Rich carried his grief and, I assume, attended the funeral and expressed his own deep sadness to the parents. It was the kind of experience that must be accepted by anyone who serves in an EMS. Growth as a leader in such situations is measured by whether the officer can recognize the importance of facing the reality, no matter how seemingly unfair, and still be ready to respond immediately if a new emergency suddenly arose. Rich showed us he could do that. He even increased his commitment to the emergency medical team. He passed the EMT-Advanced course, and asserted his leadership.

When the state funded a system of regional representatives to communicate emergency medical service regulations, evaluate departments, and promote quality EMS state wide, Rich applied for the job. It surprised me when he was appointed to the position, until I reflected on the personal characteristics that made him perfect for it. He was straightforward and unbiased in his judgments, sincere, dedicated, and still a Boy Scout in demanding high standards. The position required a strong masculine personality to gain the cooperation of a group of people who required exactly that. Rich was especially talented at persuading others to want to achieve excellence and was just the right person to work with small community volunteers. Every volunteer organization survives on the pride invested in the department, and Rich mobilized those feelings in the departments he visited. His simple straightforward language left no ambiguity, but neither did it appear to be arbitrary or motivated by self-promotion. His appointment to the position relieved our anxiety that loss of the glass factory job would result in his leaving the department.

He bridged the psychological distance inherent in moving from a job laboring on the hot production line of the window glass factory to becoming a traveling representative of the Ohio State Department of Emergency Medical Services. Instead of working five shifts a week on the line, he was now using his personality to influence those who cared for ill and injured people all over the state. He was on the road many days, and less available to us, but still was on a leader's share of the runs.

Vi remained active among the department spouses, and Debbie and Donnie ran around with the other firehouse brats at the social gatherings. Rich was a source of reflected pride for us and CTFD became known throughout the state as a department staffed with high-quality people. He was an example of the best in volunteerism, and people assumed his department must be top notch too. It was. Rich's leadership in EMS did not mean he was less interested or able as a firefighter. He was ready when our radios were toned out regardless of the type of emergency.

The Fifth of July

A late-morning fire on Sunday or a holiday is not all that unusual. Someone goes to church and forgets to turn off the fire under a skillet or does some other absent minded thing. The alarm came in, and I was late getting to the main station. All the equipment was either out the door or could not wait for me to get into my gear. I stayed in Gambier to do base-station communication.

It turned out to be a significant structure fire not too far from the Monroe substation. Because it was a day following a holiday, there were quite a few Station 2 firefighters available to respond quickly. They were there before Station 1 engines arrived. The "size up" by those on the first engine at the scene concluded that Danville Fire Department engines should be dispatched to assist. It was clear that all our equipment and personnel were needed at the fire.

It was CTFD policy to send an emergency squad to all fires, but that meant someone couldn't get on an engine and fight the fire. With so few fires per year, no one was going to be stuck on the squad if they could help it. No officer was going to risk the ire of a member by ordering someone to get off the engine, bring the emergency squad, and then sit and watch everyone else fighting the fire. The squad usually sat in the station, lonely and unwanted. At the same time it was also thought wise to have someone "sit the radio" at the station to coordinate communications. That job was the least valued of all. I was late in getting to the station, so I deserved the lousy duty, but that did not mean that I didn't imagine ten different scenarios that could justify getting into the squad and racing to the fire. It wasn't fair that an officer of my importance be stuck at the station.

By listening from my seat in the radio room I could tell that the incident commander on the scene was coordinating things well. It was also clear that it was a tenacious fire. So I sat there pouting, six miles away, imagining some way to get to one of the "best" fires we had had for months.

Assistant Chief Dave "Lightning" Williams had been assigned to coordinate water supply. In part that meant keeping the eight by eight-by-two feet canvas water tank filled so that the engines' pumps could draft water from it and feed it to the lines going to the nozzles of the attack crews. Monroe was first on the scene, and as one would expect, Rich had been first to take a crew in and had finally come out for a breather. Lightning established a relay of tanker trucks that drove to a nearby farm pond, drafted water to fill their tanks and returned to dump it in the portable tank.

Two major stressors for firefighters are on the coldest days of winter and the hottest days of summer. It was early July and as hot as it had been all season. Wearing the heavy turnout gear and manhandling an ornery charged water line is exhausting. Everyone who goes in on attack comes out drenched in sweat and in need of a rest and a cool-down.

Rich came out sweating profusely and drained of energy, but he had done exactly what a leader does. He got his crew organized and into the fight. Williams could see that Rich needed a break and asked him to come with him as they went to the nearby pond to draft water, fill a tanker, and then return. Rich removed his heavy turnout gear and helmet and joined Lightning in Tanker #5.

When they arrived at the pond the two struggled to get the gasoline-powered portable pump out of the rear compartment and start its engine to draft the water. They filled #5, and when it was ready, Rich told Lightning to go ahead. He was still pouring sweat and feeling the need for a little more cool down. He volunteered to stay and help load the next tanker, and then rejoin the fight. A Danville tanker was next in line and passed #5 on the way back to the portable tank.

Blasting through my ruminations about being left behind was the chief's voice in an uncharacteristically terse command. "We need the emergency squad to the scene now; we have a firefighter down." I was out the door in a few seconds and at the scene in the minimum time I could safely make it. I was waved in and pulled up to where firefighters were surrounding the victim. My heart sank and the "oh no" feeling spread through me. CPR was being administered. I fought back emotion and steeled myself to go into the regimented thinking and action that we had been trained to do, regardless of whether the victim was a stranger, friend, or relative: 9 months or 90 years old.

The victim was in firefighting turnout gear, so I couldn't see who it was. The backdoor of the squad was yanked open as I pulled to a stop. Another firefighter told me, "Get in the back and help, I'll drive." As I entered the squad, I saw the coal-black bushy beard and the heavily muscled chest. The twinkle in the eyes was gone. Rich was in "full arrest": no respiration and no heartbeat. Even though CPR had begun as soon as he had gone down, there was no sign of hope. The squad was in gear and on its way as soon as the doors were closed. We continued CPR, and established an intravenous line. The hospital was only a few minutes away. We did all we were capable of doing on the trip to the hospital. The people in the ER did their job in a professional way. Rich was dead. I looked at him. I did not weep. I did not curse. I crammed all those feelings into an emotional safe deposit box. I refused to let them out. I suppressed all those urges to give in by telling myself that there would be much to do in helping the department through the next days and months. (Actually, I thought those things to help myself.)

There is a prepared firefighter funeral service that was written by someone long ago. It had made its way into the department file cabinet, just in case. It was simple and sentimental, and served its purpose for our members. We all donned our dress uniforms, the navy blue ones, with Wedgwood blue shirts, clip-on ties and fire axe tie clasps. The chief read the service. Then came the public funeral. Firefighters have great funerals. Firefighters, law enforcement officers, and dignitaries from all over the state attended. Because of his popularity with his coworkers in the state capitol and his many contacts throughout the state, hundreds of people were there to pay their respects. The caravan to the cemetery was well over a mile long and contained representative fire engines, emergency squads, and law enforcement vehicles. A short interment service was offered, and Rich was placed in his grave. There were plenty of tears, though I held mine back, except for a little leaking when I looked at Vi and the kids.

Vi was strong. When I saw her, she expressed gratitude for the sympathies. I couldn't tell how the kids were doing. For the family, Rich's death was a greater sadness than we could know and, beyond that, destroyed the foundation of security his benevolence and physical strength had provided. Suddenly, their dreams for the future had disappeared into a dirt-filled hole. It was not until some years later that I learned that Debbie, who was about ten at the time, had expressed a different emotion. When the funeral was over she approached Chief Brown and, voice quavering, asked him, "Why did you kill my daddy?"

The mood at the firehouse was only somber on its good days. On all others, it was black. Lightning, emotionally beat himself up day after day for not recognizing the duration of the profuse sweating and malaise as symptoms he could have recognized. Why would he? We all had experienced being drenched in our sweat, exhausted to the point of lying down, and unable to rejoin the fire fight for a while. That is the way it is for all firefighters on hot July days at any kind of significant fire. It was years before physical exams were required before anyone could be a volunteer.

The death of one of your firefighters is about as bad as it can get for a Chief. Rich had been more than a great volunteer, he was a personal friend, a vital leader, the prototype of a hero. Add to that the words of Debbie, and Hobe discovered that losing one of his firefighters wasn't as bad as it can get; it can get worse. Of course, Debbie, the little girl, could not understand or comprehend what had occurred, nor how it affected the chief. But she had communicated to him the true depth and significance of the loss. Hobe's job now was to do something that might provide some substantive help.

One of Hobe's most prominent characteristics was perseverance and a tenacity that was unrelenting when he set out to accomplish a goal. Those qualities became focused on identifying and securing financial support for Vi and the kids. It took months of badgering the bureaucrats, making daily phone calls, and gathering medical documents, affidavits, and dozens of letters. In the end, all sources of funds for firefighters who died as a result of fighting a fire were secured for the family. Rich's name is on the honor roll at the national monument that honors firefighters who die in the line of duty. The kids went on and did well, and Vi found an interesting and useful job. Neither the kids nor Vi has had the happy life they should have had. They all deserved better. Tragedy cannot be denied no matter how hard one tries. It is no consolation that this tragedy focused attention on Rich's career and his importance to our department and the profession. I have often wondered what the department would have become if he had lived. It is not fair when a Boy Scout dies before he can realize his potential.

20

I DID NOT KNOW WHAT EVIL LURKED

In this decade, in the cities, the career firefighter/EMTs commute to work, respond to put out the fires or transport the victims, go back to the station, record the emergencies on report forms, and then file them. After their twenty four hour shift they get into their cars and drive home, sometimes for fifty miles or more. They seldom had met the people they helped before an incident and rarely ever see them again.

Volunteer firefighter/EMTs in small towns must view their experiences in a much different way than their urban colleagues. Their homes are near the fire station and they know many local families, even say hello to some of them every day. Though they know some folks well and recognize many others, they would prefer not to know the intimacies of any of those villagers' personal lives. Responding to medical emergencies removes that option. Instantly, there must be a change in role from familiar town resident to trained volunteer professional who must make decisions that affect the life of an individual or the lives of a family. That need becomes very personal, and there is no other option. After the emergency is resolved, the home town volunteer can't simply put a report in the file, wait for the next run, and then drive home to a distant residence. Volunteers remain in the community and every day they are reminded of the consequences of their actions.

If the volunteer's span of service is long, there may be opportunities to help several members of a single family. When that happens, there is a growing sense of being a constant intruder into their personal lives. It is not as if one is a voyeur, but that feeling seems inevitable when one is repeatedly immersed in the travails of the family. For me that feeling of ill ease grew with events that befell one family over a period of a couple of decades. With a different family, I detected that the sense of being an intruder was reciprocated while helping them often over a short period of time. I thought nothing much about that. We were called, came often, rendered aid, and left.

Then events brought the fates of the two families together and changed their lives forever. I might have noted the coincidence of having served each of the families on several occasions but then as the impact of the events unfolded they touched me and my family. The story makes clear how being a long-time volunteer in a small community destroys ones immunity from being immersed in the lives of its people. The origins of the tragedy began several decades prior to the convergence of events.

"Sarge"

When Will (aka "Sarge") left the military service with the rank of sergeant and returned to his home community, he probably had no idea what he really wanted to do for a living. He and Marilyn started a family, so earning an income was foremost. When I first knew him, he held a position with the college maintenance department. I don't recall what his responsibilities were. That isn't important, because Will saw an opportunity, which if it worked out, would be much more satisfying. The college had become coed in 1969. That meant different things to different people, but what was crucial to Will and Marilyn was that all those students would buy pizza somewhere. Just as important, maybe more so, yes, definitely more so, there was nowhere in the village where students felt free to party away from the watchful eyes of "Big Brother," aka The Dean (Thomas J. Edwards, Kenyon's dean of students) and "Officer Cass" (James Cass, chief of the esteemed Kenyon security force).

True, Dorothy's Lunch was still open but there were always old guys (over thirty) hanging around. Even though the college had its own beer license and a little pub in the basement of a dining hall, the specter of a "loco parentis" loomed large in the minds of the party-oriented students. Nothing about student behavior suggested that they were inhibited by college oversight of beer drinking. Still, eighteen-year-olds are adults by some definitions, and they feel they should not have to be concerned about some parental surrogate monitoring their playtime. They did not want some quasi-parent around while they tried to find out how many kinds of risky behavior they could get away with on their journey from adolescence to maturity. The students were thrilled with the idea of being able to party and eat pizza off campus. In fact, off campus, for Will's brilliant idea, was about thirty feet behind a college-owned building.

When Will and Marilyn founded what became the Pirate's Cove, it had great potential. The name celebrated the Gambier High School of old (pre-1970's) where that giant of six-man football, Banker Bill Smith, had ruled, and where Marilyn was a star student. The original decor featured a large cutout of a mean-looking pirate complete with Chuck Imel's favorite giant feather plume in his hat. It hung on the south wall of the dining area. I presume that the pirate theme was intended to broaden the base of clientele by attracting local natives. It would provide an alternative to Dorothy's Lunch for locals. I do not think many of them came to the Cove, but as it turned out, they weren't needed.

Dorothy's was the legendary hang out for students and faculty of the MEN'S college and therefore a pariah to many at the new diversely gendered coed campus. Dorothy's now had the stigma of being the bar of the "men's" college. Anyway, it was not big enough to house the brew-drinking hordes of a fourteen hundred student enrollment. It turned out that there was no need for mutual concern by the two establishments, because the Ohio legislature lowered the drinking age to eighteen. At first, the Cove flourished on the sale of pizza, but the lowering of the drinking age must have made it much easier for "Sarge" to finance construction of a bar/dining room/dance area addition. The menu grew long and strong, featuring an Italian bias. Pizzas were delivered to the dorms by teen-age kids driving rattly old Chevys and used first-generation Hondas. They roared up the alley to the kitchen door, idled audibly till the next four-topping disk was ready, and then accelerated all the way to the target dorm.

Those Ohio lawmakers ensured that it was standing room only at the "Cove" until the doors closed around two a.m. That left a couple of hours for study before the students' normal bedtime. I don't think many of those patrons registered for my eight a.m. course.

Profitability meant prosperity, and Will and family were soon able to expand their frame house on a rural road north of the village. Eventually, their elderly parents came to live with them. One by one as their children grew they too began to work at the restaurant. I think all of them had a hand in running the business, some even after they were married. Maybe Sarge made that part of their marriage vows.

Will maintained a firm grip on the business. Marilyn was the menu side and maybe the business manager; Sarge the enforcer. He retained the firm jaw and steely eyes of his military rank and whenever necessary asserted that kind of authority in the Cove. He was not tall or visibly muscular, at least not by middle age. It is the demeanor of a sergeant, especially the expressiveness of the jaw, and the laser look from his eyes that intimidated. By the time he opened the Cove, his little mustache could have misled a few into thinking him a somewhat mellowed drill master. That would have been a mistake. He could still call cadence and ream out any underage freshman with a fake ID.

As the Cove settled into a routine, the clientele divided itself into two groups. The early-evening faction consisted of local families and students who wanted a good Italian meal. That group had all cleared out before the student partiers began to arrive around ten p.m. They wedged themselves in. They were led by the smoke exhaling, laughing, screaming, jean-clad, ball-hat-wearing, sophisticated, East Coast prep school grads, but everyone in there drank beer and sweated.

For a while another form of diversity arrived when the students had left for the summer. It enabled the Cove to flourish without a three-month pause after the school year was over. The college hosted a celebrated summer theater. The construction of the new Bolton Theater on campus was aided by the support of alumnus Paul Newman and his spouse Joanne Woodward. The productions featured famous actors and directors, including the above. The Cove became a meeting site for them after the shows. The Pirate had to be satisfied with a minor role when the walls soon were covered with celebrity-autographed photos and hand-written tributes to the quality of the Cove ambiance. Cameo appearances by Jonathan Winters and Marcel Marceau assured that both the early and late sessions would produce customers hopeful of seeing a celebrity. The mime troop was a noisy boon to the bottom line.

In time, the family's second generation gradually assumed more and more of the day-to-day hosting and menu responsibilities. The eldest son was night manager and loved having the theater types around. He spent a lot of time schmoozing with them. The Kenyon Summer Theater productions were top notch and attracted audiences from all over Ohio. The theater was of such superb quality that the production costs spent it out of business.

While the summer theater was in town, however, it was not unusual to see the actors wandering through Gambier and the aisles of the Gambier Village Market. The double-takes and ogling by the faculty townies turned into flustration when a star suddenly loomed before them in the dog food aisle.

Some time after the summer theater folded, CTFD visited the Cove on business of a different kind, and our many subsequent services to Sarge's family began.

Fire!

Change is inevitable, especially in the restaurant business, and a number of events led to transitions in the history of the Cove. The first event was the fire. It started in the kitchen and threatened to destroy the whole building and the mother and daughter who lived in the second-story apartment above the restaurant. There was extensive smoke damage, and the kitchen and bar areas had to be completely renovated. The residents who lived in the apartment upstairs escaped unharmed.

The Pirate's Cove fire put an exclamation point on the importance of a rapid response time by CTFD. When the Plectrons went off that night I jumped out of bed to the dispatcher's report of a fire at the Pirate's Cove. I could feel the adrenaline surge. The Cove was within fifty feet of the new station. It was also the source of free pizza after our Tuesday evening training nights. It is a tribute to our professionalism that the thought of the potentially devastating loss of our pizza did not cause us to panic. What did cause confusion, however, was that the fire was so close to the station.

Usually, on the way to a fire there is time to think through the procedures learned during the fire training. Normally, a crew boarded an engine and radioed the Knox County sheriff's dispatcher that we were enroute to the scene of a fire somewhere in our territory. Then we spent the next minutes following the best route to the scene and debating the location of the nearest hydrant or farm pond where we could get additional water if needed. During the drive there was time to review procedures for fighting whatever kind of fire had been reported. When, for example, it is a structure fire it is essential to "spot" the engines in the best place to fight the fire: far enough away from the heat that neither the engine nor the pump operator get singed, yet accessible to other engines or tankers that supply additional water. The trip also allows the officer in charge to decide which firefighters should be assigned to ladder and rescue tasks, which to advance the hose and its nozzle, and who should regulate the pumps.

I had never thought about what the sequence of responses should be when the fire is next door to the station. Of course the veteran fire officers had thought about that possibility. Suddenly, it dawned on me that there was not the luxury of planning how to attack the fire. All I could think was "Eeeek the fire is right here. What do we do, what do we do?" Remembering my first field fire with Grandpa, I did not say that out loud. Also I remembered that real firefighters don't say "Eeek."

The chief, of course, already knew what had to be done, and had anticipated the problems. I, however, was in a state of confusion. My stream of sleep-fogged semi consciousness wrestled with all kinds of dilemmas. If the fire was next to the station, the engines had to go only a few feet, so do you need to turn on the flashing lights and siren? Where would you park the trucks so they weren't bumping into one another?

"Uh-oh, there is smoke and fire showing out the kitchen door." "What about the people who live up above the restaurant?" The building is on fire, and here we are having taken what seemed an eternity to park our cars and pickup trucks, get out, run into the station, put on the cumbersome turnout gear, climb into the cab or onto the back of the engine, wait for an officer to give the order to go, open the station doors, and sound the air horn. The engine roared out the door, traveled a few feet to a hydrant and stopped. Meanwhile, the fire continued to eat the restaurant, and we still hadn't put a drop of water on it.

The chief, his officers, and the seasoned firefighters did their jobs efficiently. In a short while, the fire was down to embers being chopped out of wall studs. When it was out, the chief talked briefly with Will, and they agreed to wait until daylight to determine the cause and assess the damage. A crew stayed at the scene to ensure that the fire did not reignite and that no one entered and obscured evidence of the fire's origin. As suspected, accumulated grease in a vent seemed the likely source. There was a noticeable elevation of respect for CTFD in the eyes of Sarge and each of us recognized his implicit gratitude from then on. He started planning for the reopening right away.

The kitchen was rebuilt and the dining room cleared of soot and redecorated. The Cove was converted from a bar with good food to a "family restaurant" with good food and a drink to go with it. The bar remained but was shielded from the direct view of diners by a wall panel. The dance floor disappeared, and patrons were seated by a host or hostess. It was very nice but not the same. I missed the pictures of the stars of stage and screen, but the Pirate still threatened guests from the south wall.

When the legislature rethought teenage drinking and raised the age, it likely did not do much damage to the well established business. The students would soon adapt to the new law and were able to produce evidence of having skipped a couple of years of maturing while on their way to the Cove. The Cove settled in to a good but maybe not quite as profitable niche. Helping to rescue the bottom line was the arrival of Pac Man and the rapid evolution of his virtual offspring. A few of the coin-collecting games were crowded into the carryout cubbyhole that was walled off from the dining area. Once patrons became addicted to the little cannibal, the machines produced a pretty fair income per hour and there was no accounting overhead for Social Security or Pac Man's worker's compensation benefits.

Visits to the Family Home

No more fires plagued the business, but we began to see the family periodically for other reasons, and we got to know well the route to the family's expanded home. The parents sustained their commitment to the establishment, but, the children ran the day-to-day operations. The food was good, student help came and went. My daughter Lizz worked there for a while after her days as "papergirl" were over. She praised the excellent tips on the weekends.

Eventually when the eldest son began to manage another tavern in the city, he spent less time directly managing the Cove. The quality of the pizza was said to have declined, but I do not know about that. In years past, my wife, Jo, and I had enjoyed regular Wednesday evening meals with our friends George and Martha Breithaupt at the Cove, but habits will change.

Sarge and Marilyn finally began enjoying a more relaxed life style with the profits of their years of hard work. He bought a nice car, and his pride in accomplishment was easy to discern as he parked it across from the family owned Gambier Deli, and sauntered over for breakfast, cooked for him by the daughter-in-law who managed the place. After working night and day for many years, he could finally enjoy the proceeds from his energies. The Deli Cranberry muffins were my favorite, and still are.

The first EMS visit to the family home was a sad one. An elderly parent could not be roused from her sleep. It was immediately apparent to us that she had died quietly in bed. Because of my cordial relationships with the family and patronage of the Cove, and because my kids enjoyed their kids, offering additional assistance was a natural adjunct to confirming the passing. Hugs and expressions of gratitude to the squad crew were offered, as if calling hours had already begun. It was not long before another parent followed.

A few years after Sarge had withdrawn from operating the Cove, he began to complain of having no energy. He was chronically tired, and though he underwent many physical exams, no cause was definitively identified. After many months there was a diagnosis. Sarge expressed relief that finally a cause could be named, and he immediately began therapy. At the Deli in late summer of that year, a colleague from the college and I sat drinking coffee. I also needed one of their famous cranberry muffins. Sarge came in. He was his usual upbeat, "good to see you" self. Whether his upbeat mood and optimism were self-deception, I don't know. What I do know is that his complexion revealed more accurately his true condition.

Weeks later came the next dispatch to the residence. I had not seen Sarge since meeting him in the deli. Arriving at the residence, we were ushered to a bedroom. Most of the children, and their spouses were there waiting in the living room. It was clear from their expressions that the family already knew that Sarge was dying.

Afterward, with the children showing less interest in the Cove, it seemed to move to the periphery of student attention, too. Pizza preferences are fickle, and as Papa John's, Domino's, and other delivery services began to cater to the college dorms, profits from the Cove likely dwindled. I assume the Cove still did okay, but it was on a downward slope, according to my friends. It might have died a natural death, but it didn't.

A Totally Different Family

College Township was created by carving out one-quarter of Pleasant Township solely to provide land for Philander Chase's college. Farming has pretty much disappeared, and houses bled from the village limits to the township boundaries. Almost all who now live here year-round, maybe a thousand people in the township and village combined, get their mail at the Gambier post office and do their banking at the Peoples Bank of Gambier. Other than the usual turnover of students every four years, local people know each other at least to say hello, and that lulled the community to assumptions begging for disproof.

If one comes down the hill from the village and college and continues south he or she will simultaneously cross the bridge over the Kokosing River and be on Laymon Road in College Township. A few hundred yards beyond the bridge is the bike path created when the railroad was abandoned and left us without most of our grass fires. Laymon Road then makes a sharp turn to the east. Another half mile and it begins to climb upward at the entry to an S curve. Make a left turn at the beginning of the S and enter Metowood Lane.

Metowood was built by a developer some years before zoning. It abuts the river and provides building sites with river frontage for some, and a good view of the stream and the country side for those on the opposite side of the street. A small number of apartment houses are near its end.

From time to time in the EMS field there are people who need assistance often, very often. In some cases the reason for calling the squad is trivial and may only require lifting an ill or aged person back into a chair or bed and making sure they have not been injured by a fall. The term "frequent flyer" is attached to those calls for help often. It is not a term of derision, because in many cases it marks the beginning of a health problem that becomes a true emergency.

Repetitious runs can, however, become a burden to a department and tempt one to be irritated when a call comes after midnight. We all groused about them but it is a professional obligation to treat each one as if it is serious and treat the victim with dignity while addressing the chronic complaint. The next time, the reason for calling may be life-threatening.

The elderly mother of a resident on Metowood Lane was one of our frequent flyers. She was diabetic and had a blood sugar level that was not well regulated. Diabetic emergencies are not trivial and must be treated promptly, but sometimes the victims are not taking proper care of themselves, or those who care for them don't monitor them well enough.

In this case the woman lived with her daughter and family in the apartment. Each time we were called, her blood sugar levels had declined, she was not responding appropriately in conversation, and was less alert. The problem can be temporarily corrected if caught early. If the blood sugar level is low and the patient alert enough, a sugar-laden soda pop can bring the person back to near normal responsiveness. Then a trip to the ER will confirm what is to be done next. Often it a two hour trip for us and no excitement.

On one occasion "Mom" was "down" halfway up a flight of stairs in a small room on the left. Getting her on the cot and making the sharp turn to descend the narrow stairwell required great care and several EMTs. They had to work in concert to assure that the cot and, even more important, the victim did not take flight and end up at the bottom of the stairs. Successful extrications of mom from the bedroom became routine with lots of practice. On one of those occasions, I stood aside. Assistant Chief Jane Kindbom used the occasion to teach new student EMTs to do the lifting and extrication. That left me at the bottom of the stairs clearing furniture that might be obstacles to the cot's route out the door. My job afforded time to look around the apartment and, as it turned out, meet other residents.

The first was a two-year-old who was toddling around, excited by all the fuss going on in the house. He was chipper and mobile and in the way. I was able to distract him through conversation, and we got along fine.

While I was entertaining the young boy, I looked up the stairs to check progress. At the top was a young man staring down at me. His facial expression seemed hostile and I speculated that he was not thrilled with all the fuss that was going on, yet again. He came down the stairs slowly, did not look into the patient's room, passed by me ignoring my comment about the cute kid, and walked on to the kitchen. I dismissed the behavior as likely irritation with a problem of "frequent-flying mother-in-law." That was the only time I saw the man, even though we had many more visits to see mom. Frequent flying for mom turned out to be seven times in six months.

Let's Try Eating at the Cove Again

A couple of years after watching CTFD burn down Dorothy's Lunch which we witnessed with our friends of fifty years, Don and Marion, they visited my wife Jo and me again. We agreed to eat at the Pirate's Cove. The place was crowded, but there was one booth available at the opposite side of the dining room. The regulars were at the bar, and I was greeted by one of them whom I knew from the college maintenance staff. At the same time, Jo was waving to a student server who was clearing the booth we would occupy. Jo knew Emily from a knitting group where a few women of the village helped a small group of coeds learn to knit. In addition to teaching knitting, the older women listened to the student gossip and shared some of their own. Emily rushed across the room and greeted Jo with a buoyant smile, and they exchanged pleasantries. Jo asked her if she could be our server for the evening, but ours was not her booth and they both expressed sincere regrets. However, our "server by rule" came rushing over, calling out an excited, "Hello, Don and Marion." The surprise was mutual. Angela had been their favorite server at "Brews," a downtown tavern in Granville, Ohio where they lived. Don and Marion were Angela's regular Wednesday customers, and over time their relationship extended into the realm of the old folks giving a young woman counseling about her confusing love life. She had left Brews to join her boyfriend in Mount Vernon and had found work at the local tavern where Sarge's son now worked. Ordinarily she would have been working there that evening but had been pressed into service at the Cove as a substitute for someone. I remember being amused by the coincidence and the love story, but I also had kind of wished Emily had been able to serve us. She was petite, perky, outgoing, and cute. She seemed genuinely fond of Jo. I thought that if this meal was okay, and it was very good, the next time we ate at the Cove we would make it a point to ask for her table. That never happened.

The Frequent Flyer's Family Secret

A number of years ago there was a teenager, Gregory McNight, who, during a robbery, killed a person. He was convicted of the crime and sentenced to the Columbus, Ohio, juvenile detention center where he was confined until he reached the age of twenty one. While at the center he came under the watchful eye of a young female guard who was only a few years his elder. After he was released, the relationship between the two resulted in their being married. They quickly bore two children.

They left Columbus in search of work, and eventually he found a job as a kitchen manager in a small community, and she received an appointment as a counselor in a youth camp for juvenile delinquents. They found an apartment in a rural subdivision, and her mother came to live with them.

On November 3, 2000, the roommate of Kenyon student Emily Murray reported that she had not returned to her room after her shift ended at three a.m. at the Pirates Cove. Emily's green Subaru Outback was missing. Her wallet, money, and credit cards were in her room. It was rumored that College authorities were alarmed when they learned that she had a history of depression. The area law enforcement agencies were notified, and a search was begun for Emily and her auto. The search was expanded throughout the state. Fearing that she had intended to do herself harm, it was speculated that she had found a way to carry out her death wish where no one could stop her. Days and then weeks passed. Planes flew over ponds where the car might have submerged. Vacant barns and buildings were searched. Local law enforcement concluded that she was not in the county, and the intensity of the search abated.

A number of us at the fire department who knew the area well conducted our own search with no success. Over the years I had responded to a substantial number of suicides. In none of those had the victims traveled any significant distance from home to carry out their plan. In most, it seemed obvious that the act was done on impulse, rather than after a rational plan that entailed a long travel time alone during which the will to end it all would have to be sustained with the passion it must take to carry it out. In short, I did not buy the idea that a young woman would go miles from the campus to commit suicide. Nor did I feel it was likely that she was sufficiently familiar with the area around the campus to have hidden in an area unfamiliar to us. She was Jo's friend. I wanted to help find her. She had not seemed at all depressed to me. But she was not found.

And Then

In the second week of December, a sheriff's deputy in a remote rural county in the southern part of Ohio was dispatched to a trailer home far off a secondary road. He was to serve a warrant to the owner who was accused of receiving stolen property and was suspected of burglary. When he arrived at the residence, he found no one home. Parked in the driveway was a Subaru with New York license plates. He thought that was odd. Few out-of-state cars are observed in that county. The subject named in the warrant was not from New York, and the remoteness of the home made finding that car there unlikely. He requested a license plate check from his dispatcher to determine to whom the car was registered. The registration was to Emily Murray, and he soon knew that she was a missing person. A search warrant enabled the officers to enter the trailer. Inside was a partially decomposed body wrapped in a rug. A single gunshot wound to the head appeared to be the cause of death.

The name on the warrant was Gregory McKnight, kitchen manager of the Pirate's Cove and son-in-law of diabetic, frequent flyer, mom, who lived with her daughter and children on Metowood Lane. McKnight and his wife were arrested for possession of the auto, and bail was set at one million dollars apiece. Positive identification confirmed that the body was that of Emily. In carrying out the investigation of this murder, authorities uncovered bones of a second body, buried at the trailer site. That turned out to be a former friend of Gregory's. On October 10, 2003, Gregory McKnight was convicted of Emily's murder and sentenced to death. His sentence was upheld in December 2005. Further appeals are pending.

When Emily disappeared McKnight was questioned by local deputies, but they did not pursue the matter when he told them that he was not there when she clocked out. It is reported that a comparison of their time cards would have shown differently. Apparently, no background check was conducted before McKnight was hired.

As sometimes happens, the grief that permeates a campus after a student's death also generates anger. Shortly after Emily's body was found, that anger was directed at the proprietors of the Pirate's Cove. Why hadn't they done a background check?

I think the academic environment leads students to a cessation of normal caution in dealing with others who live here. Ignoring the fact that there are evil people of all colors, genders, and fraternity affiliations is comforting; but dangerous. It is also true that those of us who have lived here so long and may publicly express skepticism about the "goodness" of others did not imagine or consider that someone who lived in Gambier or College Township could be evil incarnate. I had thought when McKnight glowered from the head of the stairs that he was just mad at his mother-in-law.

He now sits in prison awaiting the outcome of his next appeal of the death sentence. His wife lived here quietly in the apartment with the children and her mother for a while. We continued to "fly frequently" but only a few more times before they moved away. It seems likely that his wife provided evidence to the prosecution though reports in the paper suggested otherwise. Withholding incriminating evidence would have resulted in her being imprisoned and unable to care for her mother or children. I suspect too that she was very uncomfortable with her husband's history of killing people who were "friends."

The apartment has been vacant since they moved out. Neighbors are mounting a plea to have the disintegrating building bulldozed. CTFD may be asked to declare it a firetrap. Maybe they can use it for fire training and burn it down.

The Cove continued to operate for a while. In part that was because the hint of danger that now stuck to the place. A bit of an enticing "Friday the Thirteenth" aura was attached to eating there. But the figurative handwriting on the wall had replaced the tangible mural of the Gambier High School Pirate. The college, having a vested interest in what would happen next, bought the place.

Since the sale, it is named the Gambier Grill. For a while it was managed by a couple of Kenyon graduates, one a former CTFD firefighter, the other a refugee from a 9/11 financial firm. It is an open hall with wooden tables, a bar, and student servers. It attracts students but some locals too. The latest proprietor is Danny Ralston, Kenyon student firefighter in the 1970s, Kenyon alumnus, retired Marine Corps colonel, son of the former head of maintenance, Dick Ralston, and grandson of Paul Ralston, the maintenance supervisor at the time of the Old Kenyon fire. Danny is the husband of educational software salesperson and former student of mine, Liz. Dan rejoined CTFD upon his return to the village.

Years have passed since Emily was murdered. That means that there are no students here who knew her or shared in the horror and sadness of her murder. The new generations will know about that from oral history, and they and their parents will know that Kenyon College lost some of the qualities that led former provost Bruce Haywood to speak of Kenyon as a place akin to Thomas Mann's "Magic Mountain." It is no longer a place far from the "real world" where students can learn vicariously about life, safe from its dangers, before having to solve the empirical dilemmas of their own lives. Bishop Chase would have approved of Haywood's analogy and would have reminded us that he was right about the importance of having the college isolated from the urban world.

Gambier was a place where everyone was assumed to be honest and moral, unless a member of the wrong political party. But the fate of the Cove instructs us that Chase was correct in placing the College far from the sinful cities but neither he nor Haywood, nor the volunteers of CTFD could keep the sinners from finding the village in the twenty first century.

21

IMAGES THAT WILL NOT DISAPPEAR FROM MY HEAD

We were volunteers, local members of the community with families and jobs, We knew the grocers, the postal employees, the restaurant proprietors, the little league kids, their parents and their coaches, the school teachers, the deputies, the village mayor, the town maintenance crew. We also knew many of the college's students, its president, his wife, the faculty, and the support staff. Our kids knew everyone else's kids who lived in the village. We would have known all of them even if we had not been members of CTFD.

Because we were firefighters and EMTs, however, our relationships with any local person, friend, relative, acquaintance, or stranger could change in an instant. When suddenly someone had a medical emergency, we had to abandon the informal personal relationships and assume the professional role of EMT. To avoid that intimacy would be diving into a swimming pool and not getting wet. For better or worse those incidents indelibly affected all subsequent interactions between victim and volunteer.

Some of those experiences were seared into my memory, sometimes in curious ways. Whether responding to the emergency of a close friend, acquaintance, or a local person I did not know, a memory was created that punctured the barrier that normally would have insulated me from their personal lives. I did not want to see inside their bedrooms, remove their clothing, invade their bodies with needles and tubes, hear them say a family member was a drug addict, know their basement was a garbage dump, or see their faces when they were dying. The reality of being a volunteer who is an EMT is not filled with romantic heroism. It is the ripping off of the camouflage of interpersonal superficiality. The images of some events remain attached in memory and carry an emotional valence. Some of them return to awareness from time to time. Now, years later my memory may even have shaped them differently, but the images seem as clear as ever.

Two incidents pop up in my memory as visual icons that have no relationship to their outcomes. Some might speculate that they insulate the events from their sadness and frustration. The two images seem inexplicable, yet they have lasted for many years. One is a pair of bare legs, the other a pair of plaid socks.

Legs

Mr.Ransom had been at Kenyon for more than a decade before I arrived at the all-male college in 1955 as the assistant director of admissions. I had never heard of the literary magazine <u>The Kenyon Review</u>. Walt Whitman was the only author whose work I recalled from English class at Denison. That was only because I couldn't understand how someone who wrote so abstractly could be so admired. My undergraduate brain was preoccupied by fraternity, intramural sports, and beer drinking, but not necessarily in that order.

It was made clear to me that I had better learn about The Kenyon Review, and especially its editor John Crowe Ransom, if I were to represent the college properly when recruiting new students at secondary schools. Those names were important in the vocabularies of headmasters at the prep schools that sent to Kenyon students who ranked in the lower third and fourth quarter of their graduating class. Their parents would pay full tuition. Perhaps, under the proper tutelage, the young man would become a famous writer, or at least graduate.

My office was just down the hall from The Kenyon Review offices, but I didn't get to know Mr. Ransom. I was in awe of him, and he likely recognized me for what I was, if he noticed me at all. But, a superficial flavor of the man would be easy to caricature. Not tall, soft, graying, straight hair, parted and always combed. A slightly bemused expression on his face, and a voice clearly colored "southern gentleman." His office was spacious. The windows looked out at an eight-foot-wide, ten-foot-deep window well, more like a dry moat, which let light in from the campus green above. He held classes there in the afternoon for a few students. They sat in a circle, with his seat facing the open door. It was a quiet group with voices seldom rising to audibility from the hallway. He always seemed to be enjoying his teaching.

In those two plus years I worked at Kenyon, President Gordon Chalmers, who almost single-handedly built the college into a prestigious liberal arts college, died. In that two-year period three members of the English Department, Ransom's right-hand-man, and five students also died. In a college of forty five faculty and five hundred students, the losses, especially Chalmers', demoralized the college.

Chalmers's replacement arrived about a year later. As I listened the poor man quoted, but mispronounced, William Butler Yeats ("Yeets") in his inaugural address. Whether it was that gaffe or an unleashing of pent-up frustration after the authoritarian Chalmers, the new president elicited the dark side of Ransom the Southern Gentleman. At a dinner held to celebrate the inauguration of the new president, Ransom informed his new boss and a stunned crowd that the faculty, not the president, would be running the college. The motive for his pronouncement was not clear to most of the stunned diners. I was reminded that other soft-spoken southern gentlemen had shown a hostile side less than a century before that.

By the time I returned to Kenyon in 1969, Mr. Ransom had retired. He was honored at a celebration attended by many of the most notable of his colleagues and students, down at Dorothy's Lunch. He remained in Gambier along with his spouse of many years, a daughter, and a granddaughter. The last was among the first and best students at the Kenyon attended by both women and men.

On my return as a faculty member, my interactions with Ransom were limited to occasional Sunday mornings before inspection at the firehouse. I doubt that he remembered me from the earlier years and my publications in Science were not on his list of important contemporary writings.

My daughter Lizz, then about age ten, had insisted on becoming the Sunday morning sales girl for the Columbus Dispatch newspaper. It was a job held over the years by any number of faculty brats. The papers were dropped off in a couple of heavy bundles by the delivery truck between seven thirty and eight o'clock Sunday mornings. The little girl had to lug the bundles onto the covered porch of Farr Hall in the heart of downtown Gambier. In reality, the heart comprised the totality of downtown Gambier, and it was not quite a block long. Farr is a college-owned building that once held a destination book store but now houses Kenyon tee shirts, soda pop, ice cream cones, and textbooks. The Gambier Deli, and the Village Market remain as the other commercial tenants. A few student dorm rooms are on the second floor. Sunday newspaper sales were made at fifty cents per paper to loyal customers who drove up to the curb, got out, and approached a round cement table where they were displayed. Within forty feet of the display was the front door of the book store where one could enter and buy the same paper for the same price, and a much warmer edition in December and January. Locals and faculty preferred the kid concession, students the warmer edition. I had been concerned when tiny Lizz took the job but not enough to miss the start of inspection at the firehouse.

On one particularly nasty day I drove Lizz up to her newsstand, expecting to drop her off and go back to the fire station. I saw the size of the heavy bales of news and wondered how she was managing to get them out of the elements and onto the sales table. I got out, lifted them for her, and was from then on an admirer of her industry and tenacity. After that, I helped to get the latest news ready every Sunday. Occasionally, it was necessary for me to substitute as sales agent. Then I would see many of my friends, colleagues, neighbors, and acquaintances. They would pull up to the curb and remark about the tough circumstances that had led me to take a second job, but the cheapskates never tipped me.

The Ransoms were regular customers. Mrs. Ransom drove Mr. Ransom down to the news stand and he alighted to fetch the paper. The hair was still combed as it was in the 1950s, the same soft southern voice, polite but remote, slow gait, up the step to the stack of papers fifty cents in hand, a pleasant exchange of good mornings, "See you next week, Mr. Ransom", a 180-degree turn, back to the car, open the door, get in, and up Gaskin Street to the one-story frame home that stood behind the college infirmary; same sequence every Sunday.

The routine remained the same, but Mr. Ransom did not. Progressively it became obvious that his great mind was no longer faultlessly mediating his interactions with his long familiar surroundings. He arrived at the same time, got out of the car, and with obvious effort to concentrate searched for the next step in the sequence of the programmed Sunday morning ritual. Verbal interaction ceased, and he offered the coins, awaiting whatever came next, but was not able to solve that puzzle until the paper was placed in his hands. Then he wandered back to the car, found the door and got in. On his last few Sundays, he arrived as usual, fumbled with the door handle, opened it, got out facing the post office across the street, and stumbled, stepped, turned, reversed, looked at the money in his hand, trying to remember why it was there and what he was supposed to do next. As his progressive decline became unbearably sad we began to meet him halfway, then at the curb, and finally delivered the paper to the car. Then he came no more.

One morning quite a while after he had ceased coming to Farr on Sunday the tone alert sounded at the fire station for a squad run to the Ransom residence on a possible DOA. Our crew arrived at their home within a few minutes and we were directed into the bedroom. Mr. Ransom was lying supine in the bed. He looked very much as if he were sleeping; peaceful, hair barely mussed, his face placid.

The family knew he was gone, and in those early days, just as today, there is some doubt as to what comes next even for those who had known that death is coming. They have not anticipated the steps that must come immediately after the final breath. Then, more than now, the next step was to call the emergency squad. To us this was often an opportunity to serve the family by providing them with a dignified caring transport to the funeral home by fellow villagers who had volunteered to help in such times. It was an important obligation. I had seen a funeral director and his assistant grab the feet and shoulders of a family member and toss the body onto a gurney with a thump while loved ones watched. That was not going to happen to families in our village and townships.

The family expressed their preference of funeral home. We positioned the ambulance cot where we could lift him onto it. We gently uncovered him and prepared for the four-man lift that would support him from head to toe while we moved him to the cot. When the covers were down, a curious phenomenon occurred. For reasons I cannot understand, a visual image burned into my memory and resides there even today. I was struck by the appearance of Mr. Ransom's legs. They looked firm, smooth, youthful, and strong. They did not look like the limbs of a man in his mid-eighties, more like they might still run a mile without fatigue.

Maybe by focusing on the legs, not the aura of a great literary figure, I was able to avoid showing emotions that would undermine the obligation to the family in mourning. Sometimes death's greatest injustice is when the mind does not wait for the heart to stop. Mind and body are one, but they may die at different rates.

That was 34 years ago. I still see his Kenyon graduate granddaughter quite often in the village. She is a stalwart of the village government and a faithful dog walker.

Socks

The dispatcher called us to provide mutual aid to the Danville Fire Department on a vehicle accident involving injury. We left the station and headed East on the U.S. highway that winds its picturesque way along the Kokosing River curving left and right and up and down through rural eastern Knox County. The river is on its way to feed the Walhonding, the Muskingum, the Ohio, and finally the Mississippi and the Gulf of Mexico. The accident was at an area where there were frequent crashes. The road curved fairly sharply and at the same time rose steeply from riverside, up a grade to higher ground. As we arrived on the scene, we could see that a long flatbed truck and auto had collided. It was not head-on. The car hit the side of the truck well behind the cab. Conclusions about the cause of the wreck were the responsibility of the Ohio State Patrol, and a trooper was already there to begin the investigation.

As expected in such impacts, the auto bore the worst of the damage. The Danville squad was busy separating the car from the two victims, both of them in the front seat. We were assigned the driver, who remained pinned by the steering wheel. He appeared to be a teenager. The passenger was a middle-aged woman who was being rescued from the passenger's side door. A Danville firefighter offered the opinion that the young man was beyond help.

We never accepted the death of a child even when there was evidence that it is too late. Young people have more survivability in some instances. Kids should fulfill their dreams and ambitions and the hopes and visions of their parents. Parents need to know that we tried everything possible to save their child.

We expedited the extrication of the young man, laid him on the cot, and applied the leads of the electrocardiograph. There was what is referred to as an agonal rhythm on the monitor. It can be interpreted as a heart that is not pumping blood, and it is caused by residual, final, neural activity that can endure after recovery is no longer to be expected. We did not accept his death. A Danville EMT, CTFD colleague Jane Kindbom, and I began the chest compressions and ventilations that are CPR. A bag-valve mask was placed over his mouth and nose, and pure oxygen was used to inflate the balloon like device. As it filled with oxygen, the bag was squeezed and the oxygen forced into his lungs. CPR and ventilations were continuous during the 10 minute travel time to the hospital. The cot bearing the boy was rolled rapidly into the emergency room, where the staff was waiting ready to try whatever else might strike a spark of life.

As the ER staff began to remove clothing to assess the injuries, I stood back, sure that there would be no future for him. As his shoes were removed, my eyes fell on his feet. Covering each was a conservatively colored plaid sock. The image of those socks remains with me.

The boy's family had just moved to the rapidly growing lakeside community east of Mount Vernon. The fun of being able to play at its lake helped ease the adjustment of leaving old friends behind and enduring the stares elicited at school as he became the "new kid."

I could not ward off a vision of the young man rising in the morning, selecting his favorite pair of socks, eager to get down to the breakfast that his mother was preparing, then hurrying out to board the school bus. This was a special day, and he would have trouble concentrating on English and math. This was the first day in which he would be behind the wheel, following the directions of his driving instructor. He would drive for the first time on a U.S. highway. I still see those socks, and they continue to remind me that even though we did everything we had been trained to do to save his young life, we failed.

It was an accident: just that. It was nothing he did, or his instructor did, or the truck driver did. Road conditions led to the impact. It means nothing that it was not someone's fault. The boy is dead. Those socks should have been worn until they fell apart.

22
LOCAL BOYS MAKE GOOD

Kids tend to idolize the firefighters of their community. Some pass through a stage in which they aspire to become one. Some actually realize that goal while others who might have held that dream have it snuffed out the first time they see their local fire department emergency squad in action.

A Solemn Four Year Old Grows Up To Be a Social Success

Tom worked at the college book store for a couple of years. Jack, the former manager, put him at the cash register because of his congeniality, and partly I suspect, to demonstrate his commitment to providing opportunities for those who may have a tough time getting an initial job interview.

No one who visited the store could have failed to notice that the carpeted floors were being vacuumed all day long. Largely silent young men and women carefully pushed their sweepers back and forth, working their way around the book laden shelves, the jewelry counters, juice drink dispensers, displays of greeting cards, and, oh yea, sundries and hardware. The store provided an olio of items that met the needs and desires of college students, their visiting parents, bibliophiles, and retired professionals, but mostly books. The designated sweepers, were well trained, conscientious, and business like, though each was from that sub set of the populace euphemistically referred to as the developmentally disadvantaged. They were reliable and conscientious workers and got the carpet clean though sometimes the Hoover's wheels followed the same track for several minutes. Jack's "disadvantaged" were gainfully employed.

Tom was from a different class of the disadvantaged. One could see from his eyes that he was alert, socially adept, and big for his age. He was a young man in his late teens. It was impossible not to notice that his right arm was withered, permanently bent at a right angle, and useless except as a means to brace objects. His left arm, hand and fingers did the manipulations required to manage the tasks of living, and of making a living. He had no trouble operating the cash register, recording entries on the student charge accounts, and bagging the cornucopia of purchases available at Jack's store. His handicap seemed not to handicap him in any way.

I didn't recognize him the first time I came in to pick up my <u>New York Times</u>, daily edition, but he seemed vaguely familiar. I couldn't recall, until someone spoke his name, where I had seen him before. More than a decade had past, and he had grown from child to young man. Then flashbulb memory suddenly recalled every detail of our earlier meeting. I did not reintroduce myself to him by reference to that day.

It was a hot day. My colleague Dick Hoppe, who lived on the state route about a mile outside the village, had staked out an area of his land to allow me to plant a garden. I had gone there to do some hoeing and weeding. I was well into the work with dirt rising up my arms toward my neck. Sweat met it and reversed the grime in little trickles of mud that dropped to the ground.

It is at such times that the volunteer EMT understands that if the pager announces a medical emergency, the filth should preempt any thought of responding to join the ambulance crew. At those moments it is also true that a medical emergency will occur. The new emergency forces the EMT to resist the reflexes which gang up against a rational decision. Common sense gets trampled in the head long charge to the station. Then the next task is to create a rationale that will justify doing what professional judgment has ruled one must not do. One could, for example, open the car window as it heads to the station, turn its air-conditioning fan on full blast to evaporate sweat, race in to the station, go directly to the sink, wash hands and face, and then dry with a bunch of paper towels before the squad can escape leaving behind one's indispensable skills. For the sake of the victim it is best if a crew has already left the station with siren clearing the roads. If not, would the victim rather have clean hands providing care or die because no EMT would respond with dirty hands and smelling of sweat? It is a volunteer's dilemma.

For me the dilemma fostered a near compulsion to keep my hands clean. Dirty jobs were postponed, and whenever possible avoided. My compulsion became a firehouse joke at my expense, and a source of teasing about being afraid to get my hands dirty. But they also knew I was willing to get my hands the bloodiest, or pukiest, or fecaliest, so my compulsion was tolerated with fire house humor. In the midst of pulling the grass and weeds from around the tomato plants, and planting the second batch of lettuce, and getting dirty because there was no way to avoid it and still have a garden, the inevitable happened. The pager beeped, and the speaker announced that there is an injured child at a house, on the same road as the garden, and half way between me and the fire station. "I can't respond I'm way too dirty, especially to aid a child." So I didn't respond. Neither did I continue with the planting. I listened for the pager to tell me the squad is enroute with a crew. I waited. I waited but heard no reassuring sound. Five minutes elapsed and there was no sound from the squad.

I got into my car and drove toward the house number given on the radio. It is the small frame house next to the cement block building that is now an apartment but was a live bait and fishing tackle store when it was built in the

50's. I pulled in the drive and parked about 100 feet from the detached garage behind the house. The emergency squad was not there yet. Three or four adults rushed toward me. They were agitated about how long it had been since they called for the squad. Beyond them, past an antiquated ringer washer, I saw a young boy seated on the ground but leaning against a garage.

He was not crying. He did not appear overtly distressed, but was pale, and seemed to be unaware of the fuss surrounding him. As I was led closer, the adults told me that the child had been playing with the old washing machine and his hand caught in the rollers that squeeze the water out of the clothes before they are hung on the clothesline to dry. I saw that his right arm was bare and red, as if burned. I knelt down beside him and softly explained that I was there to help him. He said nothing. I asked if I could look at his arm. He didn't respond but did not resist. Gently, I examined it. The skin was abraided not cut. As I cleared the clothing away I saw that the redness extended to his arm pit. Very carefully I moved the arm away from his body to examine the upper arm. My heart sank. The rollers had continued to squeeze their way up his arm until they could go no further. They did not stop turning. They rolled and rolled, ground and ground, eroding away the flesh, the muscle, the tendons, the nerves, the blood vessels. There was no bleeding from the wound. The crushing and grinding had effectively sealed the blood vessels. It had also forever damaged the nerves and tissue that would have allowed that arm to grow and function. Four year old Tom was displaying the kind of symptoms I learned to recognize in children who are seriously injured. They seem to be lost in another world, quiet, uncommunicative, perhaps disbelieving their first experience with trauma and pain they did not imagine existed. I did not touch his wound with my dirty hands. Soon the emergency squad arrived driven by new volunteer, Ron Smith. He had broken protocol by driving because he was not yet 25, the age the department required to be eligible to drive the equipment. He had demonstrated the adaptability important in emergency workers who must break a rule when conditions demand it. He knew how long it had been since the family had called and decided it was time to act. He became an outstanding EMT. When he and two other EMT's arrived we took Tom to the hospital emergency room and then to Children's Hospital in Columbus. Tom didn't complain on the way, nor when the physician examined him. I do not think I saw him again until the day I picked up my newspaper at the book store.

I can imagine his treatment was a long and painful process but obviously was not one that returned normal function to that arm. Tom the cashier seemed untroubled by his handicap. But if as a four year old he had dreamed of becoming a firefighter, that was not to be. I can imagine that his parents will always be troubled by that tragedy. Ringer washers should be recycled. Tom did not need to be a firefighter to become an admirable person.

I do not know where Tom is today. I recall that the family sold the house and must have moved to another community. Jack no longer manages the book store so there are no handicapped employees. Intellectuals do not hang out there as much either since most of the books are gone, having been replaced by the pop and ice cream cones essential to a good liberal arts education.

The EMT-P Volunteer, Sheriff's Deputy, Kid From Down the Block

The call came in that a teenager had passed out in his kitchen. The home was only a couple blocks from the station, and we arrived in just a few minutes from the time of alarm. When we entered the kitchen, we observed a young man, probably fifteen or so, who was seated in a chair, eyes open, but in a confused state. He seemed to be struggling to become oriented but was still drowsy and not responsive to our questions. He had been working on the construction of a model airplane. His mom thought maybe he had inhaled the fumes from the tube of glue used to fasten the balsam struts of the fuselage. We advised the parents to contact their family physician. It happened once more a few weeks later, again as he was model building. Something must be wrong, but the doctor and family will surely figure it out. At least he should stop messing with the glue. There were no more incidents that we knew about.

I remembered the runs, but not the boy's face or name so I did not recognize him years later as the close friend of Mayor Baer's son, Billy (now Bill). As the two of them progressed through school they both expressed interest in joining CTFD. That is how I got reacquainted with Ron Smith. My first impression was that he might be a slow learner. He seemed to have difficulty expressing himself verbally.

I did not pay much attention to him until he declared that he had ambitions of becoming an EMT and then a paramedic. I greeted that with skepticism and wondered how he would handle the sophisticated medical terminology and procedures. He graduated near the top of his class. That did catch my attention and I began to plan an increasingly important role for him in the department. His judgment and decisions matured rapidly as he accumulated experience. A sign of that was his decision to bring the squad for little Tom when an eligible driver did not appear. Billy followed the same path and they both became among the most reliable responders and hardest workers around the station. They were just what the department needed. They were young and lived in the village close to the fire station. It seemed likely that they would reside in Gambier for many years. The more volunteers who live in the village, especially young ones, the quicker will be the response time from alarm to the scene of the emergency

They both accumulated experience rapidly because they lived close to the station. Ron's skills attracted the attention of others and resulted in a job in the hospital emergency department. But in youthful years, experience can also lead to the conclusion that the line of work you thought you wanted, wasn't what you really wanted and a career law enforcement seemed to hold a more exciting future. With a little help via a recommendation to Sheriff P. K. Rowe, Ron became a fledgling deputy. He passed the arduous period of learning with flying colors and was gradually introduced to his new profession.

After Ron had jumped through all the department's initial hoops, he asked for duty "on the road." That translates to being in a sheriff's department black car out on patrol throughout the county. Soon his car could be seen on the roads, mostly after midnight. During the daytime he remained an active CTFD volunteer.

Ron and Billy were still best friends, and Billy had been hired as a paramedic in a neighboring county. They still liked to hang out together, but Ron was a little more interested in, or at least more actively pursuing, a love life. Ron's blossomed and a wedding was the next major step in his life. The couple agreed that Gambier was the place to live, and they found an apartment on Meadow Lane not too far from the Smith's family home. They started coming to the fire station together and his spouse expressed the intention of joining. We were elated with the possibility that three talented young people who lived in the village would respond to emergencies for years to come.

As is true in many communities, the people in different aspects of emergency services, law enforcement, fire, and emergency medical see each other periodically at incidents. There are friendships that cross those professional boundaries such as with Ron and Billy. Law enforcement people often stop by a fire station and several deputies have been members of CTFD. Out of one of those contacts came a disturbing story that no one seemed able to explain.

One night Ron was discovered dazed and confused in his oddly parked cruiser. In a short while he seemed normal but could not recall what had happened. It could have been that he fell asleep, but that was not in keeping with what fellow road deputies had observed of his work habits. He had always seemed alert, conscientious, and thrilled with his new profession. P.K., however immediately suspected that Ron was "goofing off."

One morning not long after the incident a tone alert announced a squad run to the Meadow Lane Apartments to attend to a man who was unresponsive. A crew of four including Bill Baer, responded. The drive time to the apartment was less than a minute. We recognized that our destination was the unit where Ron and his new wife had started their lives together. We rushed in with the jump bag containing the emergency instruments and the oxygen equipment. Ron was was lying in bed on his back with a pillow under his head. There was no sign of life. A quick check for respirations and pulse found neither.

Defibrillators and electrocardiographs were still rare in rural ambulances. We did not have them. All we could do was begin CPR, establish an intravenous line, and get Ron to the hospital as fast as possible.

What might have made a difference was the unexpected arrival in the squad of an experienced paramedic. Larry Cullison EMT-P, Life Flight medic, emergency equipment salesman, and future Chief of CTFD arrived at the station to deliver some supplies we had ordered. He immediately came to help us. His presence had a calming influence and helped us focus on our efforts. We transmitted our Code Blue and approximate time of arrival to the hospital ER so that personnel and equipment would be ready when we arrived.

The gurney was rushed into the emergency room and the staff immediately searched for ways to restore life to Ron. They tried every option and fought death with experienced skill just as they had done with dozens of strangers. This time it was not a stranger but a friend and colleague. At age twenty five and having just reached his professional goal, Ron was pronounced dead.

We had done all that we were trained to do. In that, we could take satisfaction. Ron is dead. He was one of "my kids." He proved he could achieve much more than when I had unfairly prejudged his ability. I had seen him, and I had touched him, and he is dead. The tears began to flow. We had lost a young buddy who shared our pride in the department, the kidding, and the sick humor. There was no humor of any kind at the firehouse for a long time.

Many other volunteers had arrived at the station to learn the outcome, and by now they knew. The flag in front of the department was lowered to half staff. This would be a difficult time, but we were still the emergency service for the community and there could be another difficult incident to manage at any moment. Mourn, but be ready.

I had not recalled those two times years ago when Ron was supposed to have been overcome with the fumes of the model airplane glue. I should have connected them to his spell in his cruiser and hypothesized that maybe the seizures were due to some congenital brain abnormality. Coroner Dr. "Eddy" Blackburn and I discussed those possibilities. Now, the why was irrelevant.

P.K. gave me that look he gave when grilling a suspect. "Did you know Ron had these spells when you recommended that I hire him?" That had never occurred to me when I told P.K. that Ron would be a good deputy. It was ten years or so after those spells, and there was no indication that he was anything but healthy and strong. After Ron died, I made the connection.

P.K. had already decided that I had deceived him and nothing would change his mind. Maybe everyone in law enforcement believes that even a friend will be devious. That is their human relations burden. Ron's certificate of paramedic status from the state EMS board hung in the meeting room for a while and then went to his wife. The invisible scar on Bill Baer's heart was reflected on his saddened face for much longer.

Ron was a local boy who fulfilled his childhood ambitions to become a volunteer firefighter and deputy sheriff. CTFD and the community should still be benefiting from his talents and leadership.

23
GOOD FRIENDS WHO HAVE MOVED NORTH ON GASKIN STREET

This book is a memoir that also includes some history and maybe an essay or two. This last chapter is memoir. Its intent is also to convey how my personal life often melded with my service as a volunteer at CTFD. Long time volunteers of departments in other small communities will have experienced the same depth of immersion in the life of their village, and consequently, in the lives of many of its residents.

The Postman Never Even Rings Once in Gambier

In Gambier Village there is no free door-to-door delivery of mail. Everyone has a post office box and pays to rent it. Long-time residents usually have larger boxes near the front of the lobby. Students and new residents have to go back to the little room off the lobby. Getting a larger box requires waiting until one is vacated. That happens when a faculty member fails to receive tenure at the college or when a local resident doesn't get tenure on earth.

There is a reason why villagers have always rejected the offer of the postal service to deliver the mail door to door. The most reliable reward for coming to the post office every day is not necessarily the mail. It is the pleasure of seeing friends and acquaintances, chatting a while with them, and sharing gossip. It is a chance to say hello to Roger or Bobby from the market across the street, marathon runner Ron Dukes of the Kenyon buildings and grounds staff, Bill McConnell who delivers the mail to the college offices, or the college president. One could tell a lot about the various college presidents by whether or not they picked up their mail and then spent a few minutes chatting with friends from the college and village. Some knew almost everyone, others only those who they deemed important.

When the college is in session, it is best to come to the post office right at eleven, before the students have walked up middle path after their "ten o'clocks." From eleven fifteen to eleven thirty there is always a big crowd of students at a lobby window, where they redeem the "package too large for your box" notices from Nick the long time seller of stamps and box retriever. Postmaster Chuck Woolison, one of the last graduates of Gambier High School, used to do some of that but he recently retired. The college held a retirement reception for him.

With a few friends, it was almost uncanny how often we met there. My friend Ed and I felt there was some spiritual force that drew us to the post office simultaneously everyday. If I was late he was late. If I was early he was early. Most of the time we were both there at eleven.

Ed and I found looking down to be profitable

Every day Ed would chuckle at the coincidence of our timing and go home and tell Alice, his wife, that he ran into me again at the post office. We discovered that we shared the postural habit of looking down at the ground while walking and that each of us had that habit strengthened by the discovery of coins dropped to the pavement by students and townsfolk. They were usually pennies, but occasionally a nickel or dime, and on a few glorious occasions a quarter. On my luckiest day I found several coins, totaling fifty cents. Several faculty colleagues offered to help me find shelter. Ed reported any recent treasures destined for the piggy bank as part of our daily greeting.

Ed was raised in humble circumstances so far north in Maine that his ear was well tuned to the French language, which spilled over the border from Canada. His extraordinary intelligence soaked up the culture of the area and probably resulted in his studying languages at Harvard. At Kenyon, starting in the 1940s, he taught French, and sometimes Italian. He was as close to a real Frenchman as there was in Gambier and probably all of Knox County. He could be seen almost every day wearing a beret while walking down Middle Path to his office.

The beret, his trimmed dark mustache, and loosely fitted suit and aged necktie reminded me of those photographs of Frenchmen lining the streets of Paris as the Germans goose-stepped toward the Arc de Triomphe. Ed, however, was anything but conquered, and his life was devoted to preventing anyone else from being bullied. He was always happy to see everyone he met on his walks down Middle Path to the post office or market. His greatest pleasure was to pause and exchange gossip about the latest faculty crisis or indiscretion. He would lean forward, laugh, and in the most confidential voice, relate his latest tidbit. At the end of his revelation, he would chuckle on his next exhale and then, on the inhale, make a sound like a coin stroking across a washboard. Politically, he championed the cause of the "common man" and always considered himself to be of that class regardless of his professorial status. He was a liberal for his time. His sense of justice was guided by the blindfolded lady holding scales. He even had friends who were conservatives.

Ed loved the Kenyon students and was a strong supporter of their efforts in the classroom, athletic fields, and on stage. He was invariably good for a comment or two in faculty meetings and reveled in its politics. For many years after retirement, he faithfully attended those awful meetings so as to be up to date on the latest issues ripe for gossip.

Ed and Alice and, in their younger days, the children lived within a stone's throw of Middle Path. Their house was next door to Jim Hayes's market, which was at the opposite end of the block from rival John Wilson's store. Jim, and butcher Art Arnold sold fine wines and prime-cut meats to the faculty. John sold basic food and even bass boats to locals. After the kids grew up and left Gambier, Ed and Alice built a sturdy little frame house at the north end of Middle Path up beyond Bexley Hall the one time Episcopal divinity school, then the college business office, and for a little while longer it will be the art department. Their former house "downtown" was converted to the offices of student affairs, i.e., where the dean of students held office. It's the structure that survived the arsonist student's attack in the 1980s.

Alice taught languages at the local high school and was recognized for her rigorous instruction and accomplished students. She supervised the couple's entertaining, and the house was always neat and orderly when guests arrived for tea and cookies. Alice was conscious of Ed's professorial status and balanced his informality with fastidious management when they entertained.

They had moved to the new house after the kids were gone. For a while the cat was their only companion until one, and then the other, daughter returned to Gambier. Each of them had marriages that did not last, and they returned in middle age to live, work, and help Ed and Alice when needed. In reality, however, the opposite was the case with the eldest. She had experienced neurophysiological symptoms for many years and needed the support of the family to fend off the depressing persistence of her discomfort.

As aging progressed, Ed and Alice did begin to need the squad to come to their door occasionally, and me and my stethoscope more often. There was nothing immediately life threatening, but it helped to keep track of pulse and blood pressure and to deliver a little vicarious fun via the latest "tsk, tsks" from the college. Now that Ed was no longer driving to the post office, they relished the news from the village. They welcomed each visit, and we even tape recorded some stories of the golden age of the college, the 1940's and 1950's. Ed had a few favorite items about eccentric colleagues and their wives that just had to be preserved.

I have no doubt that the decline and eventual death of both Ed and Alice was accelerated by what happened on a single day. The pagers bebeeped around six a.m. We were dispatched to a home at the east edge of the village. I recognized the house number as being about the location where the older daughter lived. She had been seeing a local man, and Ed and Alice were encouraged that she might be enjoying companionship for the first time in several years. My hypothesis was correct. When I arrived, I could see that the garage door was partially open. A man I did not recognize was standing just outside, accompanied by several deputy sheriffs. He was her new friend. It did not take long to learn what had happened. The garage door had been shut and the engine of the car started and allowed to run. Depression had claimed another soul. My next task was to inform Ed and Alice. Accompanied by two deputies, I traveled the several blocks to their house. The cat ran into the garage as we approached.

Shock is one common reaction when sudden death is reported to a family. Disbelief is another, and "Are you sure it is him or her?" is usually asked over and over. Sometimes acceptance of the fact only comes with seeing and touching the deceased. There was, in this case, only an instant of disbelief. There was logic that led them to accept suicide as a believable end. They knew that the agony of the long-suffering child was over.

I am not good at consoling people with words when their loved ones die. It helps me to handle the awkwardness by doing some deed that seems helpful. Because I have had to be the first to know and then first to inform, I discovered ways to help. In part it helps me to show that I do care and want to help.

The deceased needs to be transported to a funeral service. That call can be made for the family. When some of my friends have been struck by tragedy, I have helped write an obituary, called a minister, served as a pallbearer, and just been available to assist with the details of death.

As communities progress toward staffing EMS departments with career professionals, the option for EMTs to help in those ways declines. I felt honored to be able to help Ed and Alice that day and on subsequent days. There weren't as many of those as I would have liked.

Not too long after, Ed began to demonstrate some confusion. His aging accelerated. Both Ed and Alice required attention and sometimes a trip to the ER. When those led to a few days confined to the easy chair in the tiny TV den at the west end of the little frame house, I dropped by to chat, check the blood pressure, unobtrusively look for symptoms of improvement or alarm, and let the cat in or out. Age and dementia eventually conquered both Ed and Alice. One of the squad's last meetings with Ed was at midnight one cold early winter night as he wandered around the streets in his nightclothes, trying to find the door to his house.

Visiting Ed and Alice and Other Friends at Oak Grove

In the mid-nineteenth century, the Gambier villagers had acted on their desire to reduce their dependence on the college. One of their decisions was to create the Oak Grove cemetery at the north side of town. They did not want to spend eternity in the college's cemetery. Today we might refer to their declaration of independence from the college as a town-and-gown conflict. The names that have been etched into the granite grave stones of Oak Grove verify that some families have stayed close to the village for many generations.

We attended Ed's funeral, and soon after, Alice went to a nursing home. She joined Ed in the family plot at Oak Grove cemetery. Ed wanted to be buried there, not in the college cemetery where he certainly earned the right to claim a place. He was a man of the village as much as the college. At Oak Grove, he will still be around some of his bowling buddies from the Kenyon team, many of whom were from the college maintenance crew. Another professor/villager who preferred to be at Oak Grove is Denham Sutcliffe, educated at Oxford in England, a revered teacher at Kenyon and respected colleague of Eds. Close by, Eileen has recently joined Davey Clark a few years after his "last call."

If I walk across the cemetery turf made rugged by the years of digging and burying caskets, I can find Shoppy, Grandpa, and Ron. Twenty years later, a visitor might wonder why so young a man as Ron would be there. Just a few of us at today's CTFD remember him. Dorothy is there, too, having died ten years before her establishment was burned by CTFD. The name Dorothy's Lunch brings blank stares from this generation of students, but the old alums "glow" when they hear the name.

As I wandered around, I happened on the grave of little Andy, who was struck by a motorcycle while riding his new bike on Wiggin Street, two days after his tenth birthday. His grave is not near another. A little boy should not be in an isolated grave. I remember too well our efforts to return life to his little body. I escorted his father into the emergency room where Andy lay dead on the gurney. Back then, the volunteer's role did not end at the ER doors. I, not a doctor, led him to his son. I meet his dad on the street once in a while and feel guilty. For him, just seeing me must be like stabbing a wound that never heals.

A couple days before their son was to enter law school, I awakened my psychology department colleague and his wife to tell them that he had been killed in his bisected car. Then I helped them find the cemetery lot in Oak Grove and a granite stone to mark his grave. Later I served as a pallbearer for his mother and placed her beside him. His dad and I still relive our teaching careers and analyze college gossip over lunch at the Village Deli.

Don and Marion go to Oak Grove every year to plant flowers on the graves of family members born in the nineteenth century. Dr. Blackburn assured me that there was nothing I could have done for Marion's mother.

The cemetery is filled with familiar local names. Some I met only once as a volunteer, others were friends I saw often. They have moved to that permanent neighborhood at the end of Gaskin Street and they wait to welcome the next local resident to their subdivision. When I am there I can feel the warmth of some fond memories, like hearing Ed chuckle about his discovery of a copper-colored Lincoln head treasure. But as I stroll farther, the warmth is balanced by the fate that robbed little Andy and Ron of their chances to have their full share of fun.

The wages of the true volunteers are deposited in their memories. Most of them are on the credit side of the ledger, but some images withdraw from that balance like a tax that tempers the sense of profitable contribution.

24
FAREWELL

In the preface to the book I implied that the era of the centuries, old volunteer fire department was at sunset. That opinion has to be qualified. There will be volunteer fire departments just like ours in 1970, before emergency medical service intruded. They will exist in rural areas, be staffed by long-time residents of the district, and have secondhand engines and grass trucks that they maintain in good-enough shape to get the job done. They will drill once or twice a month and have a dozen or so fires a year, most of which will be minor. "Good old boys" will tend the equipment, joke around and tease each other, occasionally revolt against the chief, eat together, and sponsor a fund-raiser. They will be located where the tax base doesn't allow them to "get modern" and the number of fires doesn't beg for more resources than they always have had. Most will be dispatched by some 911 communications center. They will be FIRE DEPARTMENTS.

The rural citizens they protect from fire will have emergency medical service. They will be served by urban, or county funded paramedics. Isolated areas are accessible by helicopter, so chances for survival are a lot better for them than three decades ago.

Most of the rural emergency services will soon be governed by an integrated fire district rather than operated by a village or township. Many already are. Their district will be funded by its own tax levy and managed by representatives from the political subdivisions within the geographic boundaries they serve.

There are still fire departments in Knox country, like CTFD, that might still be called "volunteer," but the definition of volunteer has changed. Some members will be full-time employees, some will be paid by the run, and a few will still be of the original tradition. Those who respond to emergencies will be dual-trained and certified in fire and EMS. Their leaders likely will be salaried officers. It is certain that their rosters will now be diverse in the contemporary sense. That became most clear at CTFD in the 1990s when Jane Kindbom became an assistant chief and volunteers varied in gender and race. Those appointments were based solely on competence.

A subtle irritant is created in the minds of volunteers who receive money for their service. As soon as they are paid for their work, a conflict may arise in their self-perception. The pay is well justified but decreases their sense of doing noble deeds purely out of the goodness of their heart. Accepting the pay somehow dilutes their altruistic motive. It is just that taking a tiny bit of money, barely enough to cover their expenses, sometimes makes an abrasion in their ears when they say "I am a volunteer."

There is a continuum that leads from the original meaning of volunteer to career status in an emergency service. The farther one progresses from unpaid volunteer to paid by the run, to hourly worker, to career professional working a couple twenty four hour shifts a week, the closer one gets to the egocentrism of business and industry. Volunteers can, and still do, squabble with the chief or the governing body, and if they find their situation too stressful, they quit. Career professionals do not usually quit. They organize a union, set work rules, have shop stewards, and can appeal to the National Labor Relations Board. In each form the sense of altruism can get bent but it does not break under the strain of the disputes. Whether a volunteer or career emergency worker, pride in doing one's best to help others is not compromised. The career professionals who also serve as volunteers on their days off are still very close to the original volunteer in spirit.

The College Township Fire Department remains ready to respond to emergencies and is better prepared than ever. There are not, however, many volunteers like those of my era who are inextricably entwined with the life of the village and the lives of its citizens. Every year more members report for a shift as career professionals elsewhere and come to CTFD on their days off. Other volunteers drive miles to stand by at our station for a block of time, hoping to gain experience that will land them a full-time position in a city.

Of those traditional volunteers at CTFD, only my former Kenyon faculty colleague Dick Hoppe can claim years of service that span almost the whole period of the mutation. He is the last of the former Kenyon faculty members who sacrificed time and energy from his teaching and research to help his community. For many years most faculty members lived in the village and some, like economics professor Alan Batchelder and physicist Peter Collings were officers in CTFD. There are still a few at CTFD who remember and treasure the pure spirit of the old days, like former chief Bob Hooper, current chief Bill Smith, Neil Bower, Roger Hite, Lee Henthorn and Carl Day. So what about the rest of today's roster? There is not one that does not give to the community more than is received. There is not one who does not make personal sacrifices for the victims of fire and medical emergencies.

The 18-to-22 year-old Kenyon student volunteers are idealistic and altruistic in their motivation, but they never receive adequate thanks from the community. The people of the community seldom know any of their names. They serve CTFD during their college years, graduate, and then become great citizens wherever they live.

Reunion of Kenyon Student firefighter/EMTs in 2001. Alumni gathered for the first reunion of the College Township volunteers included (standing, left to right) Kenneth S. Thompson '76, Thomas B. Faulkner '84, James S. Wilson '95, James W. Caley '86, David P. Diggdon '88, Andrew E. Niles '87, Chuck Rice, Steven J. Alex '76, Amie Graves Swope '91, Philip R. Purdy '75, Michael R. Pour '73, David J. Snell '73, Daniel G. Ralston '71, Edward "Mel" Otten '73, F. Jay Andress III '75. Standing behind front row: Randolph B. Gorman '81. Seated at top: Homer R. Richards '74, Sarah E. Reading '99, Jay A Johannigman '79, David E. Williams 1985, Jason A. Creux '94, Peter A. Igneri '92. (2001) (Greenslade Special Collections and Archives, Kenyon College, Gambier, Ohio. Used by Permission.)

A major sign of progress here is that the antipathy between CTFD and the Mount Vernon Fire Department (MFD) has ended. That was helped by the fact that MFD's chief, asst. chief, many of its officers and firefighter/EMTs are former members of CTFD. Among them are mature professionals who humbly give credit to Chief Hobe Brown of CTFD for preparing them well for their careers.

I retired for the final time a couple years into the twenty first century. I did not renew my EMT certifications in 2001 at age seventy one. I still felt that my skills were strong and my experiences had prepared me to make wise decisions in most any kind of emergency a small community can have. However, once people know you are seventy, they begin to look at you as if you are seventy. When the guys witnessed my first fall on the ice at a crash scene, I was in my 50's. They derided me for complaining when I had only broken two ribs. When I slipped on ice at a scene when I was seventy and suffered a mild concussion, they did not say anything but from then on began to help me into the squad on every run. That was the clear sign that I was becoming a burden in their minds, if not in fact.

Recently I turned in my pager because I realized there were no longer occasions when my advice and experience would be helpful, and the department needed it for other volunteers. I turned in the jacket with my name stitched on it so a student firefighter/EMT could use it. I turned in my dress uniform many years ago, because I couldn't get into it. So now I am gone. But I cherish every minute of those years, good times and bad..

We were pioneers and don't you dare forget us.

My generation of volunteers knows for certain that our successors will never have the thrill of being pioneers in a period of such dynamic change. That fire department is dead. Ed Dick, John and Mike Hammond, Duane Shaw, Dick Hoppe and the rest of us who served Knox County from 1970s to the present brought into being a new era in which the sign above the station door is now more appropriately labeled "emergency services" than fire department. The people who serve there now are far better able to save lives and property than we were, but the new breed owes us. They are there because we kept demonstrating that EMTs could do more, and more, and more.

Now it is time for us old guys at CTFD to listen for the last echo of the voice of Davey Clark as he signals the end of our work session. "Last call!" Its time for a beer, but we'll have to go over and see Dan Ralston at the Gambier Grill to get it. It will cost a lot more than a quarter.

www.ingramcontent.com/pod-product-compliance
Lightning Source LLC
Chambersburg PA
CBHW071235080526
44587CB00013BA/1631